SQL Server 2017 Machine Learning Services with R

Data exploration, modeling, and advanced analytics

Tomaž Kaštrun
Julie Koesmarno

BIRMINGHAM - MUMBAI

M000286494

SQL Server 2017 Machine Learning Services with R

Copyright © 2018 Packt Publishing

All rights reserved. No part of this book may be reproduced, stored in a retrieval system, or transmitted in any form or by any means, without the prior written permission of the publisher, except in the case of brief quotations embedded in critical articles or reviews.

Every effort has been made in the preparation of this book to ensure the accuracy of the information presented. However, the information contained in this book is sold without warranty, either express or implied. Neither the authors, nor Packt Publishing or its dealers and distributors, will be held liable for any damages caused or alleged to have been caused directly or indirectly by this book.

Packt Publishing has endeavored to provide trademark information about all of the companies and products mentioned in this book by the appropriate use of capitals. However, Packt Publishing cannot guarantee the accuracy of this information.

Commissioning Editor: Amey Varangaonkar
Acquisition Editor: Prachi Bisht
Content Development Editor: Deepti Thore
Technical Editor: Nilesh Sawakhande
Copy Editors: Safis Editing, Laxmi Subramanian
Project Coordinator: Shweta H Birwatkar
Proofreader: Safis Editing
Indexer: Mariammal Chettiyar
Graphics: Tania Dutta
Production Coordinator: Shantanu Zagade

First published: February 2018

Production reference: 1260218

Published by Packt Publishing Ltd.
Livery Place
35 Livery Street
Birmingham
B3 2PB, UK.

ISBN 978-1-78728-357-2

www.packtpub.com

`mapt.io`

Mapt is an online digital library that gives you full access to over 5,000 books and videos, as well as industry leading tools to help you plan your personal development and advance your career. For more information, please visit our website.

Why subscribe?

- Spend less time learning and more time coding with practical eBooks and Videos from over 4,000 industry professionals

- Improve your learning with Skill Plans built especially for you

- Get a free eBook or video every month

- Mapt is fully searchable

- Copy and paste, print, and bookmark content

PacktPub.com

Did you know that Packt offers eBook versions of every book published, with PDF and ePub files available? You can upgrade to the eBook version at `www.PacktPub.com` and as a print book customer, you are entitled to a discount on the eBook copy. Get in touch with us at `service@packtpub.com` for more details.

At `www.PacktPub.com`, you can also read a collection of free technical articles, sign up for a range of free newsletters, and receive exclusive discounts and offers on Packt books and eBooks.

Contributors

About the authors

Tomaž Kaštrun is a SQL Server developer and data scientist with more than 15 years of experience in the fields of business warehousing, development, ETL, database administration, and query tuning. He holds over 15 years of experience in data analysis, data mining, statistical research, and machine learning. He is a Microsoft SQL Server MVP for data platform and has been working with Microsoft SQL Server since version 2000. He is a blogger, author of many articles, a frequent speaker at the community and Microsoft events. He is an avid coffee drinker who is passionate about fixed gear bikes.

I would firstly like to thank my dear friend and co-author, Julie Koesmarno, for making this book a pleasing journey. It was also a great pleasure to work with Deepti Thore and Nilesh Sawakhande. Special thanks to my daughter, Rubi Kaštrun, for your patience while writing this book and your inspiration. Thanks to my family's support. Thanks to the SQL Server community and friends, for kindling my curiosity with all the questions.

Julie Koesmarno is a senior program manager in the Database Systems Business Analytics team, at Microsoft. Currently, she leads big data analytics initiatives, driving business growth and customer success for SQL Server and Azure Data businesses. She has over 10 years of experience in data management, data warehousing, and analytics for multimillion-dollar businesses as a SQL Server developer, a system analyst, and a consultant prior to joining Microsoft. She is passionate about empowering data professionals to drive impacts for customer success and business through insights.

Special thanks to my coauthor, Tomaž Kaštrun, for his expertise, passion, and dedication to this book and to the Data Community—it has been a dream and a goal to work with him. Thanks to our editors and the team at Packt Publishing for their professionalism. Also, thanks to my husband for his support throughout this writing journey, as well as to my inspiring friend, Hamish Watson, for sharing his CI/CD best practices with me.

About the reviewers

Marlon Ribunal is a data professional primarily focusing on the Microsoft stack. His work experience includes but is not limited to database administration, SQL development, query and performance tuning, ETL, and BI. He is the primary author of *SQL Server 2012 Reporting Services Blueprints*. His love for continuous learning is leading him toward the path of big data and data science, which he is gearing up for in his next adventure.

> *Thank you to the SQL Server Community. #SQLFamily is the best! Let's keep inspiring and supporting one another.*

Dave Wentzel is the CTO of Capax Global, a data and cloud consultancy. For years he worked at big ISVs, dealing with the scalability limitations of traditional databases. With the advent of Hadoop and big data technologies, things that were impossible to do with data were suddenly within reach.

Prior to Capax, he worked at Microsoft, assisting customers with Azure big data solutions. Success for him is solving challenging problems at companies he respects with talented people whom he admires.

Packt is searching for authors like you

If you're interested in becoming an author for Packt, please visit authors.packtpub.com and apply today. We have worked with thousands of developers and tech professionals, just like you, to help them share their insight with the global tech community. You can make a general application, apply for a specific hot topic that we are recruiting an author for, or submit your own idea.

Table of Contents

Preface

SQL Server has supported machine learning capabilities since SQL Server 2016. Previously known as SQL Server 2016 R Services, SQL Server 2017 Machine Learning Services come in two flavors, R and Python. This book provides hands-on reference and learning materials for data professionals, DBAs, and data scientists on how to install, develop, deploy, maintain, and administer data science and advanced analytical solutions using SQL Server with R. Whether you are new to SQL Server, or an experienced SQL Server professional, *Hands-on SQL Server Machine Learning Services with R* contains practical explanations, tips, and examples to enable you to make the most of keeping analytics close to the data for better efficiency and security.

Who this book is for

This book is for data analysts, data scientists, and database administrators with some or no experience in R, and who are eager to deliver practical data science solutions easily in their day-to-day work or future projects using SQL Server.

What this book covers

Chapter 1, *Introduction to R and SQL Server*, begins our data science journey in SQL Server, prior to SQL Server 2016, and brings us to today's SQL Server R integration.

Chapter 2, *Overview of Microsoft Machine Learning Server and SQL Server*, gives a brief outline and overview of Microsoft Machine Learning Server with an emphasis on SQL Server Machine Learning Services, while exploring how it works and the different versions of R environment. This includes key discussions on the architecture behind it, different computational environments, how the integration among systems work, and how to achieve parallelism and load distribution.

Chapter 3, *Managing Machine Learning Services for SQL Server 2017 and R*, covers the installation and setup, including how to use PowerShell. It covers exploring the capabilities of a resource governor, setting up roles and security for users to work with SQL Server Machine Learning Services with R, working with sessions and logs, installing any missing or additional R packages for data analysis or predictive modeling, and taking the first steps with using the sp_execute_external_script external procedure.

Chapter 4, *Data Exploration and Data Visualization*, explores the R syntax for data browsing, analysis, munging, and wrangling for visualization and predictive analysis. Developing these techniques is essential to the next steps covered in this chapter and throughout this book. This chapter introduces various useful R packages for visualization and predictive modeling. In addition, readers will learn how to integrate R with Power BI, SQL Server Reporting Services (SSRS), and mobile reports.

Chapter 5, *RevoScaleR Package*, discusses the advantages of using RevoScaleR for scalable and distributed statistical computation over large datasets. Using RevoScaleR improves CPU and RAM utilization and improves performance. This chapter introduces readers to RevoScaleR functions on data preparation, descriptive statistics, statistical tests, and sampling, as well as predictive modeling.

Chapter 6, *Predictive Modeling*, focuses on helping readers who are stepping into the world of prediction modeling for the first time. Using SQL Server and SQL Server Machine Learning Services with R, readers will learn how to create predictions, perform data modeling, explore advanced predictive algorithms available in RevoScaleR and other packages, and how to easily deploy the models and solutions. Finally, calling and running predictions and exposing the results to different proprietary tools (such as Power BI, Excel, and SSRS) complete the world of prediction modeling.

Chapter 7, *Operationalizing R Code*, provides tips and tricks in operationalizing R code and R predictions. Readers will learn the importance as stable and reliable process flows are essential to combining R code, persistent data, and prediction models in production. In this chapter, readers will have a chance to explore ways to adopt existing and create new R code, followed by integrating this in SQL Server through various readily available client tools such as SQL Server Management Studio (SSMS) and Visual Studio. Furthermore, this chapter covers how readers can use SQL Server Agent jobs, stored procedures, CLR with .NET, and PowerShell to productized R code.

Chapter 8, *Deploying, Managing, and Monitoring Database Solutions containing R Code*, covers how to manage deployment and change control to database deployment when integrating R code. This chapter provides guidelines on how to do an integrated deployment of the solution and how to implement continuous integration, including automated deployment and how to manage the version control. Here, readers will learn efficient ways to monitor the solution, monitor the effectiveness of the code, and predictive models after the solution is deployed.

Chapter 9, *Machine Learning Services with R for DBAs*, examines and explores monitoring, performance, and troubleshooting for daily, weekly, and monthly tasks the DBAs are doing. Using simple examples showing that R Services can also be useful for other roles involved in SQL Server, this chapter shows how R Services integrated in SQL Server enables DBAs to be more empowered by evolving their rudimentary monitoring activities into more useful actionable predictions.

Chapter 10, *R and SQL Server 2016/2017 Features Extended*, covers how new features of SQL Server 2016 and 2017 and R services can be used together, such as taking advantage of the new JSON format with the R language, using new improvements to the in-memory OLTP technology to deliver almost real-time analytics, combining new features in Column store index and R, and how to get the most out of them. It also considers how to leverage PolyBase and Stretch DB to reach beyond on-premises to hybrid and cloud possibilities. Lastly, the query store holds many statistics from execution plans, and R is a perfect tool to perform deeper analysis.

To get the most out of this book

In order to work with SQL Server Machine Learning Services, and to run the code examples found in this book, the following software will be required:

- SQL Server 2016 and/or SQL Server 2017 Developer or Enterprise Edition
- SQL Server Management Studio (SSMS)
- R IDE such as R Studio or Visual Studio 2017 with RTVS extension
- Visual Studio 2017 Community edition with the following extensions installed:
    - R Tools for Visual Studio (RTVS)
    - SQL Server Data Tools (SSDT)
- VisualStudio.com online account

The chapters in this book go through the installation and configuration steps as the software is introduced.

Download the example code files

You can download the example code files for this book from your account at www.packtpub.com. If you purchased this book elsewhere, you can visit www.packtpub.com/support and register to have the files emailed directly to you.

You can download the code files by following these steps:

1. Log in or register at `www.packtpub.com`.
2. Select the **SUPPORT** tab.
3. Click on **Code Downloads & Errata**.
4. Enter the name of the book in the **Search** box and follow the onscreen instructions.

Once the file is downloaded, please make sure that you unzip or extract the folder using the latest version of:

- WinRAR/7-Zip for Windows
- Zipeg/iZip/UnRarX for Mac
- 7-Zip/PeaZip for Linux

The code bundle for the book is also hosted on GitHub at `https://github.com/PacktPublishing/SQL-Server-2017-Machine-Learning-Services-wi th-R`. We also have other code bundles from our rich catalog of books and videos available at `https://github.com/PacktPublishing/`. Check them out!

Download the color images

We also provide a PDF file that has color images of the screenshots/diagrams used in this book. You can download it here: `http://www.packtpub.com/sites/default/files/downloads/SQLServer2017MachineLearningServiceswithR_ColorImages.pdf`.

Conventions used

There are a number of text conventions used throughout this book.

`CodeInText`: Indicates code words in text, database table names, folder names, filenames, file extensions, pathnames, dummy URLs, user input, and Twitter handles. Here is an example: "To calculate crosstabulations – the relationship between two (or more) variables – we will use two functions: `rxCrossTabs` and `rxMargins`."

A block of code is set as follows:

```
> df <- data.frame(unlist(var_info))
> df
```

Any command-line input or output is written as follows:

```
EXECsp_execute_external_script
        @language = N'R'
        ,@script = N'
                    library(RevoScaleR)
                    df_sql <- InputDataSet
                    var_info <- rxGetInfo(df_sql)
                    OutputDataSet <- data.frame(unlist(var_info))'
        ,@input_data_1 = N'
        SELECT
         BusinessEntityID
        ,[Name]
        ,SalesPersonID
        FROM [Sales].[Store]'
```

Bold: Indicates a new term, an important word, or words that you see onscreen. For example, words in menus or dialog boxes appear in the text like this. Here is an example: "You can always check the run_value of **external scripts enabled** if it is set to **1**."

Warnings or important notes appear like this.

Tips and tricks appear like this.

Get in touch

Feedback from our readers is always welcome.

General feedback: Email feedback@packtpub.com and mention the book title in the subject of your message. If you have questions about any aspect of this book, please email us at questions@packtpub.com.

Errata: Although we have taken every care to ensure the accuracy of our content, mistakes do happen. If you have found a mistake in this book, we would be grateful if you would report this to us. Please visit www.packtpub.com/submit-errata, selecting your book, clicking on the Errata Submission Form link, and entering the details.

Piracy: If you come across any illegal copies of our works in any form on the Internet, we would be grateful if you would provide us with the location address or website name. Please contact us at copyright@packtpub.com with a link to the material.

If you are interested in becoming an author: If there is a topic that you have expertise in and you are interested in either writing or contributing to a book, please visit authors.packtpub.com.

Reviews

Please leave a review. Once you have read and used this book, why not leave a review on the site that you purchased it from? Potential readers can then see and use your unbiased opinion to make purchase decisions, we at Packt can understand what you think about our products, and our authors can see your feedback on their book. Thank you!

For more information about Packt, please visit packtpub.com.

1
Introduction to R and SQL Server

SQL Server 2016 came with great new features, and among them was R integration into SQL Server, partly with advanced analytics and partly with new programmability capabilities. Microsoft R Services for SQL Server is part of the family of new extensibilities for highly scalable and parallel advanced analytics. R Services allows you to perform advanced analytics (statistical, multivariate statistics, predictive analytics, machine learning, and deep learning) on large quantities of data stored in the database. Microsoft published R Services as part of **Microsoft R Server** (**MRS**), which was specially designed for reading data directly from the SQL Server database within the same SQL Server computational context.

We will cover the following aspects in this chapter:

- Using R prior to SQL Server 2016
- Microsoft's commitment on open source R language
- Boosting analytics with SQL Server R integration
- Outline of the book

Using R prior to SQL Server 2016

The R language has been in the community since the 90's (even though it was developed a decade before). With its open source GNU license, R gained popularity for its no-fuss installation and ability to evoke any available package for additional statistical learning functions. This was a clear advantage to R as there were not that many statistical programs available on the market in the '80s and '90s; in addition, most of them were not free. The extensibility with emerging new packages for the core R engine gave a broader community and users more and more abilities to use the R language for multiple purposes, in addition to its strong statistical analysis and predictive modeling capabilities.

SQL Server 2005 introduced **SQL Server Analysis Services (SSAS)** data mining features to be applied against the customer's existing rich data stored in SQL Server and SSAS OLAP cubes. This feature allows users to use **Data Mining eXpression (DMX)** for creating predictive queries. In the next couple of years, several questions, requests, and ideas emerged on SQL forums, blogs, and community websites regarding additional statistical and predictive methods and approaches.

Back in 2011, I started working on the idea of extending the capabilities of statistical analysis in SQL Server 2008 R2 with the help of open source R language. One reason for that decision was to have flexibility of running statistical analysis (from data provisioning to multivariate analysis) without feeding the data into OLAP cube first, and another reason was more business orientated, with the need to get faster, statistical insights from all the people involved in data preparing, data munging, and data cleaning.

I kicked in and started working on a framework that was based on a combination of T-SQL stored procedure and R package RODBC (`https://cran.r-project.org/web/packages/ RODBC`). The idea was simple; get the transactional or OLAP data, select the columns you want to perform analysis against, and the analysis itself (from simple to predictive analytics, which would stretch beyond SSAS, T-SQL, or CLR capabilities):

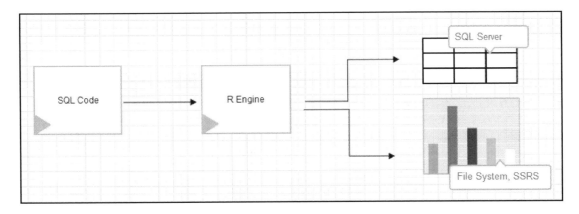

Figure 1: Process flow of a framework

The framework was far from simple, and calling the procedure considered calling a mixture of R code, T-SQL select statements, and configurations to your R engine.

The stored procedure with all its parameters looked like this:

```
EXECUTE AdventureWorks2012.dbo.sp_getStatistics
         @TargetTable = '[vStoreWithAddresses]'
        ,@Variables = 'Name'
        ,@Statistics = '8'
        ,@ServerName = 'WORKSTATION-31'
        ,@DatabaseName = 'AdventureWorks2012'
        ,@WorkingDirectory = 'C:\DataTK'
        ,@RPath = 'C:\Program Files\R\R-3.0.3\bin';
```

The nuts and bolts explanation is outside the scope of this book and is well-documented at: http://www.sqlservercentral.com/articles/R+Language/106760/.

Looking back on this framework and the feedback from the community and people on forums, it was accepted positively and many commented that they needed something similar for their daily business.

The framework in general had, besides pioneering the idea and bringing R engine one step closer to SQL Server, many flaws. The major one was security. Because it needed access to a working local directory for generating R files to be run by the vanilla R engine, it needed xp_cmdshell enabled. The following reconfiguration was mandatory and many sysadmins would not approve of it:

```
EXECUTE SP_CONFIGURE 'xp_cmdshell', 1;
GO
RECONFIGURE;
```

```
GO
EXECUTE SP_CONFIGURE 'Ole Automation Procedures', 1;
GO
RECONFIGURE;
GO
```

In addition, the framework needed to have access to R engine installation, together with R packages to execute the desired code. Installing open source programs and providing read/write access was again a drawback in terms of security and corporate software decisions. Nevertheless, one of the bigger issues—later when everything was installed and put into production—was performance and memory issues. R is memory-based, meaning all the computations are done in the memory. So, if your dataset is bigger than the size of the available memory, the only result you will get will be error messages. Another aspect of performance issues was also the speed. With no parallel and distributive computations, the framework was bound to dexterity of an author of the package. For example, if the package was written in C or C++, rather than in Fortran, the framework performed better, respectively.

The great part of this framework was the ability to deliver results from statistical analysis or predictive modeling much faster, because it could take OLTP or any other data that needed statistical analysis. Furthermore, statisticians and data scientists could prepare the R code that was stored in the table, which was later run by data wranglers, data analysts, or data stewards. Therefore, one version of truth is maintained, because there was no need for data movement or data copying and all users were reading the same data source. In terms of predictive modeling, the framework also enabled users to take advantage of various additional predictive algorithms (for example, decision forest, glm, CNN, SVM, and word cloud) that were not part of SSAS Data Mining at that time.

Besides the pros and cons, the framework was a successful initial attempt to get more data insights that were easily distributable among different business units through pushing visualizations in SQL Server Reporting Services. In the years prior to the release of SQL Server 2016, I had met people from the SQL Server community that developed similar frameworks, in order to push predictions to the SQL Server database to support business applications and solutions. With SQL Server 2016, many such similar solutions were internalized and brought closer to the SQL Server engine to achieve better performance and to address many of the issues and cons.

Microsoft's commitment to the open source R language

With a growing popularity and community, R has become and continues to be a big player in the field of advanced analytics and data visualization. R and machine learning servers (or services) are not just buzzword that will be forgotten in the next cycle of SQL Server, but it is infiltrating more and more into different layers of open source and corporate software. In the past five years, many big analytical players have introduced R integration, interpreters, and wrappers for the R language, because of the language's practicality, usability, and inter-disciplinarily and open source orientation. As Microsoft's making a bold and strategic move toward being open source friendly, the use cases for integrating R in SQL Server are growing, making this move even more natural and at the right point in time. This move had been very well appreciated in the SQL community and the business as well.

In comparison to other big analytical tools, Microsoft took integration very seriously. It addressed many of the issues and limitations of the language itself, and created complete integration of R with the SQL Server in order to give the best user experience. Many competitors (such as SAS, IBM, SAP, and Oracle) have done similar integration, but failed to take into account many aspects that contribute to a holistic user experience. Microsoft has announced that joining the R consortium will give them the ability to help the development of the R language and to support future development. In addition, Microsoft has created its own package repository called MRAN (from CRAN, where M stands for Microsoft) and is giving support and SLA agreement for R as well, even though the language and engine is based on Open R (a free, open-sourced version). All these steps tell us how dedicated Microsoft is in bringing an open source, statistical and programming language into the SQL Server environment.

We can only expect more R integration into other services. For example, Power BI supports native R visuals (`https://powerbi.microsoft.com/en-us/blog/r-powered-custom-visuals`) since October 2016, and R language since December 2015. Therefore, I am a strong believer that R will soon be part of the whole SQL Server ecosystem such as SSAS, SSIS, and SSRS natively as well. With Azure Analysis Services, R is again one step closer to analysis services.

Boosting analytics with SQL Server R integration

Data science is in the forefront of the SQL Server and R integration. Every task performed by DBA, sysadmin, the analyst, wrangler, or any other role that is working with SQL server can have these tasks supported with any kind of statistics, data correlation, data analysis, or data prediction. R integration should not be restricted only to the fields of data science. Instead, it should be explored and used in all tasks. DBA can gain from R integration by using switching from monitoring tasks to understanding and predicting what might or will happen next. Likewise, this idea can be applied to sysadmin, data wranglers, and so on. R integration also brings different roles of people closer to understand statistics, metrics, measures, and learn how to improve them by using statistical analysis and predictions.

Besides bringing siloed individual teamwork into more coherent and cohesive teams, R integration also brings less data movement, because different users can now—with the help of R code—execute, drill down, and feel the data, instead of waiting to have data first prepared, exported, and imported again. With smoother workflows comes faster time to deployment, whether it is a simple report, a predictive model, or analysis. This allows the boundaries of data ownership to shift into insights ownership, which is a positive aspect of faster reactions to business needs.

In the past year, we have also seen much more interest in data science in Microsoft stack. With R integration, Azure Machine Learning, and Power BI, all users who want to learn new skills and virtues have great starting points from the available products.

Summary

Starting with SQL Server 2016, R integration became a very important part of the SQL Server platform. Since the public release of SQL server 2016, until February 2018 (the time of writing this), the community had embraced R as well as Python very well, making data exploration and data analysis part of the general database task. Microsoft addressed many of the issues, and broadened the SQL Server as a product. With SQL Server 2017, Python was added as a secondary analytical language, reaching to an even broader community as well as businesses, and at the same time, taking are of data scalability, performance, and security.

In the next chapter, we will cover different R distributions and IDE tools for using R as a standalone or within the SQL Server, and what the differences among them are when deciding which one to choose.

2
Overview of Microsoft Machine Learning Server and SQL Server

In this chapter, we will look into the reasons why Microsoft decided to add the R language to SQL Server 2016 and what burdens this integration has overcome. We will cover the following topics in this chapter:

- Addressing analytical barriers and R limitations
- The Microsoft R Server platform
- The Microsoft R Services architecture
- Exploring computational contexts

Analytical barriers

Many companies encounter barriers when trying to analyse their data. These barriers are usually knowledge scarcity (not all departments have the knowledge to analyse the data) and data dispersity (usually data arrives from different sources).

Enterprises divide responsibilities according to the roles or functions of the employees. Such division of work has a positive effect, especially when an enterprise is large. Usually, small to mid-sized enterprises adopt such roles as well, but they are normally granulated on a higher level due to a smaller number of employees.

With rapid market changes, the emergence of new technologies, and the need for faster adaptation, many experts have noticed many of the following barriers:

- Data scarcity and data dispersity
- Complex (and many times outdated) architecture
- Lack of knowledge
- Low productivity
- Slow adaptation to market changes (long time to market)

Many enterprises are facing at least one (if not more) of these barriers and Microsoft has addressed these barriers by opening the R language to SQL Server. Embracing an open source language and open source technology, it broadens the pool of knowledge, enabling the enterprises to use community knowledge and community solutions, as well as opening and democratizing analytics. Rather than suffering and waiting on data scientists and specialists with the subject-matter academic knowledge, now this pool of knowledge can be easily shared and many of the data munging and data engineering tasks can be offloaded to other roles and people. This offload process also bridges the traditional gap between IT and statisticians that resulted in low and slow productivity in the past. This gap in knowledge and skills can now be overcome by mixing different roles and tasks using R in SQL Server (meaning that data wranglers or data stewards can have R code at their perusal that would help them in getting data insight, without actually needing to understand the complexity of the statistics). There are no surprises for understanding or knowing different platforms, now, as many IT people can use the R language provided by statisticians and data scientists. Also, data scientists can start learning skills and languages that one finds in IT.

Such interconnected and shared knowledge between two or more different departments of people will also increase productivity. When productivity is increased, statistical and predictive models can be deployed faster, changed, or adapted to consumer and market changes and enabled for data engineers, wranglers, and analysts. This certainly is the way for an enterprise to improve the innovation path and maximize the potential of open source, and broaden the sandbox of experiments using different methods and models.

The last step in addressing these barriers is addressing the issues of data scarcity and complex infrastructure. The rule is that the bigger the enterprise, the higher the likelihood that the infrastructure will be complex. With complex infrastructure, we can understand that data resides on different layers or different granularity, on different platforms, on different vendors, and on different silos, making data analysis an additional step further from realization. With an introduction to R, this complexity can be overridden with simpler data connectors, an easier way to extract the data.

As the R language is becoming more and more popular and important in the field of analytics, it can be ready for enterprises on different scales and can be designed to anticipate beyond vendors, regardless of whether you have your solution on-premises or in the cloud. The need for data movement also decreases because of the ability to access and read data directly from any hybrid system and extract only what is needed. All barriers that are present in enterprises can now be addressed faster with less bureaucracy, better integration, and less effort.

Another important aspect of embracing open source language, with which many big enterprises are still struggling, is the general providence of open source solutions. This aspect shall not be overlooked and must be taken into consideration. Microsoft took the R language on-board with several steps:

1. Being on board in the R Consortium, which is responsible for supporting the R Foundation and key organizations working tightly on developing, distributing, and maintaining R engine and supporting R-related infrastructure projects. One of the projects was the RHub project (lead by *Gabor Csardi*) that delivered a service for developing, testing, and validating R packages.

2. Creating an MRAN repository of R packages under the CC license and making CRAN packages to Microsoft R engine distribution available and compatible with R distributions.

3. Making Intel **MKL (Math Kernel Library)** computational functions to improve the performance of the R statistical computation, available out of the box when you download the R engine from the MRAN repository. **Basic Linear Algebra Subprograms (BLAS)** and **Linear Algebra Package (LAPACK)** are a family of functions for linear algebra that is enhanced for parallel computations. Such functions are matrix factorization, Cholesky matrix decomposition, vector and matrix additions, scalar multiplications, and so on.

4. Rewriting many R functions from Fortran to C++ language to improve the performances.

We can quickly support the theory of the MKL computational functions, when we compare the R engine distribution available on the CRAN and R engine distribution available on MRAN. As we have already seen, BLAS and LAPACK are vector or matrix superseded, so we will compare (benchmark) the computations on a matrix between two R engine distributions.

The comparison is made on CRAN R 3.3.0 and MRAN R Open 3.3.0, with the following code:

```
# Matrix creation
set.seed (2908)
M <- 20000
n <- 100
Mat <- matrix (runif (M*n),M,n)


# Matrix multiply
system.time (
   Mat_MM <- Mat%*% t(Mat), gcFirst=TRUE
) [1]

# Matrix multiply with crossprod
system.time (
   Mat_CP <- crossprod(Mat), gcFirst=TRUE
) [1]
```

The following are the results with the following time (in seconds):

Time (seconds)	CRAN 3.3.2	MRAN 3.3.2
MM	26,69	2,75
CP	0,19	0,01

In the following figure, you can see the difference in performance between CRAN and MRAN R engine:

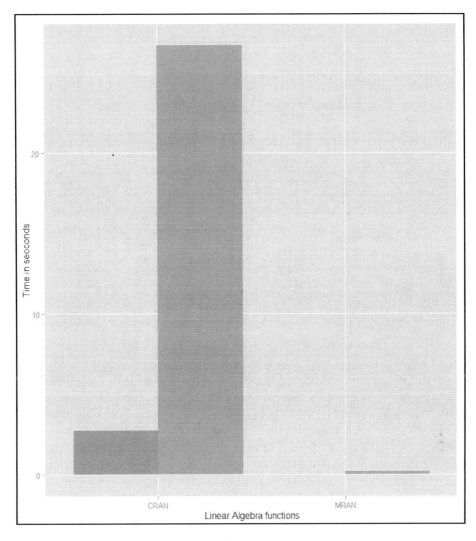

Figure 1

The graph shows a simple linear algebra that uses matrices or vectors and performs faster for a factor of 10 (tested on my local client-Inter I7, 4 CPU, 20 GB RAM). Note that, when you run this test on your local machine, you should observe the RAM and disk storage consumption; you will see that the MRAN operation is very lightweight in comparison to the CRAN operation when it comes to the RAM consumption.

When you download the MRAN distribution of R Open, note that there will be additional information on MKL multithreaded performance functions available:

Figure 2: Source: `https://mran.microsoft.com/download/`

Many more steps were taken that would reassure consumers, developers, wranglers, and managers from bigger enterprises that the R language is here to stay. Microsoft promised that, besides this provision, there is also support for general governance and if the company decides, it can also receive R support on an enterprise level.

Furthermore, to support the idea of using open source R language, one must understand the general architecture of R. The R engine is written by the core group of roughly 20 people with access to the source code of the R engine (even though only six are working on day-to-day R development). This group of people not only maintains the code, but they themselves are also contributors, bug fixers, and developers. So, the R engine is open source, which means that it is free software (under a GNU license), but the engine is not maintained that openly. On the other hand, R libraries (or packages) are mostly community-driven contributions, which mean that people in the community are free to develop and create a variety of functions to support statistical calculations, visualizations, working with datasets, and many other aspects.

In the months following the release of SQL Server 2016 (from summer 2016 onward), Microsoft also changed what is available in different editions of SQL Server. If you visit the SQL Server 2016 editions overview at `https://www.microsoft.com/en-us/sql-server/sql-server-2016-editions`, you can see that under advanced analytics, basic R integration is available in all editions of SQL Server 2016, and advanced R Integration (with full parallelism of ScaleR functions in `RevoScaleR` package) is available only in the Enterprise and Developer editions.

The Microsoft Machine learning R Server platform

We have already touched on the concept of R Open and R for enterprise environment briefly. Microsoft Machine Learning R Server is an enterprise server that delivers high dimensional and large datasets that can be processed in parallel, and the workload can be distributed across nodes. R Server can process these parallel and distributed workloads on Windows, Linux servers, or HDFS systems, such as Hadoop, Spark, Teradata, and HD Insight. R Server can achieve parallel and distributed workloads using Microsoft R packages designed to do just that. The RevoScaleR package will give the ability to do highly parallel and distributed computations, statistical analysis, and predictive analytics, as well as machine learning and deep learning.

With the acquisition of the company Revolution Analytics, Microsoft rebranded their two main products, Revolution R Open and Revolution R Enterprise, to Microsoft R Open and Microsoft R Server and Microsoft SQL Server R Services. In addition to these two flavors, they also added Microsoft R Client as an additional standalone product:

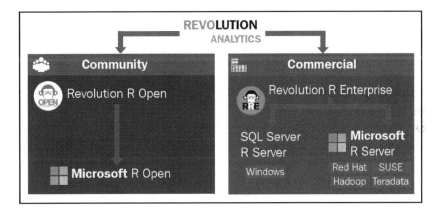

Figure 3

Based on different flavors and enterprise ecosystems, companies can choose the type of usage they will need (community, or non-commercial, and commercial) and, based on their business needs and where they want their analytical server to be set up, they can choose what suits them the most. In the commercial version, a standalone machine learning R Server (or simply R server) is available, as well as in-database machine learning services (or SQL Server R services).

In the version of SQL Server 2017, Microsoft R Server has been changed to Machine Learning Server (both in-database and as a standalone; the rebranding from in-database R Services to Machine Learning R Services was introduced in the CTP version of SQL Server VNext that later changed to SQL Server 2017). In *Figure 4*, one can see the naming available when installing SQL Server 2016 (left-print screen) and the names that will be available in SQL Server 2017 (right-print screen):

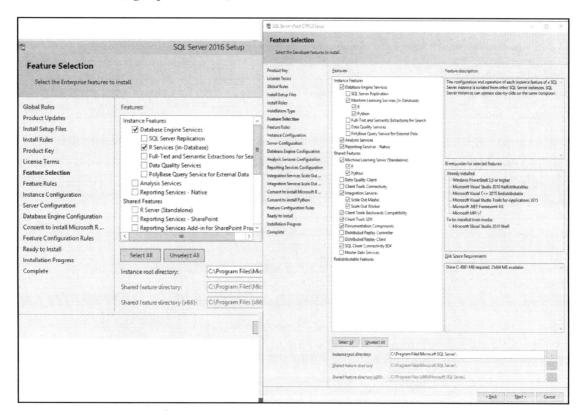

Figure 4

The reason given for the change in the naming was the fact that Microsoft introduced Python in SQL Server 2017. Python is a powerful statistical, analytical, and machine learning language, and therefore, the name was unified. The R-part of the Machine Learning Server will not change internally, but it will gain useful additional packages and improved functions, as follows:

```
serialize/unserialize -> rxSerializeModel/rxUnserializeModel
InstallPackages -> rxInstallPackages
Histogram -> rxHistogram
```

All these functions have been rewritten either for working on large datasets in parallel and distributed workloads, or to support R and SQL Server work.

In the Microsoft R platform, the following products are available:

- Microsoft Machine Learning R Server
- Microsoft R Client
- Microsoft R Open
- R Tools for Visual Studio

Product description has been summarized based on Microsoft Docs descriptions and based on an article published on SQLServerCentral in September of 2016 (http://www. sqlservercentral.com/articles/Microsoft/145393/).

Microsoft R Open (MRO)

Microsoft R Open is an open source R distribution that is 100% free and generally available. Microsoft has enhanced this R Open distribution with an additional high-performance multi-threaded feature of **Math Kernel Library** (**MKL**) that is optimized for vector and matrix-based mathematical and statistical computations; otherwise, this distribution is fully compatible with legacy R objects and R code.

R Open is also compatible with the CRAN repository, GitHub packages, or any other repository, making MRO widely usable. On the other hand, R Open has some limitations. It is memory bound, which means that it can only handle the datasets that will fit into the memory (client) available. Proprietary ScaleR functions (available in the RevoScaleR package) will not be available under R Open and it will run on all SQL Server 2017 editions, except on Express or Express with Tools, whereas Microsoft R Client/Server will run only on the Enterprise or Developer editions of SQL Server 2017.

Microsoft R Client is the same R distribution as Microsoft R Open and it is built on top of 100% open source R version. Microsoft R Client is the first version from the Microsoft family of R versions that introduces the RevoScaleR package (ScaleR functions). A data wrangler, data scientist, or data engineer (or any other profile) who installs this version will have the ability to use the parallelization and multi-threaded computing, as well as the use of proprietary functions from ScaleR.

There are some limitations to the R Client version. The memory will be limited to a local client machine with the same limitations as Microsoft R Open—data must fit into the local memory in order to be computed. The ScaleR functions will be installed alongside this version, but the processing will be limited to only two threads simultaneously (regardless of the technical specifications of the client machine) and to the local disk and CPU speed. Otherwise, any legacy R packages or R code will be compatible.

Microsoft R Client also brings the possibility to change the computational environment, which means that the computational load can be pushed to Microsoft R Server or SQL Server R Services and any HDFS system to achieve maximum performance. Building the ecosystem with many R Clients and one (or a few) R Servers will give a high-performance analytical environment without having the need for Microsoft R Server being installed locally. It is compatible with the following flavors of R Server: Microsoft R server for Linux, Microsoft R Server for Teradata DB, Microsoft R Server for Hadoop, Microsoft R HDInsight, and both versions of Microsoft R Server-Standalone and SQL Server R Services.

Microsoft Machine Learning R Server

Microsoft R Server is a standalone server version of the R engine, built on top of the R open source platform but modified to suit the needs of the enterprise environment and heavy usage of analytical purposes, from statistical analysis and data mining to machine learning and any big data tasks.

It is fully compatible with CRAN/MRAN/GitHub repositories and any R legacy code. The ScaleR functions and algorithms available in the `RevoScaleR` package are capable of parallel and multi-threated data processing with no limitations known to R Open or R Client. Computations are prepared for large datasets—in most cases, datasets that easily exceed the server memory size. This can be done due to a special external data frame format that enables multi-threaded computations and enables R-based applications that can perform parallel computations and deployable solutions across multi-platforms with the help of ConnectR and DeployR. Disk scalability is also available with Microsoft R Server.

Microsoft SQL Server Machine Learning R Services

The in-database flavor of R Open distribution is available as Machine Learning R Services for Microsoft SQL Server, and covers all the ScaleR algorithms that are available in the `RevoScaleR` package.

The memory and disk, in this case, will be managed by your installation of SQL Server, and the R execution is done using the `SQL Server Trusted Launchpad` service that governs the communication between SQL Server and R engine.

Also, users can connect to R Services using R Client but the `DeployR` and `ConnectR` functions will be limited.

Microsoft SQL Server R Services is an in-database version for SQL Server 2016 and onwards, and this will be the main focus of this book. These in-database services can be installed when a new instance of SQL Server is installed. *Figure 4* shows that R in-database service (or machine learning services (in-database) as a part of SQL Server 2017) are installed as an instance feature, and when ticking this feature, the R service (or the Python service) will be installed. One must also understand that Microsoft R Server is a standalone component that is not installed when R Services are installed. One must explicitly put a tick next to **R Server (Machine Learning Server)** under shared services. However, R services (in-database) will not install R Server.

R Services (in-database) is a standalone source of R language and R programming with full stack and capabilities of SQL Server, including the tools and technologies for governance, security, reliability, and performance. In SSMS, one can invoke and call R functions making R analysis or predictions using transact SQL with an R script. This can be achieved using a system external procedure: `sp_execute_external_script`.

The ScaleR libraries that are a part of the R Service (in-database) installation allow data scientists, developers, or database administrators to securely execute an R script from a SQL Server computer or on Microsoft R Server. By defining the computational context, a user can choose where to push the computations and load, either to stay in-database R runtime or use the ScaleR library to enhance connectivity and parallelism and push the load to Microsoft R Server.

To close the circle, with the installation of client R that comes available as a standalone and separate installer, you can develop your R code and deploy the solution to R Services or to Microsoft R Server running on Windows or Linux.

Figure 5 depicts how data scientists or data analysts can push the load from client/workstation to a cloud-based solution, a virtual machine, an R Server, or R services (in-database). From a client's perspective, one can also easily choose a hybrid solution, especially when the need for data integration and data consolidation between different systems is needed. This concept will most certainly give the enterprise an immediate boost and lift in performance, as well as faster and better solutions adaptation almost instantly:

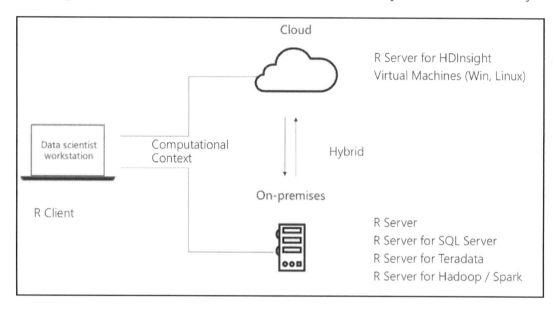

Figure 5

R Tools for Visual Studio (RTVS)

RTVS is a Microsoft free version (distributed under a GNU license) of IDE for writing, validating, and running an R code within Visual Studio. RTVS is supported on the Community, Professional, and Enterprise editions of Visual Studio 2015 and Visual Studio 2017.

R Tools (https://www.visualstudio.com/vs/rtvs/) will help developers, analysts, and data scientists to operate and perform statistical computations, visualizations, and data management. R Tools bring graphical interface to R Engine, workspace for rich editing, interactive windows, variable and visuals explorer, help, IntelliSense, and much more. It also binds local and remote workspaces (on-premises or in the cloud), so that data analysts can switch between computational environments very easily.

The view of workspaces in RTVS is made simple and graphical for a user to switch between different R environments:

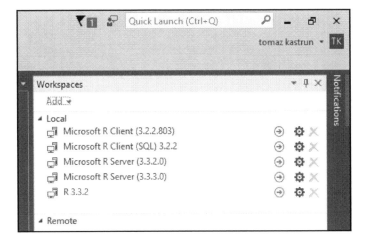

Figure 6

It resembles the famous and powerful RStudio (`www.rstudio.com`), but still offers all the necessities that community and time brought into the development of RStudio, Emacs, Vim, Eclipse, or others. Microsoft has also addressed the community with questionnaires to ask what the users of RTVS are still missing. They can contribute and add their wishes at `https://www.surveymonkey.com/r/RTVS1`.

RTVS was announced and released (as a beta version) in early 2016 but only got version 1 in 2017.

The Microsoft Machine Learning R Services architecture

The architecture of R Server covers many components needed in order for the communication between R IDE or SQL Server and R engine to work properly.

Several components are involved in order to properly execute Transact SQL, R script, and return all the results back to T-SQL:

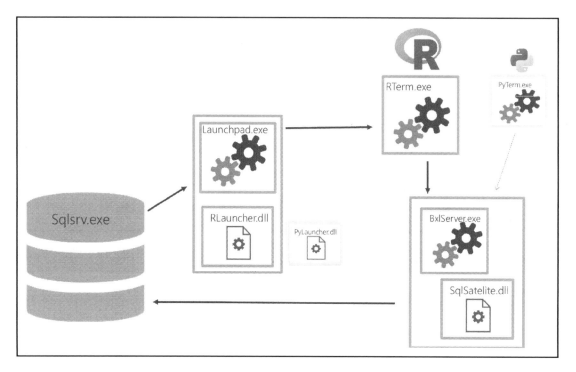

Figure 7

Launchpad is a new service in SQL Server 2016 that supports execution of external scripts using the external stored procedure from SQL Server. However, in SQL Server 2017, the Python launcher has also been introduced, making Launchpad generally available to the second non-SQL Server language. The idea behind Launchpad is that since the infrastructure is already prepared, the SQL Server should, in the future, support other languages as well, such as JavaScript and C++, opening this service not only to predictive analytics and machine learning, but also to other standalone languages.

The Launchpad service (service name: MSSQLLaunchpad) is dependent on the SQL Server service (service name: MSSQLSERVER), which means that, when restarting or stopping a SQL Server service, the Launchpad service will be restarted or stopped also.

In addition, the R language has also brought two additional services: R Terminal service (abbreviated as RTerm) and BxlServer, which use SQL Satellite, an additional extension to SQL server that communicates between external runtime (correlating to the Launchpad service) and SQL Server; both can be found as processes.

For easier understanding of these correlations, let's start a simple PowerShell script to see all the components of `Launchpad` and `BxlServer`:

```
Get-Process -Name Launchpad | Select-Object *
Get-Process -Name BxlServer | Select-Object *
```

Additionally, with a simple T-SQL code, we can include the R script:

```
EXEC sp_execute_external_script
    @language = N'R'
   ,@script = N'library(RevoScaleR)
OutputDataSet <- data.frame(rxInstalledPackages())'
```

Additionally, observe the Process Explorer and Launchpad Process:

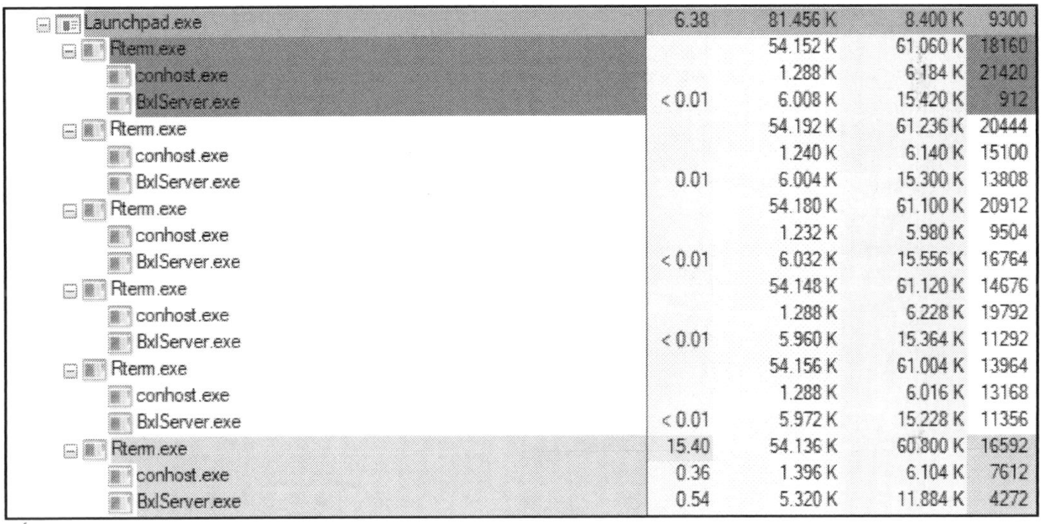

Launchpad.exe	6.38	81.456 K	8.400 K	9300
Rterm.exe		54.152 K	61.060 K	18160
conhost.exe		1.288 K	6.184 K	21420
BxlServer.exe	< 0.01	6.008 K	15.420 K	912
Rterm.exe		54.192 K	61.236 K	20444
conhost.exe		1.240 K	6.140 K	15100
BxlServer.exe	0.01	6.004 K	15.300 K	13808
Rterm.exe		54.180 K	61.100 K	20912
conhost.exe		1.232 K	5.980 K	9504
BxlServer.exe	< 0.01	6.032 K	15.556 K	16764
Rterm.exe		54.148 K	61.120 K	14676
conhost.exe		1.288 K	6.228 K	19792
BxlServer.exe	< 0.01	5.960 K	15.364 K	11292
Rterm.exe		54.156 K	61.004 K	13964
conhost.exe		1.288 K	6.016 K	13168
BxlServer.exe	< 0.01	5.972 K	15.228 K	11356
Rterm.exe	15.40	54.136 K	60.800 K	16592
conhost.exe	0.36	1.396 K	6.104 K	7612
BxlServer.exe	0.54	5.320 K	11.884 K	4272

Figure 8

It is obvious how communication creates the entire circle from SQL Server to R and back.

Furthermore, the Command Line also reveals that the Launchpad process uses the `RLauncher.dll` library and launches `sqlsatelitelaunch` using `sqlsatellite.dll`:

```
CommandLine: "C:\Program Files\Microsoft SQL
Server\MSSQL14.MSSQLSERVER\MSSQL\bin\launchpad.exe" -launcher RLauncher.dll
-pipename sqlsatellitelaunch -timeout 600000 -logPath "C:\Program
Files\Microsoft  SQL Server\MSSQL14.MSSQLSERVER\MSSQL\LOG\ExtensibilityLog"
-workingDir "C:\Program Files\Microsoft SQL
Server\MSSQL14.MSSQLSERVER\MSSQL\ExtensibilityData" -satelliteDllPath
```

```
"C:\Program Files\Microsoft SQL
Server\MSSQL14.MSSQLSERVER\MSSQL\Binn\sqlsatellite.dll"
```

Many more configurations will tell you where and how communication in this architecture is set up. Opening the RLauncher.config file will show you the following configuration:

```
RHOME=C:\Program Files\Microsoft SQL Server\MSSQL14.MSSQLSERVER\MSSQL\R_SERVICES
MPI_HOME=C:\Program Files\Microsoft MPI
INSTANCE_NAME=MSSQLSERVER
TRACE_LEVEL=1
JOB_CLEANUP_ON_EXIT=1
USER_POOL_SIZE=0
WORKING_DIRECTORY=C:\Program Files\Microsoft SQL Server\MSSQL14.MSSQLSERVER\MSSQL\ExtensibilityData
PKG_MGMT_MODE=0
```

Figure 9

Additionally, by changing the TRACE_LEVEL parameter, it can also reveal potential logs, showing same path and communication between the systems, as the RevoScaleR log also shows information on each worker session:

```
library(RevoScaleR); sessionDirectory <-
'C:\\PROGRA~1\\MICROS~3\\MSSQL1~1.MSS\\MSSQL\\EXTENS~1\\MSSQLSERVER01\\0FEB
1004-867F-4AB6-B9CC-E1C824596645';sessionId <- '0FEB1004-867F-4AB6-B9CC-
E1C824596645';scriptFile <- file.path(sessionDirectory, paste(sessionId,
'.R', sep=''));rxIgnoreCallResult <- .Call('RxSqlSessionStart',
list(sessionDirectory=sessionDirectory, sessionId=sessionId,
waitTime=-1));source(scriptFile)
```

R Limitations

Community blogs and forums, as well as package authors and contributors, are debating over the long list of R limitations the language has. Many are murky and some are based solemnly on a particular group of user experience, but the following limitations can be agreed upon:

- Performance issues
- Memory limitations
- Security aspects
- Language syntax

Performance issues

Over 40% of the R code is predominantly written in C, and a little bit over 20% still in Fortran (the rest in C++, Java, and R), making some common computational tasks very costly. Microsoft (and, before, Revolution analytics) did rewrite some of the most frequently used functions from old Fortran to C/C++ in order to address performance issues.

Many package authors did very similar things. For example, Matt Dowle—the main author of the `data.table` R package—did several language performance lift-ups to speed up most common data wrangling steps.

When comparing similar operations on the same dataset using different packages, such as `dplyr`, `plyr`, `data.table`, and `sqldf`, one can see the difference in the time performance with the same results.

The following R sample shows roughly a 80 MiB big object with a simple grouping function of how much difference there is in the computation time. Packages `dpylr` and `data.table` stand out and have performance gain over 25x times better in comparison to `plyr` and `sqldf`. `data.table`, especially, is extremely efficient and this is mainly due to Matt's extreme impetus to optimize the code of the `data.table` package in order to gain performance:

```
set.seed(6546)
nobs <- 1e+07
df <- data.frame("group" = as.factor(sample(1:1e+05, nobs, replace =
TRUE)), "variable" = rpois(nobs, 100))

# Calculate mean of variable within each group using plyr - ddply
library(plyr)
system.time(grpmean <- ddply(
  df,
  .(group),
  summarize,
  grpmean = mean(variable)))


# Calcualte mean of variable within each group using dplyr
detach("package:plyr", unload=TRUE)
library(dplyr)

system.time(
  grpmean2 <- df %>%
              group_by(group) %>%
              summarise(group_mean = mean(variable)))
```

```
# Calcualte mean of variable within each group using data.table
library(data.table)
system.time(
  grpmean3 <- data.table(df)[
    #i
    ,mean(variable)
    ,by=(group)] )

# Calcualte mean of variable within each group using sqldf
library(sqldf)
system.time(grpmean4 <- sqldf("SELECT avg(variable), [group] from df GROUP
BY [group]"))
```

The Microsoft RevoScaleR package, on the other hand, is optimized as well and can supersede all of these packages in terms of performance and large datasets. This is just to prove how Microsoft has made R ready for large datasets to address the performance issues.

Memory limitations

R is memory bound. This literally means that the dataset must fit into the client's RAM. From the previous example, if someone is going to run a simple algebraic operation, some matrix computation, or any kind of distance-based algorithm (that is heavy on computation), the R system would be limited to what would fit into the RAM. No spill to disk or any kind of temporary object is available, unless the user loads a package that allows otherwise.

Again, Microsoft has a solution with the RevoScaleR package that covers this limitation. With the introduction of the **eXternal Data Frame** (**XDF**) format, the package is able to store any size of the dataset (there is no recorder upper limit) in this format that is persisted on the disk, with conversion from a binary, blob, CSV, or any other format to XDF format. This limitation is made possible in Microsoft Machine Learning R Server or Machine Learning R Services.

Security aspects

The evolution of the R language as a GNU distribution has been evolving over the past couple of decades as a client-based solution and, even before the dawn of the internet, all datasets have been securely stored on one's machine. With the spread of data over the internet, cloud services, and connected systems, as well as more and more present hybrid solution systems, the security aspect of reading, writing, analyzing, and storing data has never been a question. However, in the past ten years, more and more systems have been emerging, enterprise needs have changed, people roles have changed—but the core R engine and IDE has not yet taken a step in this direction. From this aspect, it seems as if R wants to remain a university developed and driven software. With R integration into SQL Server, Microsoft has addressed these issues and has not only created database roles, but also added services that make the connection to R and all computations securely, diminishing the possibilities of security vulnerabilities.

Language syntax

R language is very flexible and allows a user to change the S4 methods and S3 objects, generic objects, and all of the user-defined objects and variables. As the R Language is still not an object-orientated language, it is a question of debate if this is true or not (because currently, R understands only three object-orientated systems) because both S3 and S4 objects are OO orientated structures.

R Syntax might be easy to learn, but it is also easy to develop some doubts. The following are a couple of syntax disagreements in the R community:

- Several different R packages give users the same functionalities (data wrangling, data analysis, data predictions). As previously displayed, when comparing the performances of these packages for data-wrangling purposes with usage, users will see which package performs better or which package suit their needs better. Idiosyncratic syntax with confusing structures is also a part of the package and can be used in many different ways.
- There are multiple ways to do the same thing (declaring a variable, constructing a class, handling data, and predicting with the same algorithm).
- Missing conventions, namespaces, and package inter-dependencies.
- Somewhat challenging error messages with lacking documentation/help.
- Case sensitivity.

It is cumbersome to list all of the issues, but one can quickly get an idea of how the language evolved, but still is embraced by the community more and more; R as a language is perceived as the most popular to date.

Summary

This chapter has given an overview on the ecosystem of the new R Service and the family of R Engine products offered by Microsoft.

When thinking about R and SQL Server, one must keep in mind what the needs in the enterprise will be and how the infrastructure will be prepared in order to leverage the maximum performance from powerful `RevoScaleR` packages.

In the next chapter, we will see how to use these ScaleR computational functions to deliver better performance results, and how to set up your ecosystem.

3
Managing Machine Learning Services for SQL Server 2017 and R

This chapter will tackle managing R Services and the steps necessary to get R Services running from a SQL Server database. In detail, this chapter will cover the following topics:

- Installing SQL Server with R services
- Configuring the environment and installing **R Tools for Visual Studio** (**RTVS**)
- Resource Governor
- Security
- Sessions and logs
- Installing new R packages
- Managing SQL Server R services with PowerShell
- Getting to know the `sp_execute_external_script` external procedure

With SQL Server 2017 installation, configuration, and setting up the working environment aren't that much different, compared with how SQL Server 2016 operated when R was originally introduced. If there are differences between the versions, they will be pointed out.

Installing SQL Server with machine learning R Services using SQL Server 2016 and 2017 has minimal hardware requirements that depend on the edition of SQL Server you will be installing. SQL Server comes in several editions. More information is available on the Microsoft webpage:

```
https://www.microsoft.com/en-us/sql-server/sql-server-2017-editions
```

Minimum requirements

Basic R integration is available in almost all SQL Server editions, except the Express edition (unless it is Express with Advanced Services). This means that a standard SQL Server will support R services to the extent of using vanilla and native R code, but no advanced R integration or pushing computations to other computational contexts. The same logic will apply to SQL Server 2017 (at the time of writing), and editions and features are already made public at the following URL:

```
https://docs.microsoft.com/en-us/sql/sql-server/editions-and-components-of-sql-
server-2017
```

In terms of the operating system, many Microsoft OS versions (such as Windows Server 2012 and higher, Windows 8 and higher) are supported and, starting with SQL Server 2016 and higher, Linux is also supported. To have R Services running, a minimum of 1 GB is required, but 4 GB would be recommended, and 2.0 GHz or a faster processor (x64 processor type) speed would do the job. In addition, 6 GB hard drive space would do for the principal installation, but more disk space will be required based on any additional features or SQL Server services.

Choosing the edition

SQL Server is no longer just a database, but has grown into a database platform - an ecosystem - which consists of many additional services (such as SSRS, SSAS, and SSIS) that supports and also extends the capabilities of modern database usage. When installing Machine Learning R Services (in a database), one should think about the ecosystem environment and which additional services would be used along with R Services. If the business need requires advanced R (or Python) integration and analytics, the Enterprise edition is the right one. If only basic R integration is needed, the standard version will cover the needs. Also, think along the lines of other analytical tools if you need analysis services or reporting services, and which developments tools would also be needed for that (for example, MDX on top of OLAP cubes and running R code against the same data mart).

When you have decided on the version, download the ISO or CAB installation file of SQL Server 2017(or 2016) and start the installation. I will install the Developer edition of SQL Server 2017 (which is, from the installation perspective, almost the same as the 2016 version):

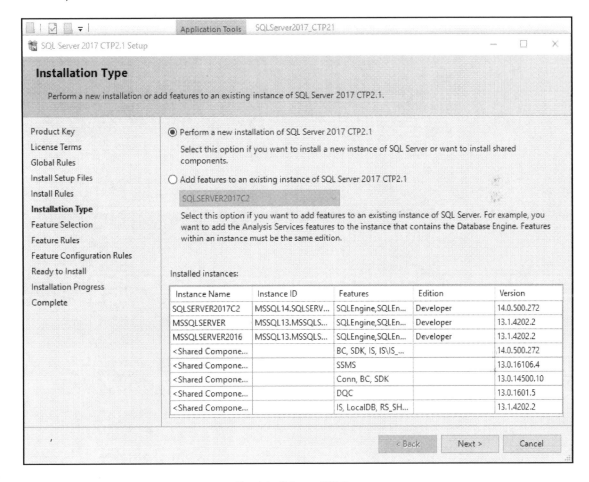

Figure 1: Installation type of SQL Server

Installing a new installation of SQL Server will guarantee that the Machine Learning Services with R (or in-database service) are correctly installed.

In the next step, the installation features must be installed. To have R Services installed, a tick must be placed on **R** for **SQL Server Services (in-database),** while for SQL Server 2017, a tick must be placed on **R** in the **Machine Learning Services (in-database)** section:

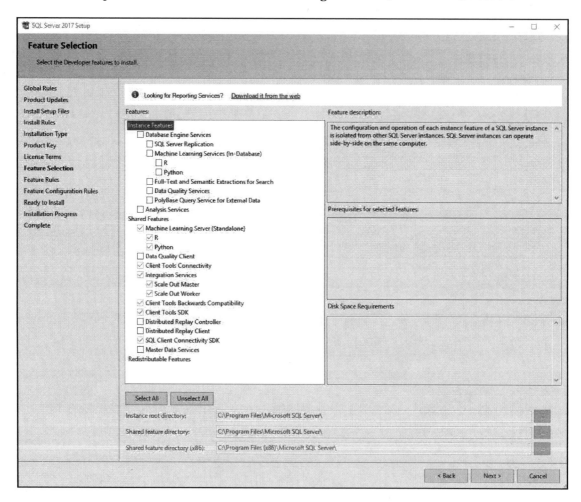

Figure 2: Feature selection for SQL Server

In the following server configuration step, you must check the users and accounts that will have access to services. For R Services (in-database), the SQL Server Launchpad service will be installed and automatically started. This service can be started or stopped after the installation through Windows Application-Services:

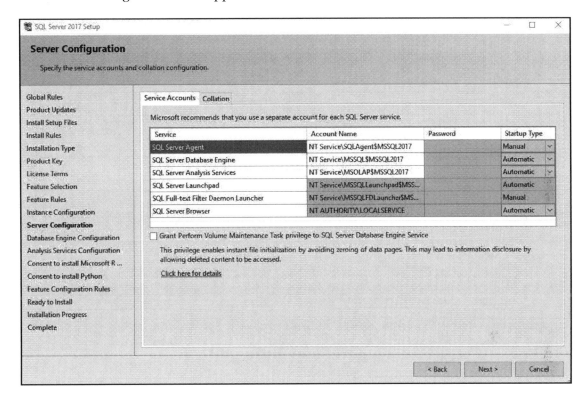

Figure 3: Server configuration for SQL Server

After the database engine is configured, you will be prompted to accept the agreement to install Microsoft R Open, making sure that you are aware of the fact that R is under GNU License. By requesting this consent, Microsoft just wants to make sure that the administrator agrees and that all new updates and patches to R Open version will be in accordance with the SQL Server update preferences:

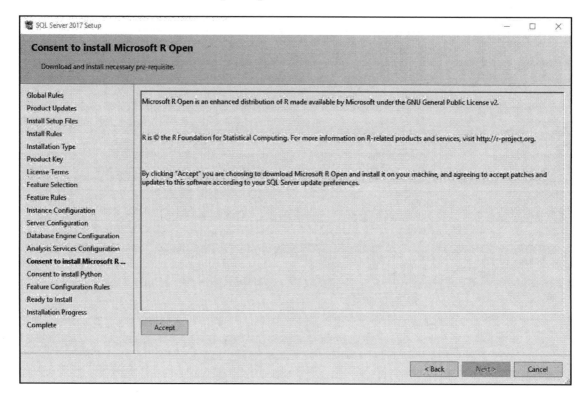

Figure 4: Prompting the content for installing Microsoft R Open

In addition to agreeing to R's agreement, please note that the life cycle of Microsoft R Server is two years. If MRS 8.0 was released in January 2016, the official support ended in January 2018; to be more precise, security and critical updates will come in for a period of one year (until January 2017) and, after that, only the security updates will continue until January 2018. During the year, upgrades will also be received. Please note that it is relevant for the standalone product-Microsoft Machine Learning Server, but it is worth mentioning how long the support timeline will be held.

If you are also installing Python, the same consent will be requested:

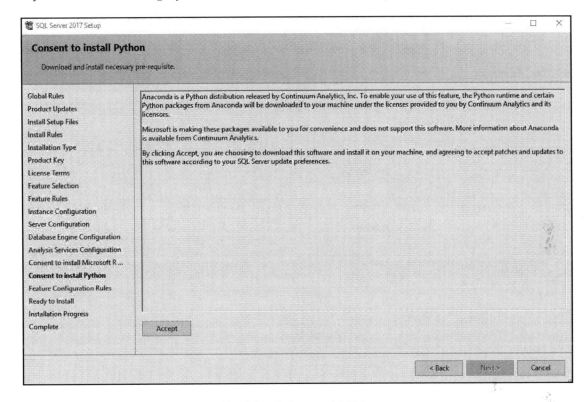

Figure 5: Prompting the content to install Python

Once you have selected all of the features, configurations, and consents, you will be presented with an overview of the services and features to be installed:

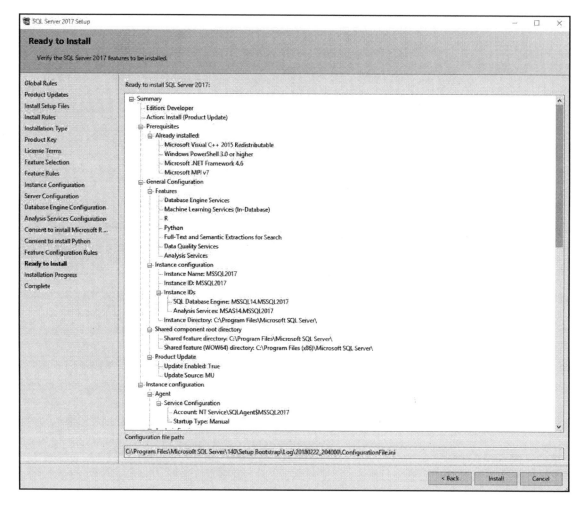

Figure 6: Selected features ready to be installed

Once the installation is completed, you will have the R Engine for Machine Learning Services and Microsoft Machine Learning Server with R (if selected) installed. Please note that R Engine for R Services (in-database) will have a different R installation, as the standalone Microsoft R Server, and also all the installed packages will be different, under different paths, rights, and security settings.

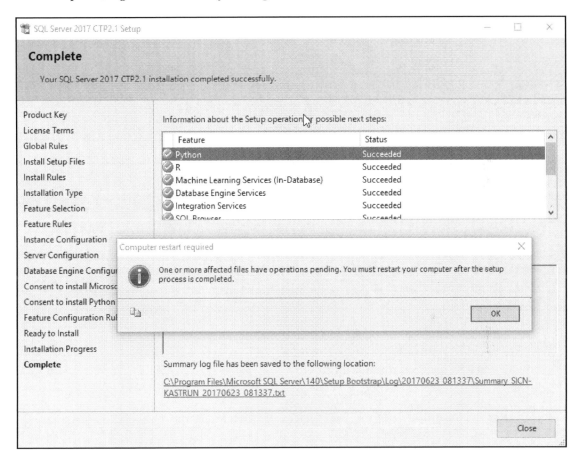

Figure 7: Completing the installation process

Configuring the database

During the postinstallation process, database configuration will be the next task. Think about database collation, because the R language is case-sensitive, and it matters what kind of data you will be feeding to SQL Server engine and pushing onward to Launchpad.Some languages differentiate the small from capital caps (for example, the Turkish language; the letter L in particular) and this might be an additional challenge when pairing SQL Server and R data types. In addition, based on your ecosystem, authentication should also play an important role in setting up the environment.

With real-time data scoring available with SQL Server 2016 and improved in SQL Server 2017, it is worth giving it a try. Also, for any extended use of Machine Learning Services, file database might be a very useful and powerful way to store graphs and results for later analysis, or results that can be exposed to Power BI, SSRS, or external applications. If you have a filestream included for tackling unstructured data in your business, this is also another service where the database configuration needs additional attention.

Configuring the environment and installing R Tools for Visual Studio (RTVS)

Once the installation is completed, there are some post installation processes that need to be executed.

The external script server must be enabled so that stored procedures can call external script. In order to do so, run the following command against your SQL Server instance, where you have installed R Services (in-database):

```
EXEC sp_configure 'show advanced options',1;
GO
RECONFIGURE;
GO
EXEC sp_configure 'external scripts enabled';
GO
```

If you are running this for the first time, it is disabled by default so enabling it is a must; otherwise, running the sp_execute_external_script procedure will not be possible:

```
EXEC sp_configure 'external scripts enabled', 1;
GO
RECONFIGURE WITH OVERRIDE;
GO
```

You can always check whether the run_value of **external scripts enabled** is set to **1**, as follows:

name	minimum	maximum	config_value	run_value
external scripts enabled	0	1	1	1

Figure 8: Setting up sp_configure

If the server configuration does not take effect, you need to restart the SQL Server service.Under services, find your MSSQLSERVER Service name and restart it (**Stop** and **Start**):

Figure 9: Checking MSSQLSERVER service

Restarting the MSSQLSERVER service will automatically restart all the dependent services, along with the MSSQLLaunchpad service. After the restart of the server, the external script will be enabled.

After the post installation process has finished, security can be set. It is optional, as the default database readers are already set, but, based on your company's environment you are advised to look into this and set it up properly.

In addition, you will need to install **R Tools for Visual Studio** (**RTVS**). To do this, Visual Studio 2015 or higher is needed and, once VS2015+ is installed, you need to download the RTVS itself from the Visual Studio website (https://www.visualstudio.com/vs/rtvs/). The installation process from that point is straightforward and does not need any further instructions now.

Security

After configuring the database and any other additional settings used in your ecosystem, you will want to think about security, in terms of who will have access to run sp_execute_external_script.

You can directly create security settings on the external procedure. In this case, you will need to add database permissions to execute external script to the user.

A simple SQL login will look like this:

```
USE [master]
GO
CREATE LOGIN [RR1] WITH PASSWORD=N'Read!2$17', DEFAULT_DATABASE=[SQLR],
CHECK_EXPIRATION=ON, CHECK_POLICY=ON
GO
ALTER SERVER ROLE [sysadmin] ADD MEMBER [RR1]
GO
CREATE DATABASE SQLR;
GO
USE [SQLR]
GO
CREATE USER [RR1] FOR LOGIN [RR1]
GO
USE [SQLR]
GO
ALTER USER [RR1] WITH DEFAULT_SCHEMA=[dbo]
GO
```

And now, let's start the external procedure:

```
EXECUTE AS USER = 'RR1';
GO
EXEC sp_execute_external_script
        @language = N'R'
        ,@script = N'OutputDataSet<- InputDataSet'
        ,@input_data_1 = N'SELECT 1 AS Numb UNION ALL SELECT 2;'
WITH RESULT SETS
((
    Res INT
))
REVERT;
GO
```

And the error message will be, that the user RR1 does not have permissions:

```
Msg 297, Level 16, State 101, Procedure sp_execute_external_script, Line 1
[Batch Start Line 34]
The user does not have permission to perform this action.
```

You also have to grant the database a datareader role in order to execute the sp_execute_external_script command:

```
USE [SQLR]
GO
ALTER ROLE [db_datareader] ADD MEMBER [RR1]
GO
```

You should also check that executing external scripts is enabled:

```
GRANT EXECUTE ANY EXTERNAL SCRIPT TO [RR1];
GO
```

After setting the database role and granting execute permissions, rerun the sp_execute_external_script procedure and the result of executing the external script should be as follows:

Figure 10: The results of the external procedure

How to manage user authentication (Windows or SQL) and primary security principles; it should be aligned using local DBA, SysAdmin, and architect to help you delegate who will have access to the system.

A rule of thumb is to prepare stored procedures for dealing with different levels of data manipulation and granting access on the level of the stored procedure. Clean the data using this commands:

```
DROP USER RR1;
GO
USE [master];
GO
DROP LOGIN RR1;
GO
--DROP TABLE IF EXISTS SQLR;
GO
```

Resource Governor

Resource Governor is a very welcome feature of R Services (in-database), as it enables the Govern workload against the server with a simple dataset that is available with the accompanying code-database `RevoTestDB`, it needs to be restored first:

```
USE [master]
RESTORE DATABASE [RevoTestDB] FROM  DISK =
N'C:\SQLServer2017MLServicesR\CH03\RevoTestDB.bak';
GO
```

After the restore, we will see the loads against the database and how to govern resources:

```
USE RevoTestDB;
GO

-- TEST query
EXECUTE   sp_execute_external_script
               @language = N'R'
               ,@script = N'
          library(RevoScaleR)
f <- formula(as.numeric(ArrDelay) ~ as.numeric(DayOfWeek) + CRSDepTime)
s <- system.time(mod <- rxLinMod(formula = f, data = AirLine))
          OutputDataSet <-  data.frame(system_time = s[3]);'
               ,@input_data_1 = N'SELECT * FROM AirlineDemoSmall'
               ,@input_data_1_name = N'AirLine'
WITH RESULT SETS ((Elapsed_time FLOAT));
```

With this test query on my computer, the whole running time was 21 seconds and with elapsed time returned from R Engine, of 1.43 seconds.

Setting up the Resource Governer to tackle picks and spikes. To have execution operations running faster when needed or when running a higher amount of data, we need to configure the external resource pool and the resource pool to grant the resources:

```
-- Default value
ALTER EXTERNAL RESOURCE POOL [default]
WITH (AFFINITY CPU = AUTO)
GO

CREATE EXTERNAL RESOURCE POOL RService_Resource_Pool
WITH (
      MAX_CPU_PERCENT = 10
      ,MAX_MEMORY_PERCENT = 5
);

ALTER RESOURCE POOL [default] WITH (max_memory_percent = 60,
max_cpu_percent=90);
ALTER EXTERNAL RESOURCE POOL [default] WITH (max_memory_percent = 40,
max_cpu_percent=10);
ALTER RESOURCE GOVERNOR reconfigure;

ALTER RESOURCE GOVERNOR RECONFIGURE;
GO
```

In the last step, a classification function must be created and reconfigured:

```
CREATE FUNCTION RG_Class_function()
RETURNS sysname
WITH schemabinding
AS
BEGIN
    IF program_name() in ('Microsoft R Host', 'RStudio') RETURN
'R_workgroup';
    RETURN 'default'
    END;
GO

ALTER RESOURCE GOVERNOR WITH  (classifier_function =
dbo.RG_Class_function);
ALTER RESOURCE GOVERNOR reconfigure;
GO
```

After that, I can run the same query again:

```
-- TEST 2 - performance normal; with governor enabled
EXECUTE   sp_execute_external_script
                  @language = N'R'
,@script = N'
library(RevoScaleR)
f <- formula(as.numeric(ArrDelay) ~ as.numeric(DayOfWeek) + CRSDepTime)
s <- system.time(mod <- rxLinMod(formula = f, data = AirLine))
OutputDataSet<-  data.frame(system_time = s[3]);'
,@input_data_1 = N'SELECT * FROM AirlineDemoSmall'
,@input_data_1_name = N'AirLine'
WITH RESULT SETS ((Elapsed_time FLOAT));
```

In the end, the comparison in performance is obvious. In the case of my test environment, because I dedicated more CPU and RAM resources to executing R code, I get a running time of three seconds with an R elapsed time of 0.63 seconds. Results on your client might be different, but the change from the default resource governor settings to new settings should be very obvious.

Installing new R packages

An R package is a container of functions that serve a particular purpose with the relevant binary source code (usually C, C++, or Fortran), documentation, and sample data. A package is a collection of these files that reside in a library folder. If you navigate to your R library folder, you will see all the packages installed for your R Engine. A package might also be called a binary package or a tarball, depending on the operating system.

A package is not equivalent to a library, nor should it be mistaken for one. In the R language, when installing a package the command `install.packages` is used. A `library()` is a function that loads functions in particular packages into your R environment. Deriving from the Windows OS, shared objects are called **Dynamic-link** library's (**DLLs**). Hence, the word library is used and refers to common and shared objects. So, to load a package into your R environment, the function `library()` is used, with the name of the package specified in brackets.

Referring to an R library in an R script is super easy; simply add the library or use the `require()` method. But in the system, the library must be, in the first place, installed.

Libraries are installed by installing packages available in common repositories, such as CRAN, Biocondutor, GitHub, and MRAN in the case of the Microsoft repository. In the R language, a library is installed by invoking the following command:

```
install.packages("Package_Name")
```

In SQL Server 2016, the installation of such packages was not possible by running an R script with an external stored procedure and the code returned an error, as follows:

```
--Install Package using sp_execute_external_script
EXECUTE sp_execute_external_script
        @language = N'R'
 ,@script = N'install.packages("AUC")'
```

This T-SQL code returns an error, saying that this package is not available for my R version. However, we will later see how to install the same package:

```
STDERR message(s) from external script:
Warning: unable to access index for repository https://mran.microsoft.com/snapshot/2017-05-01/src/contrib:
  cannot open URL 'https://mran.microsoft.com/snapshot/2017-05-01/src/contrib/PACKAGES'
Warning: unable to access index for repository http://www.stats.ox.ac.uk/pub/RWin/src/contrib:
  cannot open URL 'http://www.stats.ox.ac.uk/pub/RWin/src/contrib/PACKAGES'
Warning: unable to access index for repository https://mran.microsoft.com/snapshot/2017-05-01/bin/windows/contrib/3.3:
  cannot open URL 'https://mran.microsoft.com/snapshot/2017-05-01/bin/windows/contrib/3.3/PACKAGES'
Warning: unable to access index for repository http://www.stats.ox.ac.uk/pub/RWin/bin/windows/contrib/3.3:
  cannot open URL 'http://www.stats.ox.ac.uk/pub/RWin/bin/windows/contrib/3.3/PACKAGES'
Warning message:
package 'AUC' is not available (for R version 3.3.3)
```

Figure 11: Warning message while installing AUC package

So, we can extend the original stored procedure, as follows:

```
EXECUTE sp_execute_external_script
        @language = N'R'
 ,@script = N'    library(Hmisc)
                u <- unlist(rcorr(Customers_by_invoices$InvoiceV,
Customers_by_invoices$CustCat, type="spearman"))
statistical_significance<-as.character(u[10])
OutputDataSet <- data.frame(statistical_significance)'

 ,@input_data_1 = N'SELECT
SUM(il.Quantity) AS InvoiceQ
 ,SUM(il.ExtendedPrice) AS InvoiceV
 ,c.CustomerID AS Customer
 ,c.CustomerCategoryID AS CustCat


                                   FROM sales.InvoiceLines AS il
                                   INNER JOIN sales.Invoices AS i
```

```
                                      ON il.InvoiceID = i.InvoiceID
                                      INNER JOIN sales.Customers AS c
                                      ON c.CustomerID = i.CustomerID
                                      GROUP BY
        c.CustomerID
        ,c.CustomerCategoryID'

        ,@input_data_1_name = N'Customers_by_invoices'

        WITH RESULT SETS (( statistical_significance FLOAT(20) ));
        GO
```

If we do this, we will be able to calculate the statistical significance for the correlation between two variables. The point here is that we are referring to the R function library(Hmisc) with the appropriate package name. The following is the detailed part of the script:

```
        -- part of R script with reference to call method library
        ,@script = N'    library(Hmisc)
                        u <- unlist(rcorr(Customers_by_invoices$InvoiceV,
        Customers_by_invoices$CustCat, type="spearman"))
        statistical_significance <-as.character(u[10])
        OutputDataSet <- data.frame(statistical_significance)'
```

When referring to a library, we need to have the package already preinstalled; otherwise, you will receive an error stating that the package does not exist. The same error will be received if you misspell the package name and, since the R language is case-sensitive, in the case of the Hmisc package, an error will occur when mistyping it as hmisc (without the capital letter H):

```
Msg 39004, Level 16, State 20, Line 9
A 'R' script error occurred during execution of 'sp_execute_external_script' with HRESULT 0x80004004.
Msg 39019, Level 16, State 2, Line 9
An external script error occurred:
Error in library(Hmisc) : there is no package called 'Hmisc'
Calls: source -> withVisible -> eval -> eval -> library

Error in execution. Check the output for more information.
Error in eval(expr, envir, enclos) :
  Error in execution. Check the output for more information.
Calls: source -> withVisible -> eval -> eval -> .Call
Execution halted
```

Figure 12

Package information

Packages are always saved in the `library` folder but, depending on your version of R (Open, Client, or Server), SQL Server instance names and paths can be different.

In general, the Client or Server versions will store your libraries on your main drive. For the Client version, the default path is `C:\Program Files\Microsoft\R Client\R_SERVER\library`. You can see the folder contents in the following screenshot:

Figure 13

In the R Server version, you will find libraries on the path of your default SQL Server instance: `C:\Program Files\Microsoft SQL Server\MSSQL14.MSSQLSERVER\R_SERVICES\library`. The following are the contents of a Server installation:

Figure 14

Sub-folders represent the name of installed and available packages. To find the default path to your packages, you can execute the following code:

```
-- Path to libraries on your computer/server
EXECUTE sp_execute_external_script
        @language = N'R'
,@script = N'OutputDataSet <- data.frame(.libPaths());'
WITH RESULT SETS (([DefaultLibraryName] VARCHAR(MAX) NOT NULL));
GO
```

In my case, the following is the default path for R packages in the R Server edition:

Figure 15

Much more information can be retrieved using the R function `installed.packages()`. In this example, we extract much more information on packages and insert the information into a SQL Server table:

```
-- You can create a table for libraries and populate all the necessary
information
CREATE TABLE dbo.Libraries
        (
                ID INT IDENTITY NOT NULL CONSTRAINT PK_RLibraries PRIMARY
KEY CLUSTERED
,Package NVARCHAR(50)
,LibPath NVARCHAR(200)
,[Version] NVARCHAR(20)
,Depends NVARCHAR(200)
,Imports NVARCHAR(200)
,Suggests NVARCHAR(200)
,Built NVARCHAR(20)
        )

INSERT INTO dbo.Libraries
EXECUTE sp_execute_external_script
            @language = N'R'
,@script=N'x <- data.frame(installed.packages())
OutputDataSet <- x[,c(1:3,5,6,8,16)]'


SELECT * FROM dbo.Libraries
DROP TABLE dbo.Libraries
```

By querying this table, you get information on library dependencies, versions, imports, and builds in one execution of `sp_execute_external_script`:

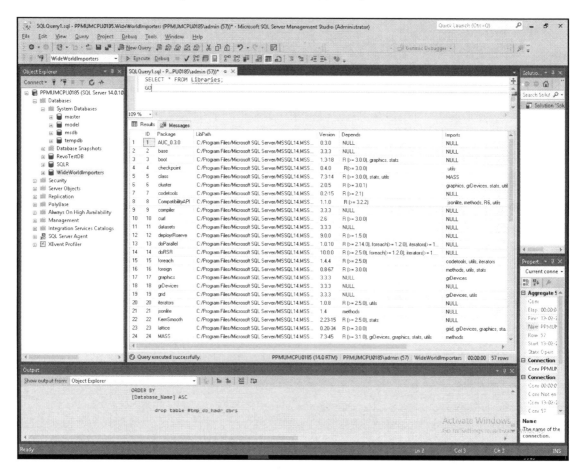

Figure 16

In the following, we will explore how to install missing R packages. With SQL Server 2016 there were several ways (official or unofficial) which will be addressed and with SQL Server 2017, we have an elegant way of using `rxInstall` package or creating an external library. Both new ways introduced in SQL Server 2017 are far better, safer, and faster ways to install missing packages.

Using R Tools for Visual Studio (RTVS) 2015 or higher

With SQL Server 2016, Microsoft recommended installing missing packages through RTVS. The user should have installed RTVS (`https://www.visualstudio.com/vs/rtvs/`) on a client in order to install packages. Check the default paths:

```
sessionInfo()
.libPaths()
```

This also returns the paths to the library folders on my machine-for R Server (by default `C:/Program Files/Microsoft SQL Server/MSSQL14.MSSQLSERVER/R_SERVICES/library`) and for the user (`C:/Users/Tomaz/Documents/R/win-library/3.2`) who is currently using RTVS:

```
locale:
[1] LC_COLLATE=Slovenian_Slovenia.1250  LC_CTYPE=Slovenian_Slovenia.852     LC_MONETARY=Slovenian_Slovenia.1250 LC_NUMERIC=C
[5] LC_TIME=Slovenian_Slovenia.1250

attached base packages:
[1] stats     graphics  grDevices utils     datasets  methods   base

other attached packages:
[1] RevoUtilsMath_8.0.3 RevoUtils_8.0.3     RevoMods_8.0.3      RevoScaleR_8.0.3    lattice_0.20-33     rpart_4.1-10

loaded via a namespace (and not attached):
[1] tools_3.2.2      codetools_0.2-14 rtvs_1.0.0.0      grid_3.2.2        iterators_1.0.8  foreach_1.4.3
[1] "C:/Users/SI01017988/Documents/R/win-library/3.2"                   "C:/Program Files/Microsoft SQL Server/MSSQL13.MSSQLSERVER/R_SERVICES/library"
>
```

Figure 17

Checking the **Options...** section:

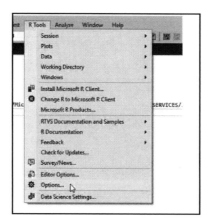

Figure 18

Then select **R Tools** | **Advanced** (as shown next):

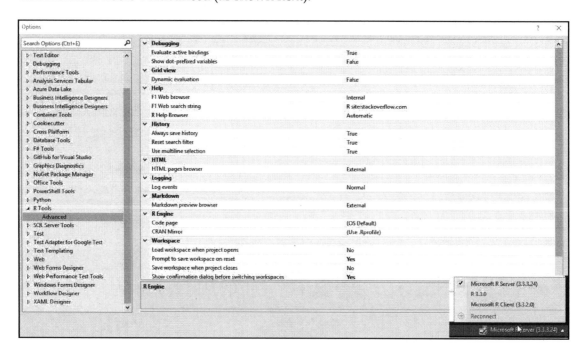

Figure 19

You will see that the **R Engine** has a path defined. This path is the root path for installing R packages. R packages are installed under the subfolder-library (`C:\Program Files\Microsoft SQL Server\MSSQL14.MSSQLSERVER\R_SERVICES\Library`).

So, by running `install.packages("AUC")`, I can see that the server path was ignored and the library was installed into the user specified folder:

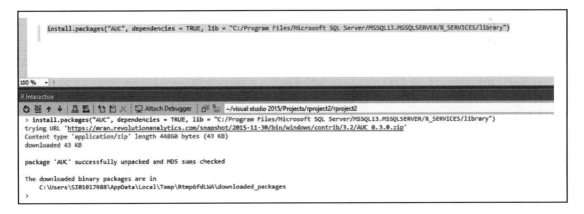

install.packages("AUC", dependencies = TRUE)

Figure 20

To install the package in the R Server folder, you need to have administrator-level access or have an administrator do it for you. Microsoft has discussed this issue on MSDN (`https://docs.microsoft.com/en-us/sql/advanced-analytics/r/installing-and-managing-r-packages`). Running Visual Studio and RTVS as an administrator does not change the result. To avoid this problem, you need to declare the path to the library folder of the R Server where you want package to be installed:

```
install.packages("AUC", dependencies = TRUE, lib = "C:/Program
Files/Microsoft SQL Server/MSSQL14.MSSQLSERVER/R_SERVICES/library")
```

The package will automatically be installed in the R Server repository folder:

install.packages("AUC", dependencies = TRUE, lib = "C:/Program Files/Microsoft SQL Server/MSSQL13.MSSQLSERVER/R_SERVICES/library")

100 %

R Interactive

Attach Debugger   ~/visual studio 2015/Projects/rproject2/rproject2

```
> install.packages("AUC", dependencies = TRUE, lib = "C:/Program Files/Microsoft SQL Server/MSSQL13.MSSQLSERVER/R_SERVICES/library")
trying URL 'https://mran.revolutionanalytics.com/snapshot/2015-11-30/bin/windows/contrib/3.2/AUC_0.3.0.zip'
Content type 'application/zip' length 44860 bytes (43 KB)
downloaded 43 KB

package 'AUC' successfully unpacked and MD5 sums checked

The downloaded binary packages are in
    C:\Users\SI01017988\AppData\Local\Temp\Rtmp6fdLWA\downloaded_packages
>
```

Figure 21

Using R.exe in CMD

When executing `R.exe` as an administrator in the binary folder of R Server (`C:\Program Files\Microsoft SQL Server\MSSQL14.MSSQLSERVER\R_SERVICES\bin`), you will be prompted with a command window:

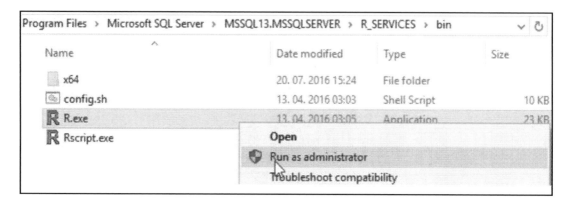

Figure 22

From there, the user can always install the missing package.

```
install.packages("AUC")
```

Using XP_CMDSHELL

This method is by far the fastest and is very useful when sharing T-SQL code, but it compromises using the command shell and many users and DBAs are not keen on this. By enabling `xp_cmdshell` in configurations and using this stored procedure, you can install any missing package. Using code with the −e switch, you can easily install the library:

```
R cmd -e install.packages("Hmisc")
```

The following code will install the missing package on the R Server:

```
-- enable xp_cmdshell
EXECUTE SP_CONFIGURE 'xp_cmdshell','1';
GO
RECONFIGURE;
GO
EXEC xp_cmdshell '"C:\Program Files\Microsoft SQL
Server\MSSQL14.MSSQLSERVER\R_SERVICES\bin\R.EXE"cmd -e
```

```
install.packages(''Hmisc'')';
GO
```

Running Vanilla R and adding the `install.packages()` function can be done if the user has been granted the permission. The results are as follows:

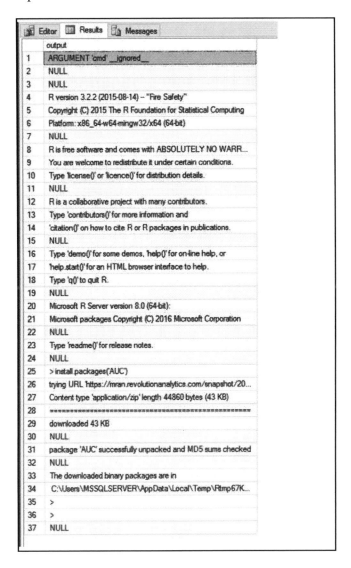

Figure 23

Using CMD and the -e switch, the deployment and computation of R code can be executed and simplified, but since this is not an official way I would not suggest using this, since it exposes security issues.

Copying files

Copying files may sound a bit strange at first glance but, for the majority of packages, copying the complete library folder to the destination folder will also do the job. Imagine being a system administrator responsible for configuring a new R environment or sandbox. In this scenario, you don't want to run hundreds of lines of code to install all the needed packages; so, you would just copy/paste the folders from an image or backup. This would be a hundred times faster and much more convenient. Also, the packages would be already tested with R Engine.

Using a simple copy/paste, drag, and drop opretion, I copied and installed the, acepack package in my R Client environment (copied from R Server):

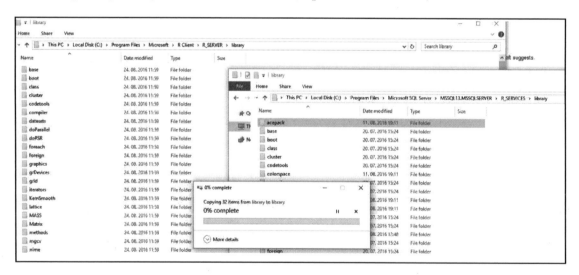

Figure 24

Using the rxInstallPackages function

With the new version of SQL Server R Services for SQL Server 2017, a very much needed R function-in the `RevoScaleR` package-has been made publicly available. With the `rxInstallPackages` function, a user will be capable of installing any additional R package for a desired computational context.

With the following code, one can really speed up the installation of packages, without worrying about workarounds, opening additional tools, or anything else.

Running code from RTVS looks as follows:

```
RSQLServicesCC <- RxInSqlServer(connectionString = "Driver=SQL
Server;Server=myServer;Database=TestDB;Trusted_Connection=True;")
rxInstallPackages("AUC", verbose = TRUE, scope = "private", computeContext
= RSQLServicesCC)
```

Running the same code from SQL Server is as follows:

```
EXECUTE sp_execute_external_script
     @language = N'R'
          ,@script = N'

          packagesToInstall <- c("caret","tree","party")
library(MicrosoftML)
          RSqlServerCC <- RxInSqlServer(connectionString = "Driver=SQL
Server; +Server=SICN-KASTRUN\\SQLSERVER2017C2;Database=SQLR;
+Trusted_Connection=True;")
          rxInstallPackages(pkgs = packagesToInstall, owner = '', +scope
= "shared", computeContext = "SqlServerCC");';
GO
```

This is way too easy to be true, but it is. Make sure to do couple of things prior to running this code:

- Set the compute environment to where your packages are installed
- Set up the correct permissions and access
- Check up on the TCP/IP protocols

In the `rxInstallPackages` function, use the `computeContext` parameter to set either `Local` or your `SqlServer` environment; you can also use scope as shared or private (the difference is that, if you install a package as shared, it can be used by different users across different databases). You can also specify the owner if you are running this command out of the `db_owner` role.

Managing SQL Server R Services with PowerShell

PowerShell is very useful for managing remote machines, virtual machines, or even Azure VM machines. Besides this common administrative work, it has many other positive and useful benefits.

One can list, schedule, or work with any task-scheduled jobs or SQL Server jobs, based on what jobs you need to be running, and how, let's say daily for fetching data or recalculating and initializing predictive models, to even running models.

Another very useful aspect of PowerShell can be API communication within different environments and systems.

For system administrators, PowerShell will be very useful for distributing and maintaining any additional R packages among client machines or even among R Server servers.

Getting to know the sp_execute_external_script external procedure

SP_EXECUTE_EXTERNAL_SCRIPT is a stored procedure that executes a provided script as an argument on an external script to a provided language (in this case, the R language). With SQL Server 2017, Python is also supported and it is said that, in the future, other languages, such as Java, C#, and C++, will be supported (through Launchpad).

sp_execute_external_script is a system procedure that evokes and sends the passed code to an external engine and returns the result to SQL Server in the form of a table. Script has a set of arguments that will navigate to T-SQL code and data to R Engine, with R code included.

The following arguments are available:

```
sp_execute_external_script
     @language = N''
,@script = N'',
,@input_data_1 =  'input_data_1'
,@input_data_1_name =  N'input_data_1_name'
,@output_data_1_name = 'output_data_1_name'
,@parallel = 0 | 1
,@params =  N''
,@parameter1 = ''
```

Arguments

- `@language`: This specifies which language will be used in the external procedure. For SQL Server 2016, the R language is available and with SQL Server 2017 Python is available. The argument is of the `sysname` build-in data type and has a limit of 128 Unicode characters. This is why we use N in front of the value, to denote the `nvarchar` type.

- `@script`: Native R or Python code is passed with this argument to the Launchpad service. This external code (external to SQL Server) must be validated and properly formatted (only in the case of Python), since SSMS or RTVS will not validate this argument. Therefore, the easiest way to do this is to use Visual Studio and validate your R code in RTVS or your Python code with **Python Tools for Visual Studio (PTVS)**. This field is of the `nvarchar` type.

- `@input_data_1`: This takes your T-SQL code as the source of data for an external procedure. This code will be validated and checked by SSMS or VS. This field is also the `nvarchar` type and can execute literally any T-SQL code. There are a few limitations as to what data types can be inputted, because of external engine (the R language) limitations. The R language itself supports fewer data types as compared with SQL Server 2016. Data types supported are logical, numeric, integer, complex, character, and raw. So immediately, one can see that the following data types (unless converted to the R data type) will deliver some problems. Let's just state a few SQL Server data types:
    - `Cursor`
    - `Timestamp` (hash format not date time format)
    - `Datetime2`, `datetimeoffset`, `time`
    - All Unicode text data types: `nvarchar`, `nchar`, `ntext`
    - `Sql_variant`
    - `Text`, `image`
    - `XML` (includingJSON, as it is an XML datatype format in SQL Server 2017)
    - `Hierarchy`, `geometry`, `geography`
    - Any CLR or assembly bound data type built using the .NET framework or any Launchpad service-supported language

In addition to some of the data types' limitations, there are also T-SQL clauses and statements that cannot be used as part of the input data argument. These are as follows:

- Stored procedure (UDF, Table value functions))
- Logical IF and WHILE, FOR loops
- Temporary variables or tables
- No updates, inserts, or deletes (only select)
- GO statements or semicolons
- OUTPUT clauses from and DML statements
- Referencing any CURSORS

The following statements (besides the SELECT statement) can be used:

- SELECT with multiple JOINS
- WITHcommontable expressions
- UNION, UNIONALL, EXCEPT, INTERSECT
- Any SET, STRING, LOGICAL, COMPARISON, BITWISE, ARITHMETIC, COMPOUND operators
- COLLATE

As already mentioned DML statements, @input_data_1 argument also does not support any DDL statement or clause.

To avoid the data type collisions between the T-SQL language and external scripts, the best practice is to do as much data preparation, wrangling, and optimization as possible prior to throwing the desired dataset into the argument. Also, many restrictions can be compromised with conversion to the R closed data type.

- @input_data_1_name:This holds the name of the dataset that will be used in the R script as an input dataset. By default, the external procedure sp_execute_external_script will be using the following:-InputDataSet for inputting data and-OutputDataSet for returning result data (both are default values). Please note that the R language is case-sensitive, so the name of your dataset provided in this argument must be written in the same manner also in R code.

- `@output_data_1_name`:This argument holds the definition of the returned result from an external script as a variable returned to any stored procedure. The returned dataset must be in the `data.frame` format in the R language. Data.frame is a set of vectors and is a representation of a table, which T-SQL Server can import and use further with any other T-SQL clause or statement: or it can store the results directly into SQL Server table. This argument is a `sysname` data type.

- `@parallel`:This is an argument that will explicitly tell the R Engine to parallelize computations in R. This parameter has been introduced with later versions of SQL Server 2016 (SP/CU) and is very welcome for any type of R code, functions, or packages that do not use parallelism for `RevoScaleR` computational functions. Of course, this is true in relation to trivial R scripts and in the case of large input datasets. R functions from a particular R package will deliver much better performance results if the package itself is written in C++ (and not the original Fortran) and, if the R script does not include relatively complex data wrangling/munching instructions, in particular and of `plyr/dplyr` or `data.table` function. Just remember the simpler, the better.

To check whether the workload can be distributed in parallel, simply observe the execution plans and look for degrees of parallelism in the plan when running T-SQL code. Also note that any local setting of MAXDOP will also have an effect on the desired parallelism. In other words, if MAXDOP is turned off, and you set your argument `@parallel = 1`, do not expect much of a distributed workload, since parallelism is by default turned off.

When running and using any of the computational functions available in the `RevoScaleR` package, Launchpad will automatically take care of parallelism, using distribute R functions, available in R Server or SQL Server R Services.

- `@params`: This is an argument where any additional variable can be declared and specified as a variable(s) that can be used in the R script. The parameters can be specified as input or output and are very handy when feeding the predictive model to your R code or when exporting additional information from R code (besides the specified results set). Using this parameter as an output can return a single value/column and not a table.

- `@parameter1`: This is an argument where the values of the parameters are specified and used within the R script in the form of an input or output variable.

Summary

This chapter has covered the installation of Machine Learning Services (in-database), the configuration of the services and how to administrate the services. It has also explored the installation of missing packages and covered security and the resource governor. In the last section, the chapter also gives an explanation of how to use external procedures and the `sp_execute_external_script` with all arguments. Several examples have been covered through digging into security issues and the installation of missing packages. The installation of missing packages was heavily dependent on the article in SQLServerCentral.

An introduction to machine learning services and using an external procedure will be the foundation for all of the following chapters, which will all heavily rely on a good understanding of configuring and using this procedure.

4

Data Exploration and Data Visualization

Data Exploration and Data Visualization techniques are essential to understanding data before one can implement predictive modeling. With existing open source R packages for statistical and mathematical algorithms, data professionals can easily explore their data and discover patterns/trends that are otherwise challenging to do in a relational database. Using SQL Server **Machine Learning Services** (**ML Services**) with R means that data exploration and data visualization are no longer siloed work, leading to faster and easier paths to predictive modeling.

This chapter outlines essential tips and tricks developers must know for data exploration and data visualization using R. You will learn how to integrate R for data exploration and data visualization in T-SQL and then stitch these techniques in SSRS and Power BI. If you are already familiar with R for data exploration and data visualization, feel free to skip to the last section of this chapter.

Understanding SQL and R data types

Before we dive into exploring data using R in T-SQL, let's get started with understanding data types to store data in R. The first and most important data type to be familiar with when working with R in T-SQL is data frame. The input and output parameters of `sp_execute_external_script` in SQL Server received and sent from R are data frames. Other data types that are important to know for data munging, and that are very similar to data frame, are matrix and data table, which are beyond the scope of this chapter.

Aside from data frame, R supports a limited number of scalar data types such as character, complex, date/time, integer, logical, numeric, and raw. Thus, when you provide data from SQL Server in R Scripts, when necessary the data will be implicitly converted to a compatible data type in R. When a conversion cannot be performed automatically, R will return Unhandled SQL data type. The following table provides a short example of data type conversion. For more information about implicit data type conversion, please visit *R Libraries and R Data Types* at https://docs.microsoft.com/en-us/sql/advanced-analytics/r/r-libraries-and-data-types#changes-in-data-types-between-sql-server-2016-and-earlier-versions:

SQL Server Data Type (input parameters to sp_execute_external_script)	R Class	RESULT SET Data Type (output parameters to sp_execute_external_script)
datetime	POSIXct	Datetime
numeric(p,s)	numeric	float
int	integer	int
varbinary(n)	raw	varbinary(max)
varchar(n)	character	varchar(max)

Data frames in R

A data frame contains rows and columns, just like a table in SQL Server, where each column can have different basic data types, for example integer, character, and so on.

Use ? to learn more about a function:
? [function]

For more information about data frames, you can type the following command in **R Tools for Visual Studio (RTVS)**, R Studio, or your other favorite R IDE:

```
> ? data.frame
```

By default, R uses memory. So once the input data frame is passed from sp_execute_external_script, R will store the input data in memory. Machine Learning Services (In-Database) is managed by Resource Governor in SQL Server as discussed in Chapter 3, *Managing Machine Learning Services for SQL Server 2017 and R*.

A general guideline is to strive for a good balance between what types of computation should be done in SQL Server VS in R. This includes whether to do data munging/manipulation in R vs in SQL Server.

There are some built-in data frames available in R, such as `mtcars` or `iris`.

Let's take a look at a data frame in R. Run the following code in RTVS:

```
> mtcars;
```

The output should be like this:

```
  mtcars;
                     mpg cyl  disp  hp drat    wt  qsec vs am gear carb
Mazda RX4           21.0   6 160.0 110 3.90 2.620 16.46  0  1    4    4
Mazda RX4 Wag       21.0   6 160.0 110 3.90 2.875 17.02  0  1    4    4
Datsun 710          22.8   4 108.0  93 3.08 2.320 18.61  1  1    4    1
Hornet 4 Drive      21.4   6 258.0 110 3.08 3.215 19.44  1  0    3    1
Hornet Sportabout   18.7   8 360.0 175 3.15 3.440 17.02  0  0    3    2
Valiant             18.1   6 225.0 105 2.76 3.460 20.22  1  0    3    1
Duster 360          14.3   8 360.0 245 3.21 3.570 15.84  0  0    3    4
Merc 240D           24.4   4 146.7  62 3.69 3.190 20.00  1  0    4    2
Merc 230            22.8   4 140.8  95 3.92 3.150 22.90  1  0    4    2
Merc 280            19.2   6 167.6 123 3.92 3.440 18.30  1  0    4    4
Merc 280C           17.8   6 167.6 123 3.92 3.440 18.90  1  0    4    4
Merc 450SE          16.4   8 275.8 180 3.07 4.070 17.40  0  0    3    3
Merc 450SL          17.3   8 275.8 180 3.07 3.730 17.60  0  0    3    3
Merc 450SLC         15.2   8 275.8 180 3.07 3.780 18.00  0  0    3    3
Cadillac Fleetwood  10.4   8 472.0 205 2.93 5.250 17.98  0  0    3    4
Lincoln Continental 10.4   8 460.0 215 3.00 5.424 17.82  0  0    3    4
Chrysler Imperial   14.7   8 440.0 230 3.23 5.345 17.42  0  0    3    4
Fiat 128            32.4   4  78.7  66 4.08 2.200 19.47  1  1    4    1
Honda Civic         30.4   4  75.7  52 4.93 1.615 18.52  1  1    4    2
Toyota Corolla      33.9   4  71.1  65 4.22 1.835 19.90  1  1    4    1
Toyota Corona       21.5   4 120.1  97 3.70 2.465 20.01  1  0    3    1
Dodge Challenger    15.5   8 318.0 150 2.76 3.520 16.87  0  0    3    2
AMC Javelin         15.2   8 304.0 150 3.15 3.435 17.30  0  0    3    2
Camaro Z28          13.3   8 350.0 245 3.73 3.840 15.41  0  0    3    4
Pontiac Firebird    19.2   8 400.0 175 3.08 3.845 17.05  0  0    3    2
Fiat X1-9           27.3   4  79.0  66 4.08 1.935 18.90  1  1    4    1
Porsche 914-2       26.0   4 120.3  91 4.43 2.140 16.70  0  1    5    2
Lotus Europa        30.4   4  95.1 113 3.77 1.513 16.90  1  1    5    2
Ford Pantera L      15.8   8 351.0 264 4.22 3.170 14.50  0  1    5    4
Ferrari Dino        19.7   6 145.0 175 3.62 2.770 15.50  0  1    5    6
Maserati Bora       15.0   8 301.0 335 3.54 3.570 14.60  0  1    5    8
Volvo 142E          21.4   4 121.0 109 4.11 2.780 18.60  1  1    4    2
```

Figure 4.1 - mtcars data

To check the data type, you can call the function `call` on the variable:

```
> class(mtcars);
[1] "data.frame"
```

Data exploration and data munging

Data munging in R can be done independently without using SQL Server. The following diagram illustrates a recommended high-level process that developers can follow when using SQL Server and R. If you have worked in R before, you are likely familiar with steps 2, 3, and 5 performed in R directly.

Please note that Steps 3 and 4 are optional and will be discussed more in `Chapter` 6, *Predictive Modeling* and `Chapter 7`, *Operationalizing R Code*:

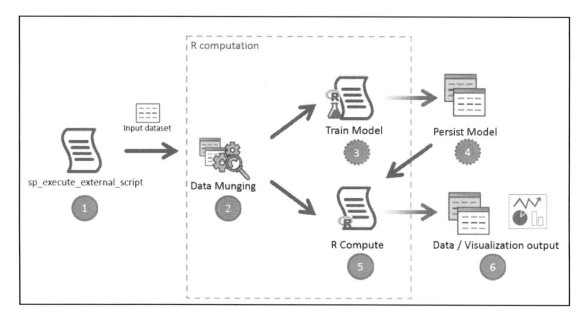

Figure 4.2 - High-Level Development Process for SQL Server Machine Learning Services with R

Let's get started with *Data Munging in R*. Specifically, in this section, we will be working with the R environment so that we know how it works in R before we stitch it together with T-SQL. If you are familiar with R, you may skip this section. Following are prerequisites for this section:

1. An R IDE, for example RTVS as part of Visual Studio 2015 or 2017. For more information about RTVS, please visit `http://aka.ms/rtvs`.

2. The `WideWorldImporters` database restored to SQL Server 2016 or above. Please refer to `http://aka.ms/wwi` to download the full SQL backup files that you can restore in your environment.

Importing SQL Server data into R

The most common way to connect to SQL Server from R is by using the RODBC package. Please note that prior to SQL Server 2016, this is the step that you'll likely need to work with.

In the example below, we want to retrieve a data set related to Sales Person Monthly Orders in 2015 from a SQL Server instance, MsSQLGirl; and a database, WideWorldImporters using a trusted connection (Windows Authentication).

Using RTVS, perform the steps mentioned as follows:

1. Create a new script called Chapter04_01.R. Ensure that the RODBC library is loaded by typing the following:

   ```
   library(RODBC);
   ```

2. Define the connection string and get the connection handle:

   ```
   connStr <- "Driver=SQL Server;Server=MsSQLGirl;
     Database=WideWorldImporters;trusted_connection=true";
   dbHandle <- odbcDriverConnect(connStr);
   ```

3. Define the query that you want to run in SQL Server. This can also be a query to call stored procedures, functions, views and so on. In this specific example, the query will get the Monthly Orders in 2015 by Sales Person:

   ```
   # Define the query to be run
   order_query =
   "SELECT DATEFROMPARTS(YEAR(o.[OrderDate]),
         MONTH(o.[OrderDate]), 1) AS OrderMonth,
       sp.[PreferredName] AS SalesPerson,
       COUNT(DISTINCT o.[OrderID]) AS OrderCount,
       SUM(ol.[Quantity] * ol.[UnitPrice]) AS TotalAmount
   FROM [Sales].[Orders] o
       INNER JOIN[Sales] .[OrderLines] ol
           ON ol.[OrderID] = o.[OrderID]
       INNER JOIN[Application] .[People] sp
           ON sp.[PersonID] = o.[SalespersonPersonID]
   WHERE sp.[ValidTo] >= GETDATE()
       AND o.[OrderDate] BETWEEN '20150101' AND '20151231'
   GROUP BY
   DATEFROMPARTS(YEAR(o.[OrderDate]),
   MONTH(o.[OrderDate]), 1),
       sp.[PreferredName];"
   ```

4. Execute the query and store the output into `orders` variable:

```
# Get the data set from SQL into the orders variable in R
orders <- sqlQuery(dbHandle, order_query);
```

5. Type the following to see the dataset in `orders`:

```
orders;
```

Or alternatively in RTVS go to the **Variable Explorer** window as shown in *Figure 4 - 2* and expand orders to see the details of the variable. Use the magnifying glass tool (🔍) to see the output as shown in *Figure 4 - 3*:

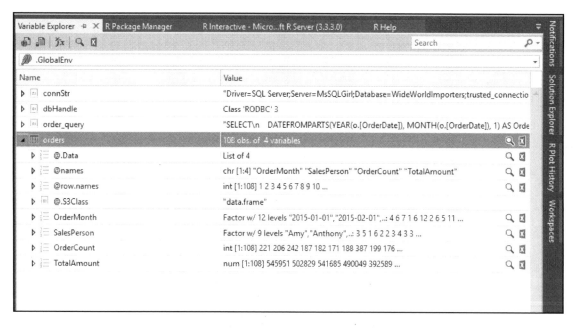

Figure 4 - 3 Variable Explorer in RTVS

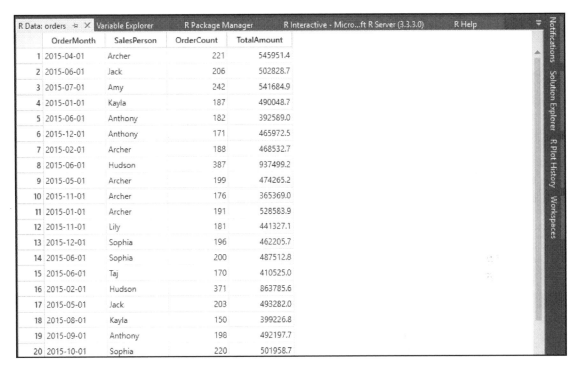

Figure 4 - 4 Viewing orders in Variable Explorer

Here is a data dictionary of the `orders` variable. It's useful to be familiar with the following columns as we will be using the orders data frame and its derived variables in this chapter:

Column Names	Description
OrderMonth	The month that the orders take place
OrderCount	The number of orders in the month for the Sales person.
TotalAmount	The order dollar amount
SalesPerson	The name of the Sales Person

Exploring data in R

There are a number of ways to explore data in R: following are some useful functions. `df` denotes a data frame variable and `col` denotes a column in `df`:

- `head(df)` returns the first few rows of the data frame `df`, by default 6.
- `tail(df)` returns the last few rows of the data frame `df`, by default 6.
- `summary(df)` provides basic summary statistics for each column in the data frame `df`.
- `names(df)` returns the column name of the data frame `df`.
- `str(df)` returns basic information about the data frame `df`.
- `describe(df$col)` describes the distribution/skewness of a set of `col` values in `df` data frame. This can be quite powerful for constructing scales and item analysis. This requires the `psych` package to be installed first.
- Following is an example of using the function `str` against the data frame `orders`:

  ```
  > str(orders)
  ```

This is how the output looks:

```
> str(orders)
'data.frame':    108 obs. of  4 variables:
 $ OrderMonth : Factor w/ 12 levels "2015-01-01","2015-02-01",..: 4 6 7 1 6 12 2 6 5 11 ...
 $ SalesPerson: Factor w/ 9 levels "Amy","Anthony",..: 3 5 1 6 2 2 3 4 3 3 ...
 $ OrderCount : int  221 206 242 187 182 171 188 387 199 176 ...
 $ TotalAmount: num  545951 502829 541685 490049 392589 ...
```

Figure 4-5 The Output of str(orders)

Unlike SQL Server, R is case-sensitive for both functions and variables. Ensure that you type them correctly.

Data munging in R

Data munging is the manual process of transforming one *raw* format into another format so that it is more consumable, either by humans or the next processes such as reporting, data visualization, statistical analysis, predictive analysis, and many more.

There are numerous R packages that are available for Data Munging. R comes preloaded with packages for simple data transformation and visualization. In this section, you will learn two super powerful packages that are commonly used for data munging: `dplyr`, `reshape`, and `lubridate`.

Adding/removing rows/columns in data frames

Adding or removing rows or columns can be achieved easily. Following is a list of examples showing how you can achieve it with R as well as using `dplyr`:

1. **Adding new rows**: Let's create a new data frame, `orders_newrows`, which contain 2 new rows that we want to append to the end of `orders`. Then we want to see the last few rows of `orders`, using the `tail` function:

```
> orders_newrows <- data.frame(
    OrderMonth = c("2015-12-01", "2015-12-01"),
    SalesPerson = c("Julie", "Tomaz"),
    OrderCount = c(201, 2017),
    TotalAmount = c(340000, 370000));

> orders <- rbind(orders, orders_newrows);
> tail(orders);
```

This will trigger the following output:

```
    OrderMonth SalesPerson OrderCount TotalAmount
105 2015-12-01        Lily        194    442645.5
106 2015-03-01      Hudson        389   1020488.6
107 2015-10-01         Taj        195    437388.4
108 2015-08-01        Lily        182    517126.3
109 2015-12-01       Julie        201    340000.0
110 2015-12-01       Tomaz       2017    370000.0
```

Using `dplyr`, you can call `bind_rows` to append multiple data frames. For example, the following displays `orders` and `orders_newrows` appended twice:

```
> bind_rows(orders, orders_newrows, orders_newrows);
```

2. **Adding new columns**: To illustrate let's create a new data frame `orders_tax` that contains a sequence id for each row and the 10% Sales Tax amount of the Total Amount. We use `cbind` function to bind the orders variable with the `orders_tax` variable:

```
> orders_discount <- data.frame(
    Discount = orders$TotalAmount * 0.25)
> orders <- cbind(orders, orders_ discount);
> names(orders)
```

This will give us the following output:

```
[1] "OrderMonth"  "SalesPerson" "OrderCount"  "TotalAmount"
[5] "Discount"
```

Using `dplyr`, you can call `bind_cols` to add a new column:

```
> orders_tax <- data.frame(
    RowID = seq(1:nrow(orders)),
    SalesTax = orders$TotalAmount * 0.1
    )
> orders <- bind_cols(orders,data.frame(orders_tax));
> names(orders)
```

The output is as follows:

```
[1] "OrderMonth"  "SalesPerson" "OrderCount"  "TotalAmount"
[5] "Discount"    "RowID"       "SalesTax"
```

Or you can add a new column called `TotalPlusTax`:

```
> mutate(orders, TotalPlusTax = TotalAmount * 0.125);
```

3. **Removing a column**: Now let's remove `RowID` from `orders`:

```
> orders <- orders[, !names(orders) == "RowID"]
```

The command `names(orders)` lists the column names in orders. So, `!names(orders) == "RowID"` excludes the column name `RowID`.

Using `dplyr`, you can call `select` to select a set of column. For example, the following excludes `RowID` from `orders`:

```
> select(orders, -RowID);
```

You can also easily select columns in orders where the column names start with `Order`:

```
> select(orders, matches("Order"));
```

Let's show `orders` with `SalesPerson` starting with `J`. First, to get the indexes of those that start with `J`, we can use the `grep` function:

```
> grep("^J.*", orders$SalesPerson);
 [1]   2  17  21  25  28  37  43  45  52  71  78 102 109
> orders[grep("^J.*", orders$SalesPerson),];
    OrderMonth SalesPerson OrderCount TotalAmount SalesTax
2   2015-06-01        Jack        206    502828.7 50282.87
17  2015-05-01        Jack        203    493282.0 49328.21
21  2015-11-01        Jack        210    473676.4 47367.64
25  2015-02-01        Jack        176    454979.3 45497.93
28  2015-10-01        Jack        205    522954.2 52295.42
37  2015-07-01        Jack        205    466244.0 46624.40
43  2015-04-01        Jack        188    520575.8 52057.58
45  2015-01-01        Jack        182    413761.0 41376.10
52  2015-12-01        Jack        209    474157.7 47415.77
71  2015-03-01        Jack        181    469591.0 46959.10
78  2015-08-01        Jack        171    359710.5 35971.06
102 2015-09-01        Jack        249    552961.4 55296.14
109 2015-12-01       Julie        201    340000.0 34000.00
```

Using `dplyr`, you can call `select` to select a set of column. For example, the following excludes `RowID` from `orders`:

```
> filter(orders, grepl("^J.*", SalesPerson));
```

You may have noticed in the last few `dplyr` examples that `dplyr` has a friendlier syntax. As an example, in the `filter` function, there is no need to specify the variable that the column belongs to.

```
> orders[grep("^J.*", orders$SalesPerson),]; # base
```

```
> filter(orders, grepl("^J.*", SalesPerson)); # dplyr
```

Also, the select function is much friendlier.

```
> orders <- orders[, !names(orders) == "RowID"] # base
```

```
> select(orders, -RowID); # dplyr
```

More data munging with dplyr

The following is a quick list of useful data munging activities, functions, and examples. df denotes a data frame variable.

Purpose	Functions
Rename columns	`rename(df, new_column_name = old_column_name)`
Sort/order data	`arrange(df, col1)` order data frame df by `col1`.

Deduplicate data	`distinct(df)`
	`distinct(df, [column names])`
	Deduplicate df for `[column names]` when provided.

Piping	*x %>% f(y)* Perform *f(x,y)*. You can nest the syntax. For example: *x %>% f(y)%>% g(z)* is equivalent to *x %>% g(f(x,y),z)*.

Finding missing values

R has a very short and simple way of finding missing values, which is `is.na(df)`. It returns row index(es) in df with missing values.

Transpose data

Transposing a dataset is not a trivial thing to do in SQL Server. Use `t(df)` in R to swap rows and columns of a data frame, df.

Pivot / Unpivot data

The `reshape` package is super useful for pivoting and unpivoting data.

Use `cast` to pivot data as follows:

```
library(reshape)
x <- data.frame(OrderMonth = orders$OrderMonth,
                SalesPerson = orders$SalesPerson,
                TotalAmount = orders$TotalAmount)
x1 <- cast(x, OrderMonth ~ SalesPerson)
names(x1)
```

Use `melt` to unpivot data as follows:

```
melt(x1,id=c(OrderMonth))
```

Example - data exploration and munging using R in T-SQL

As shown earlier, there are very nifty data munging and data exploration techniques that you can do in R. Let's now stitch it all together in T-SQL. In this following example, we want to get a statistical summary of monthly sales person order counts and the total amount, in 2015 - specifically Min, Max, 1st Quartile, Median, 3rd Quartile - to get a sense of the data range and the distribution of the monthly orders per sales person:

```
USE WideWorldImporters
GO

-- Part 1: Get Monthly Order count and Order amount
-- per Sales Person in Year 2015.
DECLARE @SQLScript NVARCHAR(MAX)
SET @SQLScript = N'SELECT DATEFROMPARTS(YEAR(o.[OrderDate]),
MONTH(o.[OrderDate]), 1) AS OrderMonth,
    sp.[PreferredName] AS SalesPerson,
    COUNT(DISTINCT o.[OrderID]) AS OrderCount,
    SUM(ol.[Quantity] * ol.[UnitPrice]) AS TotalAmount
FROM [Sales].[Orders] o
    INNER JOIN [Sales].[OrderLines] ol
        ON ol.[OrderID] = o.[OrderID]
    INNER JOIN [Application].[People] sp
        ON sp.[PersonID] = o.[SalespersonPersonID]
WHERE sp.[ValidTo] >= GETDATE()
    AND YEAR(o.[OrderDate]) = 2015
GROUP BY
DATEFROMPARTS(YEAR(o.[OrderDate]),
MONTH(o.[OrderDate]), 1),
    sp.[PreferredName];'

-- Part 2: Prepare the R-script that will summarize the dataset.
DECLARE @RScript NVARCHAR(MAX)
SET @RScript = N'OutputDataSet <- as.data.frame(t(sapply(InputDataSet[,
c("OrderCount", "TotalAmount")], summary)));
OutputDataSet <- cbind(Column = row.names(OutputDataSet), OutputDataSet);'

-- Part 3: Execute R in TSQL to get the monthly sales person's
```

```
-- order count and total amount.
EXECUTE sp_execute_external_script
    @language = N'R'
    ,@script = @RScript
    ,@input_data_1 = @SQLScript
WITH RESULT SETS ((
            [Columns] NVARCHAR(30), [Min] FLOAT,
            [Q1] FLOAT, [Median] FLOAT,
            [Mean] FLOAT,  [Q3] FLOAT,
            [Max] FLOAT));
GO
```

Data visualization in R

Good data visualization draws insights from a large amount of data and serves as a medium to communicate to the audience. Fortunately, R has powerful built-in functions as well as packages that can help you to create good data visualization. In this section, we will go through a number of built-in graphical functions and R libraries to show their capabilities. Then we'll walk through an example on how to stitch it together with T-SQL. You will also learn how to display graphics from R in SQL Operations Studio. Similar to the previous section, we will be using the orders dataset and will create a data frame **d** to narrow down the analysis for sales persons Amy, Jack, and Hudson.

Plot

The plot() function in R draws a simple scatterplot showing the relationship between two variables and distribution trends/outliers.

Here's an example of a script that visualizes the relationship between the number of orders and the monthly sales amount for Amy, Jack, and Hudson in 2015:

```
> d <- orders[orders$SalesPerson %in% c("Amy", "Jack", "Hudson"), ];
> plot(x = d$TotalAmount, y = d$OrderCount,
main = "Monthly Orders", xlab = "Total Amount ($)",
ylab = "Number of Orders", col = d$SalesPerson, pch = 19,
xaxt = "n");
> axis(side = 1, at = x <- signif(seq(from = 0,
to =  max(orders$TotalAmount), length.out = 6), 2),
labels = paste(x / 1000, "k", sep = ""));
```

The following diagram shows the Monthly Amount and the number of Orders that each Sales Person made in 2015. Using a plot like this allows us to easily see that there is a strong Sales Person denoted in blue dots:

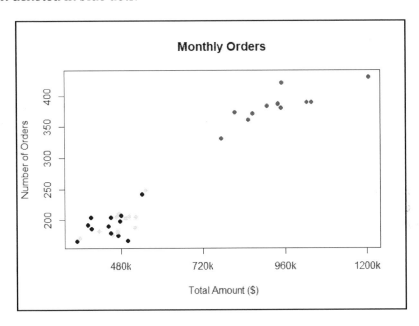

Figure 4-5 Scatterplot using the basic plot function

Obviously the preceding plot diagram takes a few steps to draw and you'll also need to add a legend() call to map the colors to the Sales Person. Following is a simpler way to draw a plot diagram with a one call.

The ggplot2 library offers an easy way to create a similar chart using the qplot function. Following script is equivalent to the previous call:

```
> library(ggplot2)
>   qplot(x = TotalAmount, y = OrderCount, data = d,
    color = SalesPerson, main = "Monthly Orders");
```

The following chart comes complete with a legend, which helps to show that **Hudson** is the top-performing **SalesPerson**:

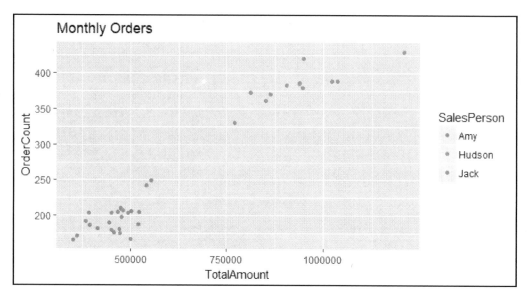

Figure 4-6 Scatterplot using the ggplot function

Histogram

The `hist()` function in R draws a histogram representing the frequency distribution of the dataset.

Here's a script that draws a frequency distribution of the monthly sales person Total Amount in 2015:

```
> hist(orders$TotalAmount, main = "Monthly Orders",
  xlab = "Total Amount ($)")
```

Using the following histogram, we can easily see that the most common monthly total amount (per sales person) is between $400 K and $500 K every month:

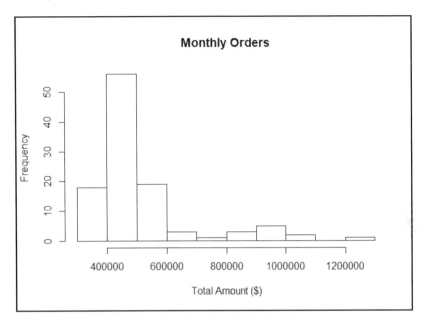

Figure 4-7 Histogram chart using basic hist function

Boxplot

The boxplot chart allows us to show outliers for each Sales Person. This can easily be achieved in R using the `boxplot()` function. However, the `ggplot` function is very easy to use and to customize. Here's an example of writing a boxplot diagram using `ggplot()`:

```
ggplot(orders,
    aes( x = SalesPerson,
        y = TotalAmount)) +
    geom_boxplot(outlier.color = "red", outlier.size = 3) +
    ggtitle(label = "Monthly Orders") +
    xlab("Sales Person") + ylab("Total Amount ($)");
```

The following diagram shows the distribution of the **Monthly Orders** that each Sales Person made in 2015:

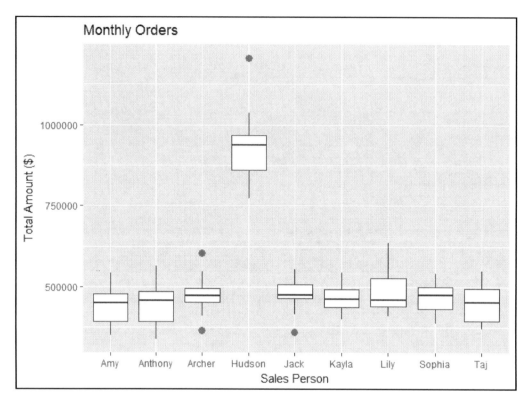

Figure 4-8 Boxplot chart using ggplot function

Scatter plot

In R, `scatterplot()` can be used to understand the relationship/trend between variables.

Following is an example of using scatterplot to understand the trend of monthly total amounts in 2015 for Amy, Hudson, and Jack:

```
library(car) # For the scatterplot function
library(RColorBrewer) # For choosing color palette more easily

# Prepare d
d$SalesPerson <- factor(d$SalesPerson);
d$OrderMonth <- as.Date(d$OrderMonth);
```

```
# Configure the palette to use
my_colors <- brewer.pal(nlevels(as.factor(d$SalesPerson)), "Set2")

# Map the monthly orders
scatterplot(TotalAmount ~ OrderMonth | SalesPerson, data = d,
    xlab = "Month", ylab = "Total Amount",
    main = "Monthly Orders", col = my_colors,
    cex = 1.5, lwd = 3)
```

Based on the following diagram, we can draw the conclusion that Hudson's monthly Total Amount is trending slightly down even though in general they are higher than Amy's and Jack. We can also see that Amy's monthly Total Amount has dropped quite sharply:

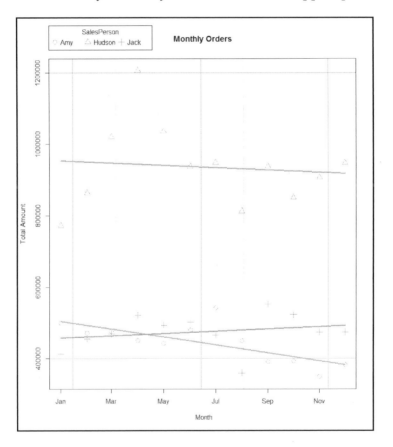

Figure 4-9 Scatterplot chart using the scatterplot function

The ggplot function can also be used to create a scatterplot and overlays it with smooth lines that show the monthly pattern of the Sales Person:

```
# Use the ggplot version
ggplot(data = d,
       aes(x = OrderMonth, y = TotalAmount, color = SalesPerson)) +
    geom_point() + geom_smooth(method = "loess") +
    scale_y_continuous(label = scales::dollar) +
    scale_color_brewer(palette = "Set2") +
    ggtitle(label = "Monthly Orders");
```

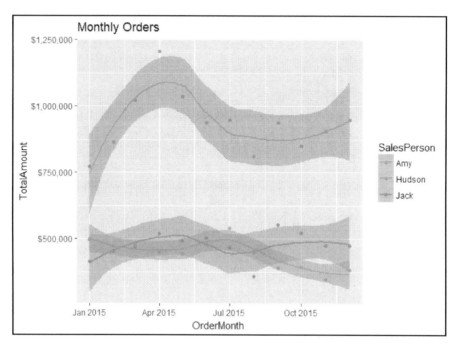

Figure 4-10 Scatterplot chart using ggplot function

Tree diagram

Data preparation for predictive modeling includes exploring the data structure and visualizing the decision rules for predicting values. These values can be categorical and continuous, represented as classification tree and regression tree respectively.

Below is an example of script to create a tree diagram depicting the decision rules for predicting the monthly Total Amount for a given Sales Person and `OrderCount`:

```
library(rpart)
library(rpart)
library(rattle)
library(rpart.plot)
fit <- rpart(TotalAmount ~ OrderCount + SalesPerson , data = d,
method="anova");
fancyRpartPlot(fit, sub = "Monthly Sales Person")
```

Running the preceding script will give a neat tree diagram with the first line on the node as the average monthly Total Amount (that is, *619e+3* in scientific notation is actually $619,000), followed by n as the number of observations and the percentage that makes up the node:

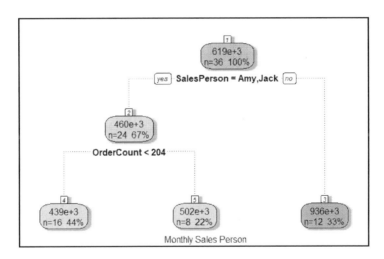

Figure 4-11 Tree Diagram using the rpart function

Example – R data visualization in T-SQL

Now that we have learned a few examples of using R for data visualization, let's stitch it all together with T-SQL in SQL Operations Studio. Please note that SSMS doesn't render the image produced by R in T-SQL.

Download SQL Operations Studio from
`https://docs.microsoft.com/en-us/sql/sql-operations-studio/downl oad`.

Perform the following steps to run R in T-SQL to produce an image that can be visualized in SQL Operations Studio.

1. Open SQL Operations Studio.
2. Connect to the `WideWorldImporters` database in your server in SQL Operations Studio.
3. Copy `Part 1` from Example: Data Visualization in T-SQL as we want to reuse the `@SQLScript` variable definition:

```
-- Part 2: Prepare the R-script that will produce the
visualization.
DECLARE @RScript NVARCHAR(MAX)
SET @RScript = N'library(ggplot2);
    image_file = tempfile();
    jpeg(filename = image_file, width=1000, height=400);
    d <- InputDataSet[InputDataSet$SalesPerson %in% c("Amy",
"Jack", "Hudson"), ];
    print(qplot(x = TotalAmount, y = OrderCount, data = d, color =
SalesPerson, main = "Monthly Orders"));
    dev.off()
    OutputDataSet <- data.frame(
            data=readBin(file(image_file,"rb"),
            what=raw(),n=1e6));'

-- Part 3: Execute R in TSQL to get the binary representation of
the image.
EXECUTE sp_execute_external_script
    @language = N'R'
    ,@script = @RScript
    ,@input_data_1 = @SQLScript
WITH RESULT SETS ((plot VARBINARY(MAX)));
```

4. In SQL Operations Studio, execute the preceding script and you will get a result set with a column called `plot`.
5. Click on **Chart Viewer**, then choose image from **Chart Type**:

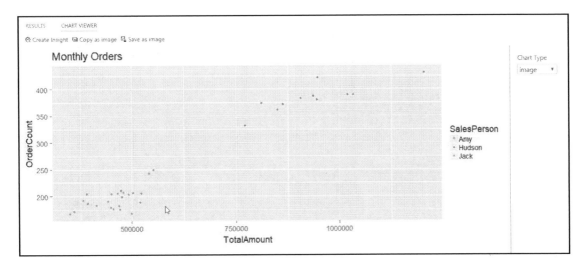

Figure 4-12 Data Visualization output from R in SQL Operations Studio

Integrating R code in reports and visualizations

In this section, we will delve into familiar reports and visualization Tools that are available in the Microsoft BI stack, such as **SQL Server Reporting Services (SSRS)**, Power BI, and Mobile Reports.

There are three main use cases for integrating R graphics with SQL Server.

1. Get a dataset output representing data / statistical analysis, training model, or predictive model:

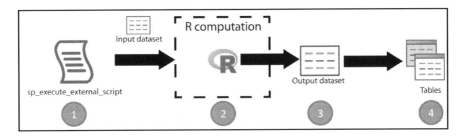

Figure 4-13 SQL Server Machine Learning Services process for data analysis in R

Execute `sp_execute_external_script` to run R to produce a dataset output as illustrated in (1) + (2) + (3). The data set output (3) could be from data/statistical analysis, a training model, predictive output, and so on. In SQL Server, we can optionally process the output further (4), for example, saving it into a table or passing it on to another stored procedure.

2. Get a dataset output containing the varbinary representation of the graphics output of R.

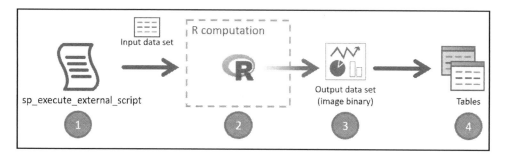

Figure 4-14 SQL Server R Services process for data visualization

Execute `sp_execute_external_script` to run R to produce a dataset output as illustrated in (1) + (2) + (3). The dataset output (3) in this case would have a varbinary (max) representation of the graphics output. In SQL Server, we can insert the output further (4), for example, saving the images as varbinary (max) into a table.

3. Save the R graphics output to files and store the file paths in the dataset output. This is ideal when offline rendering is preferred:

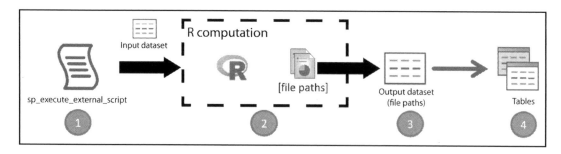

Figure 4-17 SQL Server Machine Learning Services process for data visualization to files

Execute `sp_execute_external_script` to run R to produce a dataset output as illustrated in (1) + (2) + (3). The dataset output (3) in this case contain the file paths where the graphic outputs need to reside. In SQL Server, we can optionally process the output further (4). You can also integrate Filestream for this solution as described in *Tomaž Kaštrun's* blog here:

```
https://tomaztsql.wordpress.com/2016/09/25/filetable-and-storing-
graphs-from-microsoft-r-server/
```

Integrating R in SSRS reports

SSRS reports can read datasets from either a query or a stored procedure. Essentially this gives us enough flexibility to choose how we want to incorporate the R output as part of ad-hoc or operational reports in SSRS.

Now, let's take a look at a couple of examples where we integrate R in SSRS Reports. Suppose a data analyst wants to do a quick statistical analysis to understand the strength of the relationship between Sales Person and Total Amount. It's very easy to do this using SSRS. Here's an example showing how you can achieve this.

1. Using either **Visual Studio 2017** or **SQL Server Management Studio**, connect to `WideWorldImporters`.

2. Create a new stored procedure called `dbo.usp_AnalyzeOrdersUsingAnova`:

```
CREATE PROCEDURE dbo.usp_AnalyzeOrdersUsingAnova
(
  @StartDate DATE = '20150101',
  @EndDate DATE = '20151231'
)
/**********************************************************
 * Purpose: Determine if Monthly Orders (Total Amount in $)
 *     has no dependency on Sales Person.
 * Parameters:
 *  @StartDate  - The start date of the Orders table
 *  @EndDate  - The end date of Orders table
 * Example on how to execute:
 *  EXEC dbo.usp_AnalyzeOrdersUsingAnova
 *     @StartDate = '20150101'
 *     ,@EndDate = '20151231'
 **********************************************************/
AS
BEGIN
  DECLARE @input_query NVARCHAR(MAX);
  DECLARE @RAOV NVARCHAR(MAX);
```

```
-- The SQL query representing Input data set.
-- Get the monthly orders from each Sales between
-- specific date and time.
SET @input_query = N'
SELECT
  DATEFROMPARTS(YEAR(o.[OrderDate]),
    MONTH(o.[OrderDate]), 1) AS OrderMonth,
  sp.[PreferredName] AS SalesPerson,
  COUNT(DISTINCT o.[OrderID]) AS OrderCount,
  SUM(ol.[Quantity] * ol.[UnitPrice]) AS TotalAmount
FROM [Sales].[Orders] o
  INNER JOIN[Sales] .[OrderLines] ol
    ON ol.[OrderID] = o.[OrderID]
  INNER JOIN[Application] .[People] sp
    ON sp.[PersonID] = o.[SalespersonPersonID]
WHERE sp.[ValidTo] >= GETDATE()
  AND o.[OrderDate] BETWEEN ''' +
CAST(@StartDate AS VARCHAR(30)) + ''' AND ''' +
CAST(@EndDate AS VARCHAR(30)) + '''
  GROUP BY
    DATEFROMPARTS(YEAR(o.[OrderDate]),
      MONTH(o.[OrderDate]), 1),
    sp.[PreferredName];'

-- The R code that tests if Total Amount has no strong
-- dependency to Sales Person
-- Note: Null Hypothesis (H0) in this case is Total Amount
--     has no strong dependency to Sales Person.
--     The closer p-value to 0 we can reject the H0.
SET @RAOV = N'a = aov(TotalAmount ~ SalesPerson,
 data = InputDataSet);
  m <- summary(a);
  library(plyr);
  x <- data.frame(RowID = 1:nrow(m[[1]]),
    Attribute = rownames(m[[1]]));
  OutputDataSet <- cbind(x, ldply(m, data.frame));'

-- Using R Services produce the output as a table
EXEC sp_execute_external_script @language = N'R'
  ,@script = @RAOV
  ,@input_data_1 = @input_query
  ,@input_data_1_name = N'InputDataSet'
  ,@output_data_1_name = N'OutputDataSet'
  WITH RESULT SETS (([RowID]  INT,
        [Attribute]  NVARCHAR(50),
        [DF]     NUMERIC(20,10),
        [SumSq]  NUMERIC(20,10),
        [MeanSq]  NUMERIC(20,10),
```

```
[FValue]    FLOAT,
[Pr(>F)]    FLOAT
));
```

END

3. Using Visual Studio 2017 or Report Builder, create a new report.
4. Save this file as SQL+R_Chapter04_SSRS_Anova_01.rdl by pressing *Ctrl+S*, or go to the **File** menu and click **Save**.
5. Create a new **Data Source** and save this WideWorldImporters that connects to the WideWorldImporters database on your server.
6. Then create a new **Data Set** with the following query definition, then click **Refresh Fields**:

```
EXEC dbo.usp_AnalyzeOrdersUsingAnova
```

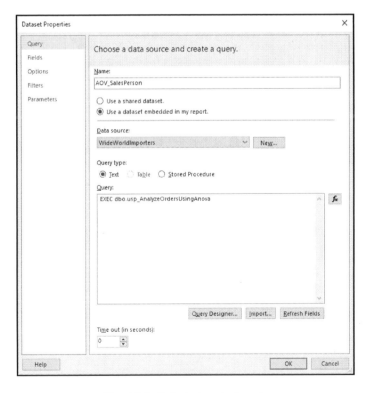

Figure 4-16 Specify the stored procedure to execute

7. Create a **Tablix** to represent AOV_SalesPerson columns:

Analysis of Variance on Monthly Orders					
Attribute	**DF**	**Sum Sq**	**Mean Sq**	**FValue**	**Pr(<F)**
[Attribute]	[Sum(DF)]	[Sum(SumSq)]	[Sum(MeanSq)]	[Sum(FValue)]	[Sum(Pr_F_)]
«Expr»					
					[&ExecutionTime]

Figure 4-17 Add a Tablix that has all the columns from AOV_SalesPerson

8. Optionally add another **Tablix** where its DataSetName is mapped to AOV_SalesPerson. On the first cell of the **Tablix** body, describe how to interpret the analysis with the following expression:

```
="Since the p-value of " & Fields!Pr__F_.Value & " is " &
IIf(Fields!Pr__F_.Value < 0.05, "less", "greater") & " than the .05
significance level, we " & IIf(Fields!Pr__F_.Value < 0.05,
"reject", "accept") & " the null hypothesis that the mean of
monthly Total Amount of " & Fields!Attribute.Value & " are all
equal. This means that there is " &  IIf(Fields!Pr__F_.Value <
0.05, "", "no") & " dependency between " &
First(Fields!Attribute.Value, "AOV_SalesPerson") & " and Monthly
Orders Total Amount"
```

9. Click **Run** to see a preview of the report:

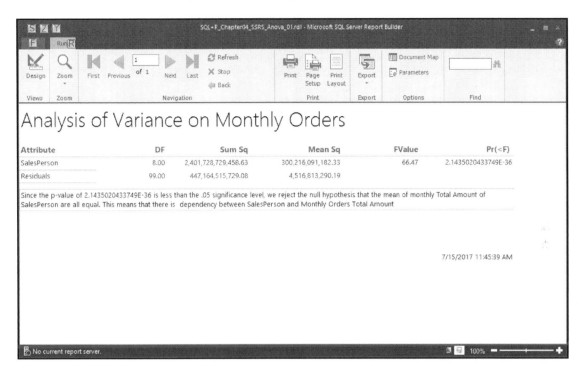

Figure 4-18 Preview the Report

Another scenario that is commonly seen for using R is to draw data visualizations. In the following example, we are going to compare how Sales Person performs in the year 2015. From here, we can see the trend of Sales Person monthly orders and how they're performing in the 12 months:

1. Using either **Visual Studio 2017** or **SQL Server Management Studio**, connect to WideWorldImporters.

2. Create a new stored procedure called dbo.usp_CreateMonthlySalesPlot:

```
CREATE PROCEDURE dbo.usp_CreateMonthlySalesPlot
(
  @StartDate DATE = '20150101',
  @EndDate DATE = '20151231'
)
/************************************************************
 * Purpose: Determine if Monthly Orders (Total Amount in $)
```

```
*        has no dependency on Sales Person.
* Parameter:
*  @StartDate  - Observation start date in the Orders table
*  @EndDate   - Observation end date in the Orders table
* Example on how to execute:
*  EXEC dbo.usp_AnalyzeOrdersUsingAnova
*      @StartDate = '20150101'
*      ,@EndDate = '20151231'
***********************************************************/
AS
BEGIN
  DECLARE @input_query NVARCHAR(MAX);
  DECLARE @RPlot NVARCHAR(MAX);

  -- The SQL query representing Input data set.
  -- Get the monthly orders from each Sales between
    specfic date and time.
  SET @input_query = N'
  SELECT
    DATEFROMPARTS(YEAR(o.[OrderDate]),
      MONTH(o.[OrderDate]), 1) AS OrderMonth,
    sp.[PreferredName] AS SalesPerson,
    COUNT(DISTINCT o.[OrderID]) AS OrderCount,
    SUM(ol.[Quantity] * ol.[UnitPrice]) AS TotalAmount
  FROM [Sales].[Orders] o
    INNER JOIN [Sales] .[OrderLines] ol
      ON ol.[OrderID] = o.[OrderID]
    INNER JOIN [Application] .[People] sp
      ON sp.[PersonID] = o.[SalespersonPersonID]
  WHERE sp.[ValidTo] >= GETDATE()
    AND o.[OrderDate] BETWEEN ''' +
      CAST(@StartDate AS VARCHAR(30)) +
      ''' AND ''' +
      CAST(@EndDate AS VARCHAR(30)) + '''
  GROUP BY
    DATEFROMPARTS(YEAR(o.[OrderDate]), MONTH(o.[OrderDate]), 1),
    sp.[PreferredName];'

  -- The R code that produces the plot.
  SET @RPlot = N'library(ggplot2);
  image_file = tempfile();
  jpeg(filename = image_file, width=600, height=800);
  a <- qplot(y = TotalAmount, x = OrderMonth,
      data = InputDataSet,
      color = SalesPerson,
      facets = ~SalesPerson,
      main = "Monthly Orders");
  a + scale_x_date(date_labels = "%b");
```

```
plot(a);
dev.off();
OutputDataSet <-  data.frame(
  data=readBin(file(image_file,"rb"),
  what=raw(),n=1e6));


EXEC sp_execute_external_script @language = N'R'
  ,@script = @RPlot
  ,@input_data_1 = @input_query
  ,@input_data_1_name = N'InputDataSet'
  ,@output_data_1_name = N'OutputDataSet'
  WITH RESULT SETS (( [plot] VARBINARY(MAX)));

END
```

3. In **Report Builder**, open SQL+R_Chapter04_SSRS_Anova_01.rdl from earlier, create a new **Data Set** with the following query definition, then click **Refresh Fields**. The field created is called Plot and there should be one row:

EXEC dbo.usp_CreateMonthlySalesPlot

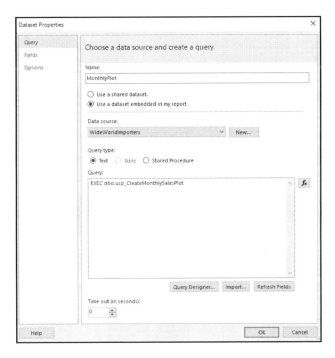

Figure 4-19 Specify the stored procedure to be executed

4. Insert a new **Image**, with the following **General** properties:

    Select the image source: Database

    Use this field: =First(Fields!plot.Value, "MonthlyPlot")

    Use this MIME type: image/jpeg

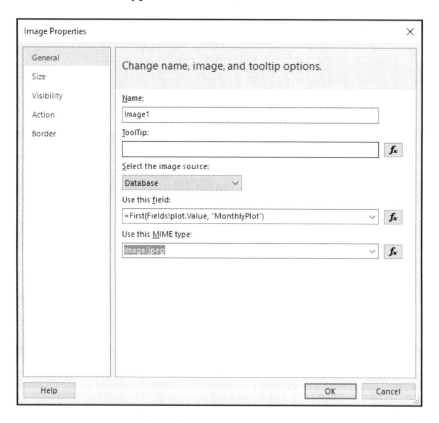

Figure 4-20 Configure Image to render the plot

5. Optionally, go to the **Size** item on the left pane and change **Display** to **Original Size**.

6. Click **Run** to see a preview of the report:

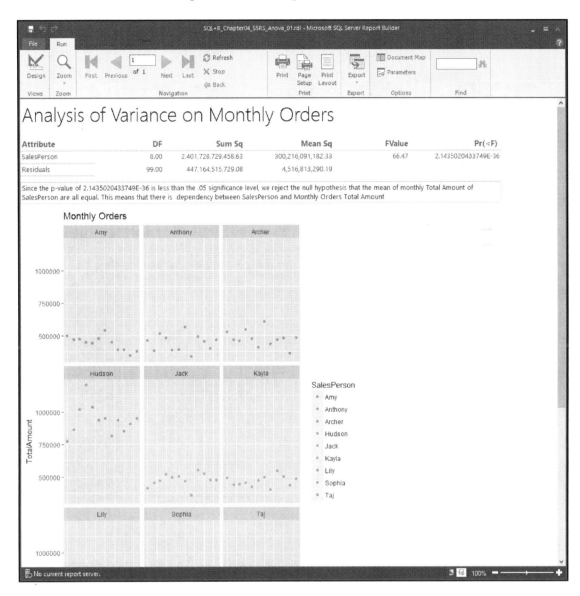

Figure 4-21 Preview the report with the plot

This RDL file can now be published to an **SSRS Report Server**.

For more information about SSRS, the following Microsoft Docs website is very useful:

```
https://docs.microsoft.com/sql/reporting-services/create-deploy-and-manage-mobi
le-and-paginated-reports
```

Integrating R in Power BI

Power BI is a powerful tool for visualizing data. Together with R, Power BI can render beautiful images with uncompromised dynamic interactivity. In this example, you'll learn how to create data visualizations similar to the one that we created in SSRS in the previous section:

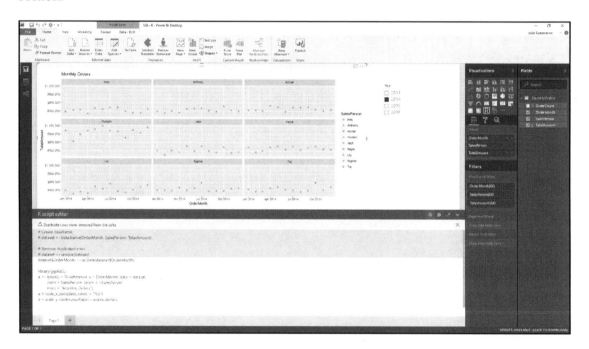

Figure 4-22 Power BI Visualization with R Script Editor

For simplicity, we will use Power BI desktop but you could just as well create one from the online `PowerBI.com` version:

1. Launch **Power BI Desktop** and create a new file.
2. From the **Home** menu, click on **Get Data** | **SQL Server**.
3. Connect to your SQL Server instance that has the `WideWorldImporters` database.
4. Then click on **Advanced Options** to provide the following query on the **SQL statement** field:

```
SELECT
    DATEFROMPARTS(YEAR(o.[OrderDate]),
    MONTH(o.[OrderDate]), 1) AS OrderMonth,
    sp.[PreferredName] AS SalesPerson,
    COUNT(DISTINCT o.[OrderID]) AS OrderCount,
    SUM(ol.[Quantity] * ol.[UnitPrice]) AS TotalAmount
FROM [Sales].[Orders] o
    INNER JOIN[Sales] .[OrderLines] ol
        ON ol.[OrderID] = o.[OrderID]
    INNER JOIN[Application] .[People] sp
        ON sp.[PersonID] = o.[SalespersonPersonID]
WHERE sp.[ValidTo] >= GETDATE()
GROUP BY
    DATEFROMPARTS(YEAR(o.[OrderDate]), MONTH(o.[OrderDate]), 1),
    sp.[PreferredName];
```

The dialog box should now look like this:

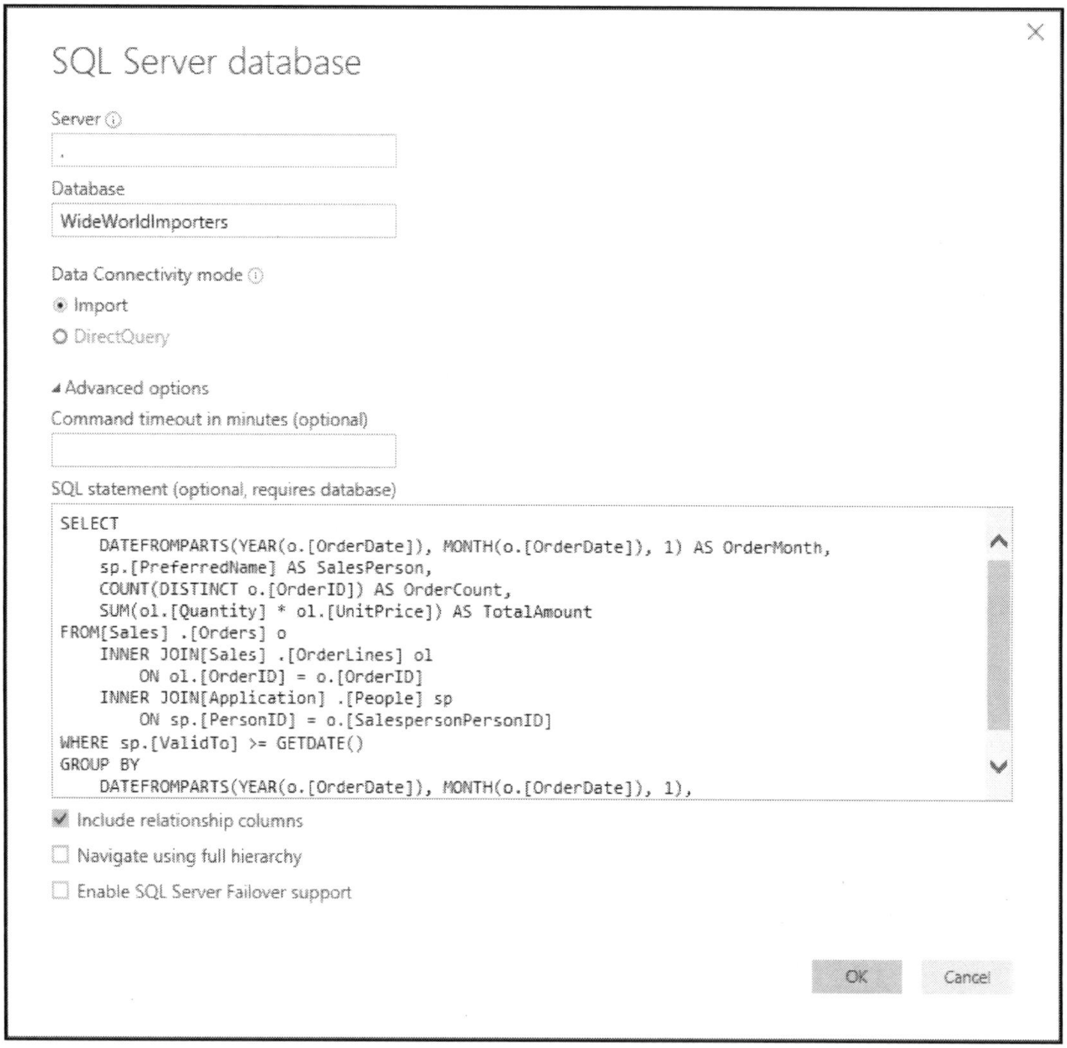

SQL Server database

Server ⓘ

⌞ . ⌟

Database

WideWorldImporters

Data Connectivity mode ⓘ

⦿ Import

○ DirectQuery

◢ Advanced options

Command timeout in minutes (optional)

SQL statement (optional, requires database)

```
SELECT
    DATEFROMPARTS(YEAR(o.[OrderDate]), MONTH(o.[OrderDate]), 1) AS OrderMonth,
    sp.[PreferredName] AS SalesPerson,
    COUNT(DISTINCT o.[OrderID]) AS OrderCount,
    SUM(ol.[Quantity] * ol.[UnitPrice]) AS TotalAmount
FROM[Sales] .[Orders] o
    INNER JOIN[Sales] .[OrderLines] ol
        ON ol.[OrderID] = o.[OrderID]
    INNER JOIN[Application] .[People] sp
        ON sp.[PersonID] = o.[SalespersonPersonID]
WHERE sp.[ValidTo] >= GETDATE()
GROUP BY
    DATEFROMPARTS(YEAR(o.[OrderDate]), MONTH(o.[OrderDate]), 1),
```

☑ Include relationship columns

☐ Navigate using full hierarchy

☐ Enable SQL Server Failover support

OK   Cancel

Figure 4-23 SQL Server database data source details

5. Click **OK** to see the preview of the query.

6. Then click **Load** on the preview window:

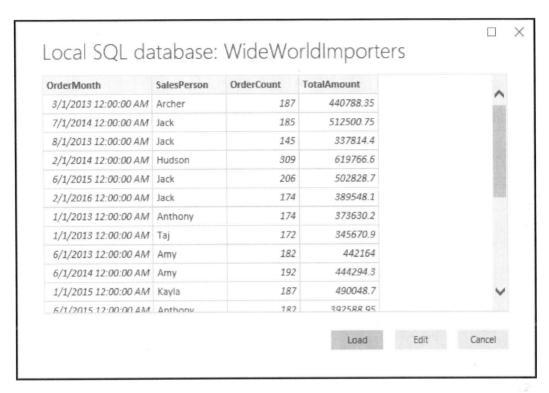

Figure 4-24 Preview of the query

7. From the **Visualizations** pane, click on the **R Script** icon.

8. Drag and drop the `OrderMonth`, `SalesPerson`, and `TotalAmount` columns from the **Fields** pane into the **Values** box.

Please note that your table might be called `Query1` and you can rename this to something more meaningful such as **MonthlyOrders**, as shown as follows:

Figure 4-25 Choose Fields as inputs to R

9. With the **OrderMonth**, instead of the default **Date Hierarchy** choose **OrderMonth** from the drop-down list in the **Values** field:

Figure 4-26 Choose Order Month instead of Data Hierarchy to display

10. Ensure that the R Script graphic box is still in focus. Optionally you can resize it to make it wider or taller:

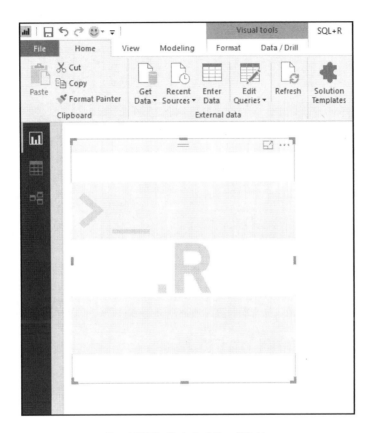

Figure 4-27 R Visualization box in Power BI Desktop

11. Then, in **R Script Editor** located on the lower half of Power BI screen, enter the following R code:

```
dataset$OrderMonth <- as.Date(dataset$OrderMonth);

library(ggplot2);
a <- qplot(y = TotalAmount, x = OrderMonth, data = dataset,
        color = SalesPerson, facets = ~SalesPerson,
        main = "Monthly Orders");
a + scale_x_date(date_labels = "%b");
a + scale_y_continuous(label = scales::dollar);
```

12. Click on the **Run Script** button located on the right of the **R Script Editor** bar.
13. Add a **Slicer**, then drag and drop **OrderMonth**.
14. Deselect all the **OrderMonth** hierarchy except for **Year**, by clicking on the **X** from the **OrderMonth** list in the **Values** filed:

Figure 4-28 Slicer for Year

15. Now your Power BI report should look something like this:

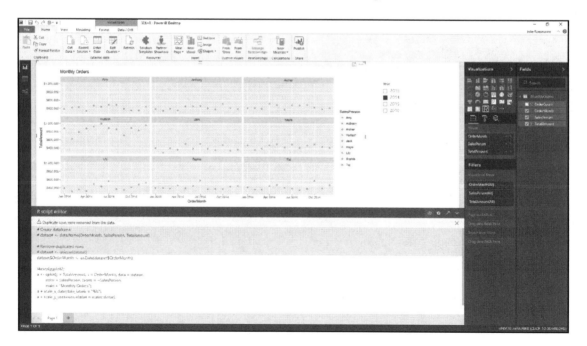

Figure 4-29 Power BI Report

Summary

In this chapter, you have learned the importance of data preparation in predictive modeling, which involves both data exploration and data visualization exercises. R has a number of open-source packages that are useful for data munging, for example `dplyr`, `reshape`, and many more. The challenge is to hit the right balance between having data munging activities in SQL Server VS in R. The beauty of SQL Server Machine Learning Services is that it allows easy integration with SQL Server Reporting Services. In addition, Power BI also supports interactive data exploration with R visualizations. In the next chapter, you will learn more about the `RevoScaleR` library for portable, scalable, and distributable R functions.

5

RevoScaleR Package

The RevoScaleR package comes with Microsoft Machine Learning R Server and R Services. It is also available with R Client, but with some limitations discussed in Chapter 2, *Overview of Microsoft Machine Learning Server and SQL Server*. Given the rapid development and constant upgrades, this chapter will cover version 8.X and version 9.X-the latter is also available with SQL Server 2017. Changes and upgrades in version 9.X are not to be overlooked and will be covered as well.

The following topics are covered in this chapter:

- Limitations of R challenged
- Scalable and distributive computational environment
- Functions for data preparation
- Functions for descriptive statistics
- Functions for statistical tests and sampling
- Functions for predictive modeling

Primarily, this R package is designed to be handled in ecosystems where clients would be connecting to Microsoft R Server in order to have R code executed against a much more powerful server, which would presumably hold whole datasets, not just a smaller portion, on which people working on client machines would be dealing with.

Overcomming R language limitations

Prior to SQL Server 2016 (and 2017) BI and data scientists had the OLAP cubes, DMX language, and all super awesome and cool Microsoft algorithms available within **SQL Server Analysis Services** (**SSAS**). But, with rapid changes and bigger market demands, the need for integration of an open-source product (whether R, Python, Perl,or any other) was practically already there. And the next logical step was to integrate it with one. Microsoft sought a solution and ended up acquiring Revolution Analytics, which has put them on track again. Revolution R has addressed major issues concerning the R language.

Microsoft addressed R's limitations. Many of these limitations were aimed at faster data exploration and parallel programming techniques in R. In addition to this, also MKL computations have been enhanced, therefore making matrix-wise calculations even faster, along with scalar calculation and also calculation resulting in cartesian-products.

The following limitations were addressed and also solved:

- Communication overhead is particularly an issue with fine-grained parallelism consisting of a very large number of relatively small tasks
- Load balance is where computing resources aren't contributing equally to the problem
- Impacts from the use of RAM and virtual memory, such as cache misses and page faults
- Network effects, such as latency and bandwidth, that impact performance and communication overhead
- Interprocess conflicts and thread scheduling
- Data access and other I/O considerations

Scalable and distributive computational environments

The RevoScaleR package has the following functions available, which will be covered in detail throughout the chapter.

To get a list of all the ScaleR functions, the following T-SQL can be used:

```
EXEC sp_execute_external_script
     @language = N'R'
     ,@script = N'require(RevoScaleR)
```

```
                     OutputDataSet <-
  data.frame(ls("package:RevoScaleR"))'
  WITH RESULT SETS
       (( Functions NVARCHAR(200)))
```

You get a table in SSMS with all the relevant `rx` functions that can be used with the `RevoScaleR` package.

Based on the list of these functions, a simpler and better overview of the functions can be prepared:

Data Preparation

*   Data import – Delimited, Fixed, SAS, SPSS, OBDC
*   Variable creation & transformation
*   Recode variables
*   Factor variables
*   Missing value handling
*   Sort, Merge, Split
*   Aggregate by category (means, sums)

Descriptive Statistics

*   Min / Max, Mean, Median (approx.)
*   Quantiles (approx.)
*   Standard Deviation
*   Variance
*   Correlation
*   Covariance
*   Sum of Squares (cross product matrix for set variables)
*   Pairwise Cross tabs
*   Risk Ratio & Odds Ratio
*   Cross-Tabulation of Data (standard tables & long form)
*   Marginal Summaries of Cross Tabulations

Statistical Tests

*   Chi Square Test
*   Kendall Rank Correlation
*   Fisher's Exact Test
*   Student's t-Test

Sampling

*   Subsample (observations & variables)
*   Random Sampling

Predictive Models

*   Sum of Squares (cross product matrix for set variables)
*   Multiple Linear Regression
*   Generalized Linear Models (GLM) exponential family distributions: binomial, Gaussian, inverse Gaussian, Poisson, Tweedie. Standard link functions: cauchit, identity, log, logit, probit. User defined distributions & link functions.
*   Covariance & Correlation Matrices
*   Logistic Regression
*   Classification & Regression Trees
*   Predictions/scoring for models
*   Residuals for all models

Variable Selection

*   Stepwise Regression

Simulation

*   Simulation (e.g. Monte Carlo)
*   Parallel Random Number Generation

Cluster Analysis

*   K-Means

Classification

*   Decision Trees
*   Decision Forests
*   Gradient Boosted Decision Trees
*   Naïve Bayes

Combination

*   rxDataStep
*   rxExec
*   PEMA-R API Custom Algorithms

Figure 1: List of RevoScaleR functions (source: Microsoft)

Functions for data preparation

Importing data is the first of the many processes in data preparation. Importing data is a process of bringing data into your system from any external system using an external file or by establishing a connection to a live data source. In the following part, we will look at importing data that is stored as SPSS or SAS files and using an ODBC connection string to connect directly to an external live database system.

Data import from SAS, SPSS, and ODBC

Importing data into R or SQL Server tables is not the main focus of `RevoScaleR` library, but since this is on the list, let's briefly look into it. In this manner, based on your data source, the `RevoScaleR` package gives many abilities to connect to different data sources. Among these are also SAS and SPSS - two very broad and common statistical programs for data analysis and predictive analytics. We will simply focus on SAS software (`https://www.sas.com/`), SPSS Statistics, acquired by IBM in 2009 (`https://www.ibm.com/products/spss-statistics`), or SPSS Modeler (`https://www.ibm.com/products/spss-modeler`).

Importing SAS data

SAS is among the popular programs for data analysis if not the most popular for statistical analysis, data mining, and machine learning. Therefore, let's create a simple SAS file and read it using the `ScaleR` function.

With the following SAS code (the code is available along with the book), you can very easily create a sample dataset:

```
DATA work.SAS_data;
INPUT income gender count;
DATALINES;
    1 1 25
    1 2 35
    2 1 30
    2 2 10
;

PROC PRINT DATA=work.SAS_data;
RUN;
```

Figure 2: Outlook of SAS code

Now, let's assume that our SAS data is stored in the file `sas_data.sas7bdat` as the code suggests in the `PROC DATA` statement.

With the following R code, we can extract and import this dataset into the R `data.frame`:

```
EXEC sp_execute_external_script
    @language = N'R'
    ,@script = N'
```

```
library(RevoScaleR)
             SampleSASFile <-
file.path(rxGetOption("sampleDataDir"), "sas_data.sas7bdat")
             #import into Dataframe
             OutputDataSet <- rxImport(SampleSASFile)
             '

WITH RESULT SETS
    ((
     income  INT
    ,gender  INT
    ,[count] INT
    ))
```

Make sure that your `sampleDataDir` holds the data sample. Also, you could specify some other path such as:

```
SampleSASFile <- file.path(("C:\\Users\\TomazK\\Documents\\CH05"),
"sas_data.sas7bdat")
```

However, you need to make sure that you have granted access to this working folder. In both ways, you should get results presented as a table, read from the SAS file as follows:

	income	gender	count
1	1	1	25
2	1	2	35
3	2	1	30
4	2	2	10

Figure 3: Outlook of SAS code result

Another way of importing the SAS file is by using `RxSasData` directly (in this case, from R):

```
SampleSASFile <- file.path(("C:\\Users\\tomazK\\CH05"),
"sas_data.sas7bdat")
sasDS <- RxSasData(SampleSASFile, stringsAsFactors = TRUE,
                colClasses = c(income = "integer", gender= "integer",
count="integer"),
rowsPerRead = 1000)
rxHistogram( ~F(gender)|F(income), data = sasDS)
```

You can easily generate a histogram from the SAS data file.

Importing SPSS data

With SPSS, the procedure is similar. The following SPSS syntax (the syntax is included with this chapter) generates the sample dataset, which is stored on your local machine:

```
DATA LIST LIST /income gender count.
Begin data
1, 1, 25
1, 2, 35
2, 1, 30
2, 2, 10
END DATA.
```

Figure 4: Outlook of SPSS syntax

This involves getting data into R Services using the SPSS save file that is generated from the preceding SPSS syntax, which is relatively the same as with the SAS file:

```
EXEC sp_execute_external_script
     @language = N'R'
     ,@script = N'
                  library(RevoScaleR)
                     SampleSPSSFile <-
file.path(rxGetOption("sampleDataDir"),  "spss_data.sav")
                     #import into Dataframe
                     OutputDataSet <- rxImport(SampleSPSSFile)
                     '
WITH RESULT SETS
     ((
      income  INT
     ,gender  INT
     ,[count] INT
     ))
```

In addition to this, the RevoScaleR package has a special function to directly read the SPSS file called RxSpssData. The following R code can accomplish the same result as the preceding T-SQL code:

```
SampleSPSSFile <- file.path(("C:\\Users\\tomazK\\CH05"),  "spss_data.sav")
spssDS <- RxSpssData(SampleSPSSFile, stringsAsFactors = TRUE,
                     colClasses = c(income = "integer", gender=
"integer", count="integer"),rowsPerRead = 1000)
rxHistogram( ~F(income)|F(count),  data = spssDS)
```

And the `RevoScaleR` histogram can be used directly with the SPSS datasource, generating a simple histogram:

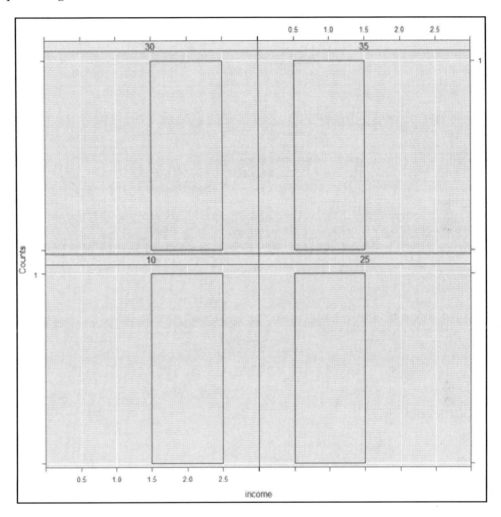

Importing data using ODBC

Using the ODBC driver extends accessibility to almost any kind of database whose driver you can obtain and that has a common RDBM model.

The `RevoScaleR` package extends the list of ODBS drivers also to support systems on Linux and other systems. Using ODBC, you can connect to MySQL, Oracle, PostgreSQL, SQL Server on Linux, Cloudera, and Teradata (which in this case is much better to use than the `RxTeradata` function).

The following example will use the ODBC driver to get data from another SQL server instance, both using the `RxOdbcData` and `RxSqlServerData` function, since they are interchangeable:

```
EXEC sp_execute_external_script
     @language = N'R'
     ,@script = N'
                library(RevoScaleR)
          sConnectStr <- "Driver={ODBC Driver 13 for SQL
Server};Server=TOMAZK\MSSQLSERVER2017;Database=AdventureWorks;Trusted_Conne
ction=Yes"
          sQuery = "SELECT TOP 10 BusinessEntityID,[Name],SalesPersonID
FROM [Sales].[Store] ORDER BY BusinessEntityID ASC"
          sDS <-RxOdbcData(sqlQuery=sQuery, connectionString=sConnectStr)
          OutputDataSet <- data.frame(rxImport(sDS))
                           '
WITH RESULT SETS
     ((
      BusinessEntityID  INT
     ,[Name]   NVARCHAR(50)
     ,SalesPersonID INT
     ));
```

This would be the same as running the following on the same server:

```
USE AdventureWorks;
GO
SELECT
TOP 10
BusinessEntityID
,[Name]
,SalesPersonID
FROM [Sales].[Store]
ORDER BY BusinessEntityID ASC
```

In the case of using the RxOdbcData function, you should check the credentials and you might also want to check which user you are using to run the script. You can also create a new login and user and use it to check and execute the script: the Adventureworks database is available to download from Microsoft's GitHub website (https://github.com/Microsoft/sql-server-samples/tree/master/samples/databases/adventure-works):

```
EXECUTE AS USER='MSSQLSERVER01'
GO
-- YOUR CODE
REVERT;
GO
```

Variable creation and data transformation

Variable creation and data transformation are two processes when defining data munging and data wrangling tasks. These tasks are important for proper data preparation and make it easier to analyze data for future tasks.

The functions that we will be exploring are as follows:

- Variable creation and recoding
- Data transformation
- Handling missing values
- Sorting, merging, and splitting datasets
- Aggregate by category (which means sums), which is similar to T-SQL aggregations and Windows functions

This part will cover some of the following functions, mainly focusing on data transformation, handling missing values, and splitting datasets:

RxDataSource, rxDataStep, rxDataStepXdf, RxFileSystem, rxFindFileInPath, rxFindPackage, rxFisherTest, RxForeachDoPar, rxGetInfo, rxGetInfoXdf, rxGetJobInfo, rxGetJobInfo, rxGetOption, rxGetVarInfo, rxGetVarNames, rxImport, rxImportToXdf, rxIsOpen, rxOdbcData, rxOptions, rxOpen, rxQuantile, rxReadXdf, rxResultsDF, rxSetFileSystem, rxSetInfo, rxSetInfoXdf, rxSort, rxSetVarInfoXdf, rxSetVarInfo, rxMarginals, rxMerge, rxMergeXdf

When using In-database R Service (or the in-database machine learning service, also counting Python for SQL Server 2017), you should keep in mind where and how to do any kind of data transformation, data wrangling, as well as sorting and/or merging. After running many performance and speed tests, it became very clear that many of the munging and wrangling tasks should be done in-database, before sending the dataset to be executed by sp_execute_external_script. This set of functions is the only set where the computation context should be considered as a very important one. All the other functions for statistical tests, descriptive statistics, and predictive statistics can easily be used with external procedure, without compromising on performance or time.

Starting with the rxDataStep function, it gives us many opportunities to extract and generate XDF files, using in-database R:

```
EXEC sp_execute_external_script
    @language = N'R'
    ,@script = N'
                 df_sql <- InputDataSet
                 df_sql4 <- data.frame(df_sql)
                 outfile <- file.path(rxGetOption("sampleDataDir"),
"df_sql4.xdf")
                 rxDataStep(inData = df_sql4, outFile = outfile, overwrite
= TRUE)'
    ,@input_data_1 = N'
                 SELECT
                  BusinessEntityID
                 ,[Name]
                 ,SalesPersonID
                 FROM [Sales].[Store]'
```

This will generate the df_sql4.xdf file on your sample data directory. If you are interested in where this folder is pointing to, you can do the following:

```
EXEC sp_execute_external_script
    @language = N'R'
    ,@script = N'
        OutputDataSet <- data.frame(path =
file.path(rxGetOption("sampleDataDir")))'
```

It will be something similar to what is shown in the following screenshot:

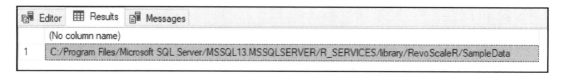

And make sure that you have granted access for the user, executing the rxDataStep code, because the code will be creating a physical XDF file on the destination location.

Variable creation and recoding

Using rxGetVarInfo will expose the information about the data.frame to the sp_execute_external_script output. It is obvious that some of these functions were never designed for presenting the output to data.frame, but were designed only for exploring the dataset. Some of these functions-for example, rxGetVarInfo-will give a nice output in the R environment, but will be hard to manipulate in data frames for outputting in the SQL Server database:

```
EXEC sp_execute_external_script
    @language = N'R'
    ,@script = N'
                library(RevoScaleR)
                df_sql <- InputDataSet
                var_info <- rxGetVarInfo(df_sql)
                OutputDataSet <- data.frame(unlist(var_info))'
    ,@input_data_1 = N'
                SELECT
                 BusinessEntityID
                , [Name]
                ,SalesPersonID
                FROM [Sales].[Store]'
```

Note that we are using the unlist function that unlists the set of lists in a single vector. Just to compare the output, we can run the same script in the R environment:

```
library(RevoScaleR)
sConnectStr <- "Driver={ODBC Driver 13 for
SQLServer};Server=TOMAZK\\MSSQLSERVER2017;Database=AdventureWorks;Trusted_C
onnection=Yes"
sQuery = "SELECT  BusinessEntityID,[Name],SalesPersonID FROM
[Sales].[Store] ORDER BY BusinessEntityID ASC"
sDS <-RxOdbcData(sqlQuery=sQuery, connectionString=sConnectStr)
df_sql <- data.frame(rxImport(sDS))
```

Now, running the `rxGetVarInfo(df_sql)` will give you a slightly different export:

```
> var_info <- rxGetVarInfo(df_sql)
> var_info
Var 1: BusinessEntityID, Type: integer, Low/High: (292, 2051)
Var 2: Name, Type: character
Var 3: SalesPersonID, Type: integer, Low/High: (275, 290)
```

And after unlisting with the `unlist()` function, we get the same information, written in a slightly different manner:

```
> df <- data.frame(unlist(var_info))
> df
                           unlist.var_info.
BusinessEntityID.varType            integer
BusinessEntityID.storage              int32
BusinessEntityID.low                    292
BusinessEntityID.high                  2051
Name.varType                      character
Name.storage                         string
SalesPersonID.varType               integer
SalesPersonID.storage                 int32
SalesPersonID.low                       275
SalesPersonID.high                      290
```

This indicates that some of these functions for variable creation and recoding were meant more for R data engineers than for T-SQL data engineers.

The `rxGetInfo()` function will get you the size of your dataset and the number of observations/variables:

```
EXEC sp_execute_external_script
     @language = N'R'
     ,@script = N'
                 library(RevoScaleR)
                 df_sql <- InputDataSet
                 var_info <- rxGetInfo(df_sql)
                 OutputDataSet <- data.frame(unlist(var_info))'
     ,@input_data_1 = N'
                 SELECT
                  BusinessEntityID
                 ,[Name]
                 ,SalesPersonID
                 FROM [Sales].[Store]'
```

The same logic applies: if you run this R environment, you will get a neater display of information:

```
> rxGetInfo(df_sql)
Data frame: df_sql
Number of observations: 701
Number of variables: 3
```

Adding some additional parameters to this function also yields a richer output, as follows:

```
> rxGetInfo(df_sql, getVarInfo = TRUE)
Data frame: df_sql
Number of observations: 701
Number of variables: 3
Variable information:
Var 1: BusinessEntityID, Type: integer, Low/High: (292, 2051)
Var 2: Name, Type: character
Var 3: SalesPersonID, Type: integer, Low/High: (275, 290)
```

A with `rxGetVarInfo`, `rxGetInfo` will create a list of elements. `rxGetVarInfo` will generate a list of lists, where the number of tuples equals the number of variables, and `rxGetInfo` will generate a list of six elements, where each list will hold information about the object:

```
◎ get_Info        List of 6                                    🔍
    objName : chr "df_sql"
    description: NULL
    class : chr "data.frame"
    numRows : int 701
    numVars : int 3
    numBlocks : num 0
    attr(*, "class")= chr "rxGetInfo"
```

Knowing this, the preceding T-SQL executions can be slightly altered so that the relevant information is displayed in a more readable format, by presenting elements (tuples) to the result set:

```
EXEC sp_execute_external_script
    @language = N'R'
    ,@script = N'
        library(RevoScaleR)
        df_sql <- InputDataSet
        get_Info <- rxGetInfo(df_sql)
        Object_names <- c("Object Name", "Number of Rows", "Number of
Variables")
        Object_values <- c(get_Info$objName, get_Info$numRows,
```

```
get_Info$numVars)
            OutputDataSet <- data.frame(Object_names, Object_values)'
      ,@input_data_1 = N'
                SELECT
                 BusinessEntityID
                ,[Name]
                ,SalesPersonID
                FROM [Sales].[Store]'
WITH RESULT SETS
      ((
       ObjectName NVARCHAR(100)
      ,ObjectValue NVARCHAR(MAX)
      ));
```

The results returned in SQL Server Management Studio:

	ObjectName	ObjectValue
1	Object Name	df_sql
2	Number of Rows	701
3	Number of Variables	3

This looks very neat and spending some extra effort will for sure give much better formatted results that will be easier to read as well as much more informative.

In this example, you have also seen how to create a new variable. This especially comes in handy when cleaning data or recoding/bucketing data.

Let's suppose that you want to recode the values of existing variables in the dataset and create a new one. It can be done using standard R code as follows:

```
EXEC sp_execute_external_script
      @language = N'R'
      ,@script = N'
            df_sql <- InputDataSet
            #first create an empty variable
            df_sql$BusinessType <- NA
            df_sql$BusinessType[df_sql$BusinessEntityID<=1000] <- "Car
Business"
            df_sql$BusinessType[df_sql$BusinessEntityID>1000] <- "Food
Business"
            OutputDataSet <- df_sql'
      ,@input_data_1 = N'
                SELECT
                 BusinessEntityID
                ,[Name]
                ,SalesPersonID
```

```
                      FROM [Sales].[Store]'
WITH RESULT SETS
        ((
         BusinessEntityID INT
        ,[Name] NVARCHAR(MAX)
        ,SalesPersonID INT
        ,TypeOfBusiness NVARCHAR(MAX)
        ));
```

Alternatively, you can do this using the `rxDataStep()` function and the `transformFunc`
parameter with an additional function for creating a new variable by transforming old
values:

```
EXEC sp_execute_external_script
        @language = N'R'
        ,@script = N'
                        library(RevoScaleR)
                        df_sql <- InputDataSet
                        df_sql$BusinessEntityID_2 <- NA

            myXformFunc <- function(dataList) {
              #dataList$BussEnt <- 100 * dataList$BusinessEntityID
              if (dataList$BusinessEntityID<=1000){dataList$BussEnt <- "Car
Business"} else {dataList$BussEnt <- "Food Business"}
                        return (dataList)
                        }

                        df_sql <- rxDataStep(inData = df_sql, transformFunc =
myXformFunc)
                        OutputDataSet <- df_sql'
        ,@input_data_1 = N'
                        SELECT
                         BusinessEntityID
                        ,[Name]
                        ,SalesPersonID
                        FROM [Sales].[Store]'
WITH RESULT SETS
        ((
         BusinessEntityID INT
        ,[Name] NVARCHAR(MAX)
        ,SalesPersonID INT
        ,TypeOfBusiness NVARCHAR(MAX)
        ));
```

`rxDataStep()` X is a very powerful function mainly for data selection, subsetting, data
transformation, and the creation of new variables for the desired dataset.

Dataset subsetting

Subsetting the data is also relatively straightforward using the rxDataStep() function:

```
EXEC sp_execute_external_script
     @language = N'R'
     ,@script = N'
                  library(RevoScaleR)
                  df_sql <- InputDataSet
                  df_sql_subset <- rxDataStep(inData = df_sql, varsToKeep =
NULL, rowSelection = (BusinessEntityID<=1000))
                  OutputDataSet <- df_sql_subset'
     ,@input_data_1 = N'
                  SELECT
                   BusinessEntityID
                  , [Name]
                  ,SalesPersonID
                  FROM [Sales].[Store]'
WITH RESULT SETS
     ((
      BusinessEntityID INT
     , [Name] NVARCHAR(MAX)
     ,SalesPersonID INT
     ));
```

Keep in mind that subsetting operations using R code might bring unnecessary memory and I/O costs, especially when pumping whole datasets into R, instead of subsetting the data beforehand. In the preceding example, using the rowSelection parameter in rxDataStep can easily be replaced with the WHERE clause in the @input_data_1 argument. So bear this in mind and always avoid unnecessary traffic.

Dataset merging

The rxMerge() function merges two datasets into one. The datasets must be a dataframe (or XDF format) and operate similarly to the JOIN clause in T-SQL (the rxMerge() function should not be confused with T-SQL's MERGE statement). Two datasets are merged based on one or more variables using the matchVars argument. In addition, when using the local compute context (which we are using in the next sample), the sorting of the data needs to be defined as well, since data.frames-as a collection of vectors-in R are not presorted or do not hold any sorts whatsoever. So, if no presorting is done, the autoSort argument must be set to true (autosort = TRUE):

```
EXEC sp_execute_external_script
```

```
      @language = N'R'
      ,@script = N'
      library(RevoScaleR)
      df_sql <- InputDataSet
      someExtraData <- data.frame(BusinessEntityID = 1:1200, department =
rep(c("a", "b", "c", "d"), 25), Eff_score = rnorm(100))
      df_sql_merged <- rxMerge(inData1 = df_sql, inData2 = someExtraData,
overwrite = TRUE, matchVars = "BusinessEntityID", type = "left" ,autoSort =
TRUE)
      OutputDataSet <- df_sql_merged'
      ,@input_data_1 = N'
                  SELECT
                   BusinessEntityID
                  , [Name]
                  ,SalesPersonID
                  FROM [Sales].[Store]'
WITH RESULT SETS
      ((
       BusinessEntityID INT
      , [Name] NVARCHAR(MAX)
      ,SalesPersonID INT
      ,Department CHAR(1)
      ,Department_score FLOAT
      ));
```

This T-SQL code creates a left join on both the datasets. Dataframe 2
(called someExtraData) is created on the fly, but it can be any other dataframe read from
an XDF file or any manually inserted dataset, and will be joined at R runtime. Also, pay
attention to which is the first and which is the second data frame in combination to which
type of join you are using. The preceding example specifies the following:

```
inData1 = df_sql, inData2 = someExtraData, type = "left"
```

However, the order of the data frames could be changed as follows:

```
inData1 = someExtraData , inData2 = df_sql, type = "left"
```

Then, the output would be presented differently (the sorting of the columns in the data
frame would be changed).

Functions for descriptive statistics

Descriptive statistics give insights into understanding data. These are summary statistics that describe a given dataset by summarizing features and measures, such as central tendency and measure of spread (or variability). Central tendency includes calculation of the mean, median, mode, whereas measures of variability include range, quartiles, minimum and maximum value, variance and standard deviation, as well as skewness and kurtosis.

These statistics are covered by rx- functions in RevoScaleR package, which means that you can use all the computational advantages of the package by calling: rxSummary, rxCrossTabs, rxMarginals, rxQuantile, rxCube, and rxHistogram, without worrying about the performance, out of memory exceptions, or which R package holds the right function.

We will be using the [Sales].[vPersonDemographics] view in the AdventureWorks database to neatly show the usability of these functions:

```
EXEC sp_execute_external_script
    @language = N'R'
    ,@script = N'
        library(RevoScaleR)
        df_sql <- InputDataSet
        summary <- rxSummary(~ TotalChildren,  df_sql, summaryStats
= c( "Mean", "StdDev", "Min", "Max","Sum","ValidObs", "MissingObs"))
        OutputDataSet <- summary$sDataFrame'
    ,@input_data_1 = N'
    SELECT * FROM [Sales].[vPersonDemographics] WHERE
[DateFirstPurchase] IS NOT NULL'
WITH RESULT SETS
    ((
      VariableName NVARCHAR(MAX)
    , "Mean"NVARCHAR(100)
    , "StdDev"NVARCHAR(100)
    , "Min"NVARCHAR(100)
    , "Max"NVARCHAR(100)
    , "Sum"NVARCHAR(100)
    , "ValidObs"NVARCHAR(100)
    , "MissingObs"NVARCHAR(100)
    ));
```

With one line of R code, you can get some summary statistics. I prefer using the `summaryStats` argument to list the statistics, but note that the order of the statistics does not mean that the order of the output will be the same. In addition, using the element `summary$sDataFrame` dataframe as a result from `rxSummary` will automatically generate the data frame that will contain all the summaries for numeric variables.

The result of the T-SQL query is as follows:

	VariableName	Mean	StdDev	Min	Max	Sum	ValidObs	MissingObs
1	TotalChildren	1.84435	1.61241	0	5	34091	18484	0

The `rxSummary()` function also holds a formula, whereby you can specify which variables the function will take into account while calculating descriptive statistics. In our case, we have used only the `TotalChildren` variable:

```
rxSummary(~ TotalChildren, ...
```

But let's assume, we want to get descriptives for all the variables; we simply write the following:

```
rxSummary(~.,   ....
```

This will give us statistics for all the variables as shown in the following screenshot:

	VariableName	Mean	StdDev	Min	Max	Sum	ValidObs	MissingObs
1	BusinessEntityID	11532,7316598139	5340,9396113817	1699	20777	213171012	18484	0
2	TotalPurchaseYTD	302.986340678424	1354,34794576823	-3578,27	9650,76	5600399,5211	18484	0
3	DateFirstPurchase	1061273459,07812	23939747,4398502	993945600	1091232000	19616578617600	18484	0
4	BirthDate	-250140143,864964	355114394,405115	-1874102400	346636800	-4623590419199,99	18484	0
5	MaritalStatus	NULL	NULL	NULL	NULL	0	18484	0
6	YearlyIncome	NULL	NULL	NULL	NULL	0	18484	0
7	Gender	NULL	NULL	NULL	NULL	0	18484	0
8	TotalChildren	1,8443518718892	1,61240793484251	0	5	34090,9999999999	18484	0
9	NumberChildrenAtHome	1,00405756329799	1,52265965841342	0	5	18559	18484	0
10	Education	NULL	NULL	NULL	NULL	0	18484	0
11	Occupation	NULL	NULL	NULL	NULL	0	18484	0
12	HomeOwnerFlag	0,676368751352521	0,467873814762749	0	1	12502	18484	0
13	NumberCarsOwned	1,50270504219866	1,13839374115481	0	4	27776	18484	0

Note that only the integer (continuous) type of variables will be taken into consideration, whereas variables such as `MaritalStatus`, `Education`, and `Occupation`, will be presented as NULL, since these variables are treated as categorical variables in R.

For this, firstly, we will need to specify the factor variable, and based on that we will be able to run the statistics:

```
EXEC sp_execute_external_script
        @language = N'R'
        ,@script = N'
        library(RevoScaleR)
        df_sql <- InputDataSet
        df_sql_r <- rxFactors(inData = df_sql, sortLevels = TRUE,
factorInfo = list(MS = list(levels = c("M","S"), otherLevel=NULL,
varName="MaritalStatus")))
                     summary <- rxSummary(~ MS,  df_sql_r)
                     OutputDataSet <- data.frame(summary$categorical)'
        ,@input_data_1 = N'
        SELECT * FROM [Sales].[vPersonDemographics] WHERE [DateFirstPurchase]
IS NOT NULL'
WITH RESULT SETS
        ((
          MS NVARCHAR(MAX)
          ,"Counts"INT
        ));
```

This function will give simple counts for the `MaritalStatus` factor:

```
MS Counts
M   10011
S    8473
```

The same logic can be applied to all other categorical variables. The formula in the `rxSummary()` function also gives users the ability to combine different variables. For example, instead of using the following code:

```
rxSummary(~ TotalChildren, df_sql_r)
```

We can also use the following code:

```
rxSummary(NumberCarsOwned ~ TotalChildren, df_sql_r)
```

This will calculate the observed statistics for both the variables together:

```
Name                                    Mean      StdDev    Min Max Sum    ValidObs
MissObs
NumberCarsOwned:TotalChildren 3.258656 4.473517 0    20  60233  18484      0
```

This can also be calculated for categorical variables. These variables need to be recoded into factors first and later the same summary statistics can be calculated:

```
rxSummary(~ TotalChildren:F(MS), df_sql_r)
```

And the complete R and T-SQL code using `sp_execute_external_script` is as follows:

```
EXEC sp_execute_external_script
      @language = N'R'
     ,@script = N'
            library(RevoScaleR)
            df_sql <- InputDataSet
            df_sql_r <- rxFactors(inData = df_sql, sortLevels =
TRUE,factorInfo = list(MS = list(levels = c("M","S"), otherLevel=NULL,
varName="MaritalStatus")))
        summary <- rxSummary(~F(MS):TotalChildren, df_sql_r, summaryStats =
c( "Mean", "StdDev", "Min", "Max", "ValidObs", "MissingObs", "Sum"),
categorical=c("MS"))
                  OutputDataSet <- data.frame(summary$categorical)'
     ,@input_data_1 = N'
     SELECT * FROM [Sales].[vPersonDemographics] WHERE [DateFirstPurchase]
IS NOT NULL'
WITH RESULT SETS
     ((
       Category NVARCHAR(MAX)
     ,"MS"NVARCHAR(MAX)
     ,"Means"FLOAT
     ,"StDev"FLOAT
     ,"Min"INT
     ,"Max"INT
     ,"Sum"INT
     ,"ValidObs"INT
     ));
```

The following are the results for each factor level:

```
Name                    Mean      StdDev   Min Max Sum    ValidObs MissingObs
 TotalChildren:F_MS 1.844352 1.612408 0    5    34091 18484       0
Statistics by category (2 categories):
Category                      F_MS Means    StdDev    Min Max Sum    ValidObs
TotalChildren for F(MS)=M M    2.080412 1.583326 0    5    20827 10011
TotalChildren for F(MS)=S S    1.565443 1.601977 0    5    13264  8473
```

Quantiles and deciles are also very useful to view the data distribution and the RevoScaleR packages provides the rxQuantile function. Using T-SQL, the result set can be returned as follows:

```
EXEC sp_execute_external_script
     @language = N'R'
     ,@script = N'
                  library(RevoScaleR)
                  df_sql <- InputDataSet
                  quan <- rxQuantile(data = df_sql, varName =
"TotalChildren")
                  quan <- data.frame(quan)
                  values <- c("0%","25%","50%","75%","100%")
                  OutputDataSet <- data.frame(values,quan)'
     ,@input_data_1 = N'
     SELECT * FROM [Sales].[vPersonDemographics] WHERE [DateFirstPurchase]
IS NOT NULL'
 WITH RESULT SETS
     ((
           Quartile NVARCHAR(100)
           ,QValue FLOAT
     ));
```

This gives us the following result:

```
0%   25%   50%   75% 100%
0    0     2     3     5
```

We can also modify and calculate deciles with a slight change to the rxQuantile() function:

```
EXEC sp_execute_external_script
     @language = N'R'
     ,@script = N'
           library(RevoScaleR)
           df_sql <- InputDataSet
           dec <- rxQuantile(data = df_sql, varName = "TotalChildren",
probs = seq(from = 0, to = 1, by = .1))
```

```
            dec <- data.frame(dec)
        values <-
c("0%","10%","20%","30%","40%","50%","60%","70%","80%","90%","100%")
            OutputDataSet <- data.frame(values,dec)'
        ,@input_data_1 = N'
        SELECT * FROM [Sales].[vPersonDemographics] WHERE [DateFirstPurchase]
IS NOT NULL'
WITH RESULT SETS
        ((
            Decile NVARCHAR(100)
            ,DValue FLOAT
        ));
```

Calculating crosstabulations-the relationship between two (or more) variables-we will use two functions: `rxCrossTabs` and `rxMargins`. Crosstabulations are usually expressed in a contingency table or any other *[n]***[m]* table format; this really depends on the number of levels each variable will have.

We will use our two variables `NumberCarsOwned` and `TotalChildren` to explore the `rxCrossTabs`:

```
EXEC sp_execute_external_script
        @language = N'R'
        ,@script = N'
                    library(RevoScaleR)
                    df_sql <- InputDataSet
                    crosstab <- rxCrossTabs(N(NumberCarsOwned) ~
F(TotalChildren),  df_sql, means=FALSE) #means=TRUE
                    children <- c(0,1,2,3,4,5)
                    OutputDataSet <- data.frame(crosstab$sums, children)'
        ,@input_data_1 = N'
        SELECT * FROM [Sales].[vPersonDemographics] WHERE [DateFirstPurchase]
IS NOT NULL'
WITH RESULT SETS
        ((
            NumberOfCarsOwnedSUM INT
            ,NumberOfChildren INT
        ));
```

Calculating crosstabulations using `rxCrossTabs` can give you two types of statistics: the count of observations and the mean of observations, given the category of intersect. This is manipulated using the means = `TRUE` or means = `FALSE` argument. The function operates in a way that will need the dependent variable(s) and independent variables(s) and in our example, the information can be retrieved from the results as follows:

```
Cross Tabulation Results for: N(NumberCarsOwned) ~ F(TotalChildren)
Data: df_sql
Dependent variable(s): N(NumberCarsOwned)
Number of valid observations: 18484
Number of missing observations: 0
Statistic: sums
```

In order to have the crosstabulation successfully calculated, independent variables must be presented as factors. In this case, the `TotalChildren` variable has a `F()` function wrapped, denoting a factor conversion in the runtime.

This can be visualized using a standard barplot in the base package or R:

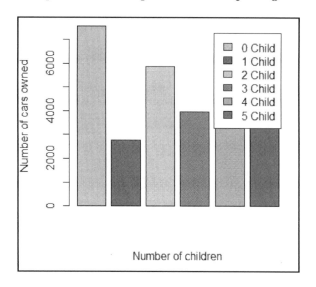

Use the following code to plot the histogram using `barplot` function:

```
library(RColorBrewer)
barplot(OutputDataSet$V1, xlab = "Number of children",ylab = "Number of
cars owned",
        legend.text = c("0 Child","1 Child","2 Child","3 Child","4
Child","5 Child"), col=brewer.pal(6, "Paired"))
```

Using variables that are categorical, there is no need for explicit conversion:

```
EXEC sp_execute_external_script
     @language = N'R'
     ,@script = N'
            library(RevoScaleR)
            df_sql <- InputDataSet
            crosstab <- rxCrossTabs(NumberCarsOwned ~ MaritalStatus,
df_sql, means=FALSE)
            status <- c("M","S")
            OutputDataSet <- data.frame(crosstab$sums, status)'
     ,@input_data_1 = N'
     SELECT * FROM [Sales].[vPersonDemographics] WHERE [DateFirstPurchase]
IS NOT NULL'
WITH RESULT SETS
     ((
            NumberOfCarsOwnedSUM INT
            ,MaritalStatus NVARCHAR(100)
     ));
```

Also, the transform argument can be used to recode, recalculate, or somehow transform any of the variables. Marginal statistics from the contingency tables deriving from rxCrossTabs can be called using the rxMarginals functions, which is simply wrapped around the rxCrossTabs.

Marginal statistics will give you the sum, counts, or mean for each of the totals per row or per column for the desired variable:

```
EXEC sp_execute_external_script
     @language = N'R'
     ,@script = N'
                   library(RevoScaleR)
                   df_sql <- InputDataSet
                   mar <- rxMarginals(rxCrossTabs(NumberCarsOwned ~
F(TotalChildren), data=df_sql, margin=TRUE, mean=FALSE))
                   OutputDataSet  <- data.frame(mar$NumberCarsOwned$grand)'
     ,@input_data_1 = N'
     SELECT * FROM [Sales].[vPersonDemographics] WHERE [DateFirstPurchase]
IS NOT NULL'
WITH RESULT SETS
     ((
            GrandTotal INT
     ));
```

The result is as follows:

```
> mar$NumberCarsOwned$grand
[1] 27776
```

Exploring the data can also be done using the graphs and the `RevoScaleR` package comes with a Line and bar plot, both designed to tackle large datasets.

The following is a simplistic preview of one of the variables:

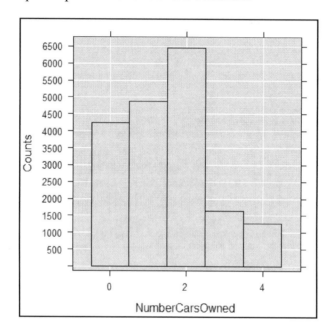

Use the following line of R code:

```
rxHistogram(~NumberCarsOwned, data=df_sql)
```

This has already been converted to marital status factor as follows:

```
rxHistogram(~F(MS), data=df_sql_r)
```

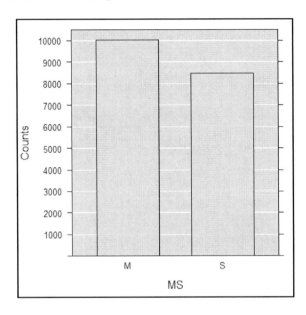

Also, variables can be combined as follows (the marital status with the number of cars owned):

```
rxHistogram(~ NumberCarsOwned | F(MS), title="Cars owned per Marital
Status",  numBreaks=10, data = df_sql_r)
```

And we get the following plot, showing marital status (**M** - married; **S** - single) and the total number of cars owned as a categorical variable (**0** - no car, **1** - 1 car owned, **2** - two cars owned, **3** - three cars owned, and **4** - four cars owned):

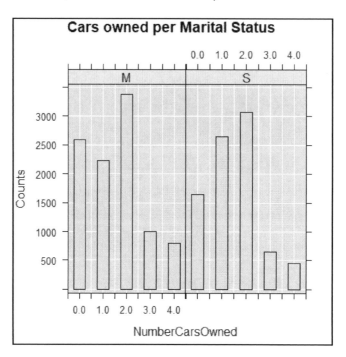

Instead of a bar plot, we can also use a Line plot, but this time with different variables:

```
rxLinePlot(as.numeric(log(TotalPurchaseYTD)) ~
as.factor(DateFirstPurchase), data = df_sql_r, rowSelection=
        DateFirstPurchase >= "2001-07-01 00:00:00.000"&amp;
DateFirstPurchase <= "2001-07-17 00:00:00.000", type="p")
```

For the time period of little over half a year (between January 01 and July 17th 2001), the plot is showing a logarithmic variable for the total amount of purchases in this time period. In this case, we need to factorize the date variable and we are also using the `log()` function to level the purchases. And instead of using `rxHistogram`, we are using `rxLinePlot`, another `RevoScaleR` function, to plot graphs for large datasets. `rxLinePlot` represents a line chart:

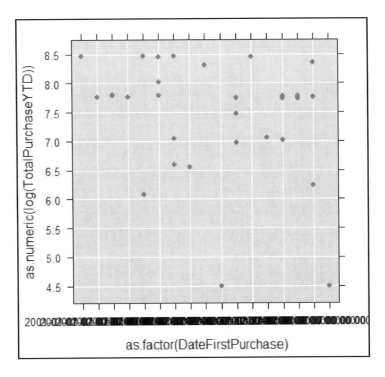

So, in the end, we can combine all three graphs using the `par()` function, arranging two columns, each having one or two graphs:

```
# combined
h1 <- rxHistogram(~NumberCarsOwned, data=df_sql)
h2 <- rxHistogram(~F(MS), data=df_sql_r)
p1 <- rxLinePlot(as.numeric(log(TotalPurchaseYTD)) ~
as.factor(DateFirstPurchase), data = df_sql_r, rowSelection=
            DateFirstPurchase >= "2001-07-01 00:00:00.000"&amp;
DateFirstPurchase <= "2001-07-17 00:00:00.000", type="p")

print(h1, position = c(0, 0.5, 0.5, 1), more = TRUE)
print(h2, position = c(0.5, 0.5, 1, 1), more = TRUE)
print(p1, position = c(0.5, 0.05, 1, 0.5))
```

Using graphs is good for storytelling, customer journey, or simply by great and fast understanding of the data, when combining the most informative variables. Another good way is to use markdown documentation and include multiple graphs in one block. An addition when using the par() function in combination with rxHistogram or rxLinePlot is that it might not always display graphs as expected. This is due to some compatibility issues with the par() function. Alternatively, using print() function and positioning each graph is another way to do it, without running into possible problems:

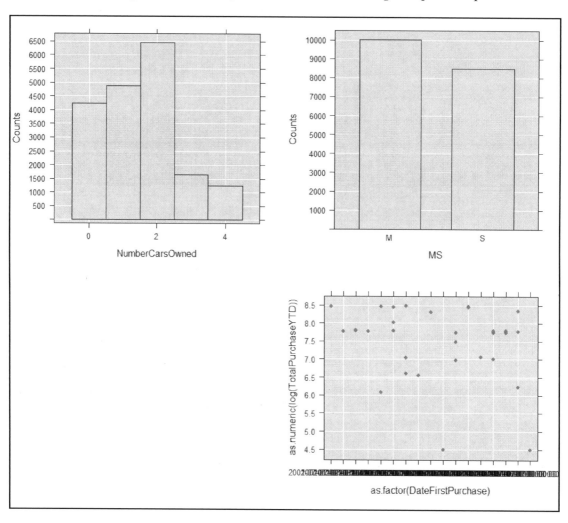

Functions for statistical tests and sampling

Statistical tests are important for determining the correlation between two (or more) variables and what is their direction of correlation (positive, neutral, or negative). Statistically speaking, the correlation is a measure of the strength of the association between two variables and their direction. The `RevoScaleR` package supports calculation of Chi-square, Fischer, and Kendall rank correlation. Based on the types of variable, you can distinguish between Kendall, Spearman, or Pearson correlation coefficient.

For Chi-Square test, we will be using the `rxChiSquareTest()` function that uses the contingency table to see if two variables are related. A small chi-square test statistic means that the observed data fits your expected data very well, denoting there is a correlation, respectively. The formula for calculating chi-square is as follows:

$$\chi_c^2 = \sum \frac{(O_i - E_i)^2}{E_i}$$

Prior to calculating this statistical independence test, we must have data in the `xCrossTab` or xCube format. Therefore, the T-SQL query will need to generate the crosstabulations first in order to calculate the chi-square coefficient.

Chi-square is generated on two categorical variables as follows:

```
EXEC sp_execute_external_script
    @language = N'R'
    ,@script = N'
        library(RevoScaleR)
        df_sql <- InputDataSet
        df_sql_r <- rxFactors(inData = df_sql, sortLevels =
TRUE,factorInfo = list(MS = list(levels = c("M","S"), otherLevel=NULL,
varName="MaritalStatus")))
        df_sql_r$Occupation <- as.factor(df_sql_r$Occupation)
        df_sql_r$MS <- df_sql_r$MS
        testData <- data.frame(Occupation = df_sql_r$Occupation,
Status=df_sql_r$MS)
        d <- rxCrossTabs(~Occupation:Status,  testData, returnXtabs =
TRUE)
        chi_q <- rxChiSquaredTest(d)
        #results
        xs <- chi_q$''X-squared''
        p <- chi_q$''p-value''
        OutputDataSet <- data.frame(xs,p)'
```

```
        ,@input_data_1 = N'
        SELECT * FROM [Sales].[vPersonDemographics] WHERE [DateFirstPurchase]
IS NOT NULL'
WITH RESULT SETS
        ((
                Chi_square_value NVARCHAR(100)
                ,Stat_significance NVARCHAR(100)
        ));
```

The following results are returned:

```
Chi-squared test of independence between Occupation and Status
 X-squared df p-value
 588.2861  4  5.312913e-126
```

With Kendall Tau you can calculate the correlation between the ranks and the result of the preceding correlation using R code:

```
rxKendallCor(d, type = "b")
```

The following are the results:

```
    estimate 1 p-value
 -0.05179647     0
   HA: two.sided
```

This same principle can be used in a T-SQL query:

```
EXEC sp_execute_external_script
        @language = N'R'
        ,@script = N'
                library(RevoScaleR)
                df_sql <- InputDataSet
                df_sql_r <- rxFactors(inData = df_sql, factorInfo = list(MS
= list(levels = c("M","S"), otherLevel=NULL, varName="MaritalStatus")))
                df_sql_r$Occupation <- as.factor(df_sql_r$Occupation)
                df_sql_r$MS <- df_sql_r$MS
                testData <- data.frame(Occupation = df_sql_r$Occupation,
Status=df_sql_r$MS)
                d <- rxCrossTabs(~Occupation:Status,  testData, returnXtabs
= TRUE)
                ken <- rxKendallCor(d, type = "b")
                k <- ken$`estimate 1`
                p <- ken$`p-value`
                #results
                OutputDataSet <- data.frame(k,p)'
        ,@input_data_1 = N'
        SELECT * FROM [Sales].[vPersonDemographics] WHERE
```

```
[DateFirstPurchase] IS NOT NULL'
    WITH RESULT SETS
        ((
                Kendall_value NVARCHAR(100)
                ,Stat_significance NVARCHAR(100)
        ));
```

Many other principles can be used to calculate correlations among variables. But this is beyond the scope of this book, and therefore we have focused only on the necessary ones.

Functions for predictive modeling will be covered in the next chapter - Chapter 6, *Predictive Modeling*.

Summary

This chapter has covered important functions (among many others) for data manipulation and data wrangling. These steps are absolutely and utterly important for understanding the structure of the dataset, the content of the dataset, and how the data is distributed. These are used to mainly understand frequencies, descriptive statistics, and also some statistical sampling, as well as statistical correlations.

These steps must be done (or should be done) prior to data cleaning and data merging in order to get a better understanding of the data. Cleaning the data is of the highest importance, as outliers might bring sensitive data (or any kind of data) to strange or false conclusions: it might also sway the results in some other direction. So, treating these steps as highly important by using the powerful rx- functions (or classes) should be the task of every data engineer, data wrangler, as well as data scientist. The next chapter will be focused on RevoScaleR functions for predictive modeling, mainly focusing on creating models and running the predictions against these models.

6

Predictive Modeling

Predictive modeling is a process that is using advanced statistics and probability algorithms to predict outcomes, based on a pretrained and built model or function. These algorithms can be groups in a family of algorithms based on the outcome of the predicted variable. The outcome is usually the forecasted value that explains the future behavior. Several variables or input data consist of a mathematical function, also called the model (hence also data modeling), and these input data are trying to explain or predict the outcome. To better understand predictive modeling, the chapter will consist of the following topics:

- Data modeling
- Advanced predictive algorithms
- Predictive analytics
- Deploying and using predictive solutions
- Performing prediction with R Services in SQL Server database

The focus in this chapter will be on delivering insight into understanding how predictive modeling can be used in SQL Server 2016/2017, using R on your typical business problem. In the enterprise environment, a business problem can be defined in a very broad aspect. For example, in medicine, a typical problem that predictive modeling can help understand and solve is, will the change of the ingredient A and B for the medicine C, help cure the disease? Furthermore, in the metallurgic industry, can we simulate how an anti-corrosion coating paint will age through time—or in retails, how can a customer select a better product in a store based on their needs or behavior? One can say, our everyday life is intertwined with predictions and forecast. Usually, every logistical problem all of us are facing is a simple question on a potentially very relevant topic: if I leave home for work 5 minutes later, will this affect my driving time if I take one shortcut and so on and so forth. Literally, we can say, our everyday decisions are the sum of all actions we take with a given output.

Data modeling

Data modeling is a process where we try to find a function (or the so-called model) with a set of independent variables or input data. Just like in data warehousing, where modeling is referring to establishing the conceptual framework based on the physical data structure and with the help of ORM or UML (even CRC) diagrams one explores the structures in data the same is seen with exploring the structures when doing predictive analysis. In case of the latter, data modeling is exploring the structures (or relations) between two or more variables. These relations can be presented as a function and are essentially stored as a model.

To start modeling, we will use some of the Microsoft data available at the following GitHub repository:

```
https://github.com/Microsoft/sql-server-samples/tree/master/samples/features/
machine-learning-services/python/getting-started/rental-prediction
```

Do not get confused at this Python example:

> ## Before you begin
>
> To run this sample, you need the following prerequisites:
> Download this DB backup file and restore it using Setup.sql.

Downloading this database will download the `TutorialDB.bak` file, which you simply restore to your SQL Server instance, where R in-database is installed. This database is included as part of the accompanying code that comes with this chapter.

Part of modeling data is to set up the understanding of how predictions at a later phase will work. Therefore, in this phase, we will create an understanding of the variables and their relation to each other. Create restore from the downloaded file and run the following restore from the backup T-SQL command:

```
USE [master]
BACKUP LOG [TutorialDB] TO DISK = N'C:\Program Files\Microsoft SQL
Server\MSSQL14.MSSQLSERVER\MSSQL\Backup\TutorialDB_LogBackup_2018-01-01_23-
59-09.bak'
```

```
WITH NOFORMAT, NOINIT, NAME = N'TutorialDB_LogBackup_2018-01-01_23-59-09',
NOSKIP, NOREWIND, NOUNLOAD, NORECOVERY , STATS = 5

RESTORE DATABASE [TutorialDB] FROM DISK = N'C:\Program Files\Microsoft SQL
Server\MSSQL14.MSSQLSERVER\MSSQL\Backup\TutorialDB.bak'
WITH FILE = 2, MOVE N'TutorialDB' TO N'C:\Program Files\Microsoft SQL
Server\MSSQL14.MSSQLSERVER\MSSQL\DATA\TutorialDB.mdf',
MOVE N'TutorialDB_log' TO N'C:\Program Files\Microsoft SQL
Server\MSSQL14.MSSQLSERVER\MSSQL\DATA\TutorialDB_log.ldf', NOUNLOAD, STATS
= 5

GO
```

Alternatively, you can simply use the RESTORE command in SSMS:

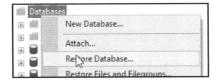

You will now have the database restored and the dbo.rental_data table at your use. For now, this will be enough.

With the dataset ready, we can now start modeling the data by exploring and understanding the variables and the relations among them. This quick exploration can be performed in SQL Operation Studio (link to download: https://docs.microsoft.com/en-us/sql/sql-operations-studio/download), where we will use a simple query:

```
SELECT RentalCount,Day,Month, Holiday, Snow FROM rental_data
```

Besides the standard table view of the results, this will also give a nice chart viewer, where a simple graphical representation of variables will give you better insights into the data:

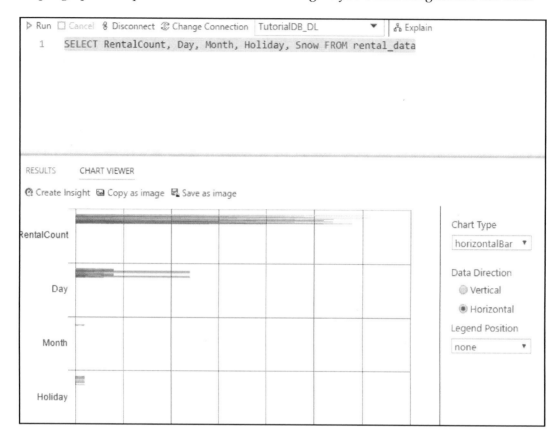

But without the general understanding of descriptive statistics, we will not continue. So, using the rxSummary function from the RevoScaleR package will give the desired results:

```
EXEC sp_execute_external_Script
@LANGUAGE = N'R'
,@script = N'
    dr_rent <- InputDataSet
    dr_rent <- data.frame(dr_rent)
    summary <- rxSummary(~ RentalCount  + Year + Month + Day  + WeekDay +
Snow + Holiday , data = dr_rent)
    OutputDataSet <- summary$sDataFrame'
,@input_data_1 = N'SELECT  RentalCount, Year, Month, Day, WeekDay, Snow,
Holiday FROM rental_data'
WITH RESULT SETS ((
```

```
     [Name]    NVARCHAR(100)
     ,Mean     NUMERIC(16,3)
     ,StdDev   NUMERIC(16,3)
     ,[Min]    INT
     ,[Max]    INT
     ,ValidObs    INT
     ,MissingObs INT
));
GO
```

The following are the results as a simple descriptive statistics table:

	Name	Mean	StdDev	Min	Max	ValidObs	MissingObs
1	RentalCount	158.437	195.155	20	846	453	0
2	Year	2014.000	0.817	2013	2015	453	0
3	Month	4.450	3.971	1	12	453	0
4	Day	15.623	8.761	1	31	453	0
5	Week Day	3.980	1.988	1	7	453	0
6	Snow	0.344	0.476	0	1	453	0
7	Holiday	0.026	0.161	0	1	453	0

Exploring the uni- and bi-variate statistics was part of the previous `Chapter 5`, *RevoScaleR Package,* but here we will focus more on bi- and multi-variate statistics. Before we begin, let's explore the correlations some more. Based on exploring the variable names and descriptive statistics, common sense will tell us that during the holidays, the rental count should be higher. Checking this can be done using the correlation coefficient. The following is a simple example:

```
EXEC sp_execute_external_Script
@LANGUAGE = N'R'
,@script = N'
      dr_rent <- InputDataSet
      OutputDataSet <- data.frame(cor(dr_rent$Holiday,
dr_rent$RentalCount))
'
,@input_data_1 = N'SELECT  Holiday, RentalCount FROM rental_data'
WITH RESULT SETS ((
    cor NUMERIC(10,3)
    ));
GO
```

This will give you the idea of the bi-variate relationship of 0.332. This is a weak correlation but a positive one:

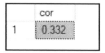

This simply means that if the `RentalCount` variable gets higher, the number of holidays also increases. This indeed makes sense, since if more holidays are coming, more rentals are expected.

Now we can continue exploring and searching for the correlations by combining each of the variables. This is similar to making a CROSS JOIN, but there are easier ways to do this. One is, of course, by using common sense and selecting the meaningful correlations:

```
EXEC sp_execute_external_Script
@LANGUAGE = N'R'
,@script = N'
    dr_rent <- InputDataSet
    dr_rent <- data.frame(dr_rent)
    cor_HR <- cor(dr_rent$Holiday, dr_rent$RentalCount)
    cor_FR <- cor(as.numeric(dr_rent$FWeekDay), dr_rent$RentalCount)
    cor_MR <- cor(dr_rent$Month, dr_rent$RentalCount)
    cor_YR <- cor(dr_rent$Year,dr_rent$RentalCount)
    d <- data.frame(cbind(cor_HR, cor_FR, cor_MR, cor_YR))
    OutputDataSet <- d'
    ,@input_data_1 = N'SELECT  Holiday, RentalCount,Month,FWeekDay, Year
FROM rental_data'
WITH RESULT SETS ((
    cor_HR NUMERIC(10,3)
,cor_FR NUMERIC(10,3)
,cor_MR NUMERIC(10,3)
,cor_YR NUMERIC(10,3)
));
GO
```

And we get the following results as shown in the figure below. Interpretation and understanding of the results is of high importance. So, the holiday time is by far the most correlative variable with rental count variable. Neither the day of the week, nor the year, play any significant role. There is a very tiny, yet negative correlation of -0.110 between `Month` and `RentalCount`, which can be understood as higher months might have lower rental counts and vice versa. Since this correlation is so weak, it is meaningless to make a fuss over of this particular correlation (even if it makes or does not make any sense):

Similarly, one can explore the distribution of the values within each variable by plotting the boxplots:

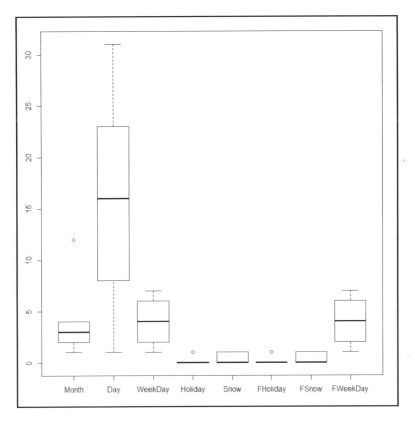

The second way is to plot the diagram of correlations between the variables. One way to do it is to invoke the `corrplot` R library, which gives you a very powerful and useful visualization of correlation. I tend to create the following code:

```
EXEC sp_execute_external_Script
@LANGUAGE = N'R'
,@script = N'
    library(corrplot)  # * footnote
    dr_rent <- InputDataSet
            dr_rent$FWeekDay <- as.numeric(dr_rent$FWeekDay)
            dr_rent$FHoliday <- as.numeric(dr_rent$FHoliday)
            dr_rent$FSnow <- as.numeric(dr_rent$FSnow)
    cor.mtest <- function(mat, ...) {
        mat <- as.matrix(mat)
        n <- ncol(mat)
        p.mat<- matrix(NA, n, n)
        diag(p.mat) <- 0
        for (i in 1:(n - 1)) {
            for (j in (i + 1):n) {
            tmp <- cor.test(mat[, i], mat[, j], ...)
            p.mat[i, j] <- p.mat[j, i] <- tmp$p.value
            }
        }
        colnames(p.mat) <- rownames(p.mat) <- colnames(mat)
        p.mat
        }
    p.mat <- cor.mtest(dr_rent)
    R<-cor(dr_rent)
    col <- colorRampPalette(c("#BB4444", "#EE9988", "#FFFFFF", "#77AADD",
"#4477AA"))
    image_file = tempfile();
    jpeg(filename = image_file);
plot_corr <- corrplot(R, method="color", col=col(200),
                type="upper", order="hclust",
                addCoef.col = "black", # Add coefficient of correlation
                tl.col="black", tl.srt=45, #Text label color and rotation
                # Combine with significance
                p.mat = p.mat, sig.level = 0.01, insig = "blank",
                # hide correlation coefficient on the principal diagonal
                diag=FALSE)
    dev.off();
OutputDataSet <- data.frame(data=readBin(file(image_file, "rb"),
what=raw(), n=1e6));  '
,@input_data_1 = N'SELECT  *  FROM rental_data'
WITH RESULT SETS ((
  correlation_plot varbinary(max)
```

```
));
GO
```

Code copied and slightly changed from the corrplot lattice documentation.

This procedure can be directly implemented and used in SSRS or in Power BI suit or Excel; the visual is as follows:

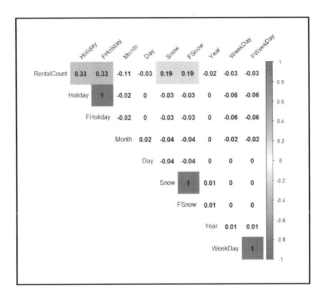

In a single graph, a trained eye will immediately see the correlations and their statistical significance. So, the 0.33 RentalCount and Holiday is visible here, but also the RentalCount and Snow is of 0.19 positive correlation. But if we want to explore the behavior of the values dispersion (variance), we can also include the analysis of variance.

If you are working with large datasets or XDF data formats, RevoScaleR package also comes equipped with functions that compute and calculate correlation matrixes. Here is an R code using rxCovCor (or, alternatively, one can use rxCor or rxCov):

```
Formula_correlation =  ~ RentalCount + Year + Month + Day  + WeekDay + Snow
+ Holiday
allCor <- rxCovCor(Formula_correlation, data = dr_rent, type = "Cor")
allCor
```

This gives the same results as all the previous calculation of correlations:

```
rxCovCor(formula = Formula_correlation, data = dr_rent, type = "Cor")

Data: dr_rent
Number of valid observations: 453
Number of missing observations: 0
Statistic: COR

             RentalCount         Year       Month          Day      weekDay        Snow      Holiday
RentalCount   1.00000000 -2.145545e-02 -0.10955985 -0.029875704 -0.027557065  0.186194501  0.332185334
Year         -0.02145545  1.000000e+00  0.00000000  0.000000000  0.010890454  0.005689906  0.000000000
Month        -0.10955985  3.174240e-13  1.00000000  0.020925350 -0.024926650 -0.036606201 -0.018729468
Day          -0.02987570  0.000000e+00  0.02092535  1.000000000  0.002235798 -0.043061766  0.002403086
weekDay      -0.02755706  1.089045e-02 -0.02492665  0.002235798  1.000000000  0.002571575 -0.060643119
Snow          0.18619450  5.689906e-03 -0.03660620 -0.043061766  0.002571575  1.000000000 -0.032761737
Holiday       0.33218533  0.000000e+00 -0.01872947  0.002403086 -0.060643119 -0.032761737  1.000000000
```

This output also has the ability to see the standard deviations, means and sum of weights, but the best part is that it stores the results in a data frame, which can be easily imported or used with other T-SQL tables. The results can be invoked using `allCov$CovCor` (R language stores the results as an object of lists and each list can be retrieved by using a dollar sign $ and referencing the name of the list—in this case, `CovCor`).

When we want to further investigate our so-far highest correlation between the `RentalCount` and `Holiday`, **Analysis Of Variance (ANOVA)** will be the appropriate method. We will compare two groups (or levels) of variable `Holiday` (0 is not a holiday while 1 is a holiday) and whether there is a difference between the rental counts. By doing so, calculating F-statistics and its significance will tell us the ratio of between-group variance to within-group variance:

```
EXEC sp_execute_external_Script
@LANGUAGE = N'R'
,@script = N'
            #ANOVA
            ANOVA <- aov(RentalCount ~ Holiday, data = InputDataSet)
            F_Stat<- unlist(summary(ANOVA))[7]
            F_Stat_Sig <- unlist(summary(ANOVA))[9]
            df <- cbind(F_Stat, F_Stat_Sig)
OutputDataSet <- data.frame(df)'
,@input_data_1 = N'SELECT  RentalCount,Holiday FROM rental_data'
WITH RESULT SETS ((
    F_Statistic NVARCHAR(200)
,Statistical_Significance NUMERIC(16,5)
));
GO
```

After running the T-SQL code with R code for statistical calculation of ANOVA, the output result is created in such manner that it returns the F-Statistic and statistical significance. The following figure shows results returned:

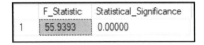

	F_Statistic	Statistical_Significance
1	55.9393	0.00000

Results tell us that the F-Statistic is statistically significant—even though it is small—and this means that the means are most likely not equal (and we would be, in this case, rejecting the null hypothesis). To find where the difference lies, `TukeyHDS` test would give us further information.

Just to illustrate the difference, since we will not go into the details, we can use the `stripchart` visualization of the difference between the holiday distribution of the rentals:

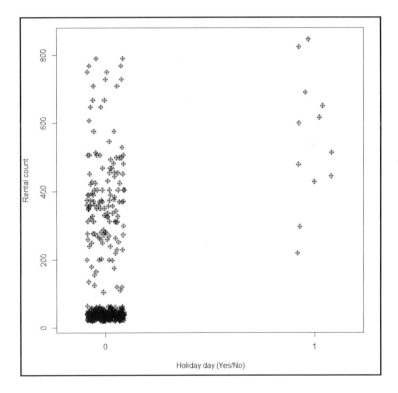

With the R code:

```
stripchart(RentalCount ~ Holiday, vertical=TRUE, pch=9,
                data=dr_rent_ANOVA, xlab="Holiday day (Yes/No)",
ylab="Rental count", method="jitter", jitter=0.09)
```

The distribution of the cases can tell us that on holidays an average of 400 or higher rental counts are made, whereas on a normal day, there is a huge density of counts between 10 and 50.

When determining which features (variables) are good for further analysis and predictive algorithms, we can use the Decrease Gini mean calculation. One of the Gini mean functions is available in `randomForest` package, so, let's call the function and see which variables are to be used:

```
EXEC sp_execute_external_Script
@LANGUAGE = N'R'
,@script = N'
   library(randomForest)
    dr_rent   <- InputDataSet
    fit_RF <- randomForest(factor(dr_rent$RentalCount)~., data=dr_rent)
     vp_rf <- importance(fit_RF)
      vp_rf<- data.frame(vp_rf)
      imena <- row.names(vp_rf)
      vp_rf <- data.frame(cbind(imena, vp_rf))
    OutputDataSet <- vp_rf'
,@input_data_1 = N'SELECT  *  FROM rental_data'
WITH RESULT SETS ((
    Variable NVARCHAR(200)
,MeanDecreaseGini NUMERIC(16,5)
));
GO
```

With T-SQL code we are returning the decreased Gini coefficient:

	Variable	MeanDecreaseGini
1	Year	39.34362
2	Month	46.37933
3	Day	89.72434
4	WeekDay	32.72640
5	Holiday	3.56413
6	Snow	10.27519
7	FHoliday	2.12951
8	FSnow	6.49198
9	FWeekDay	33.30637

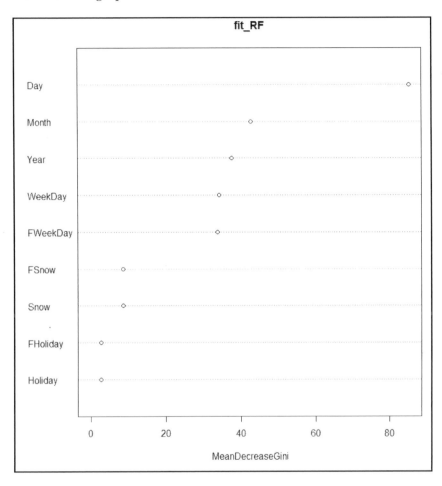

`Gini` coefficient can also be represented visually as a scatter plot, so that the user can immediately determine which variables contribute most to the model. For the sake of brevity, the code for this graph is included in the code but not in the book.

One can now determine, which of the following variables play any role or contribute gain in the model. The **MeanDecreaseGini** was drawn as `varImpPlot(fit_RF)`. Technically, this is how one can determine which variables or input parameters have the least or most impact, but each of these techniques will give you some of the aspects—what can be good in the model, and what may not. Comparing the `Holiday` variable in the correlation matrix and mean decrease plot, you can see that it gives different methods and different results. Most significant are the ones where particular variables do not play any importance whatsoever through several different methods.

Advanced predictive algorithms and analytics

So far, we have examined the data preparation and data exploration functions available in the `RevoScaleR` package. Besides these functions, predicting classification or regression problems can also be done, especially when dealing with large datasets.

I will mention only few of these. The complete list is available online (`https://docs.microsoft.com/en-us/machine-learning-server/r-reference/revoscaler/revoscaler`) and some of the points are as follows:

- `rxLinMod`: This is used for building and predicting a linear model
- `rxLogit`: This is used for building and predicting the logistic regression model
- `rxGlm`: This is used for creating a generalized linear model
- `rxDTree`: This is used for creating a classification or regression tree
- `rxBTrees`: This is used for building a classification or regression decision forest—that is using a stochastic gradient boosting algorithm
- `rxDForest`: This is used for building a classification or regression decision forest model
- `rxNaiveBayes`: This is used for building a Naive Bayes classification model

All these algorithms are part of a family of supervised algorithms, where the only unsupervised (or undirected) algorithm available in `RevoScaleR` package is `rxKMeans`, which is used for dealing with clustering.

Using the same dataset as we did earlier, we plug in and start using `rxLinMod` and `rxGlm` for demonstrating how this can be used within T-SQL:

```
USE RentalDB;
GO

-- rxLinMod

EXEC sp_execute_external_Script
@LANGUAGE = N'R'
,@script = N'
          library(RevoScaleR)
          dr_rent <- InputDataSet
          Formula_supervised =  RentalCount ~ Year + Month + Day  +
WeekDay + Snow + Holiday
          #Create Linear Model
          rent_lm <- rxLinMod(formula=Formula_supervised, data = dr_rent)

          #PREDICT
          rent_Pred <- rxPredict(modelObject = rent_lm, data = dr_rent,
extraVarsToWrite = c("RentalCount","Year","Month","Day"), writeModelVars =
TRUE)
          OutputDataSet <- data.frame(rent_Pred)
'
,@input_data_1 = N'SELECT RentalCount,Year, Month, Day,
WeekDay,Snow,Holiday  FROM rental_data'
WITH RESULT SETS ((
 RentalCount_Pred    NUMERIC(16,3)
,RentalCount  NUMERIC(16,3)
,YearINT
,MonthINT
,DayINT
,WeekDayINT
,Snow   INT
,Holiday INT
));
GO



-- rxGlm

EXEC sp_execute_external_Script
@LANGUAGE = N'R'
,@script = N'
          library(RevoScaleR)
          dr_rent <- InputDataSet
```

```
            Formula_supervised =  RentalCount ~ Year + Month + Day  +
WeekDay + Snow + Holiday

        #PREDICT
            rent_glm <- rxGlm(formula = Formula_supervised, family =
Gamma, dropFirst = TRUE, data = dr_rent)
            rent_Pred <- rxPredict(modelObject = rent_glm, data =
dr_rent, extraVarsToWrite=c("RentalCount","Year","Month","Day"),
writeModelVars = TRUE)
        OutputDataSet <- data.frame(rent_Pred)'
,@input_data_1 = N'SELECT RentalCount,Year, Month, Day,
WeekDay,Snow,Holiday  FROM rental_data'
WITH RESULT SETS ((
 RentalCount_Pred     NUMERIC(16,3)
,RentalCount   NUMERIC(16,3)
,YearINT
,MonthINT
,DayINT
,WeekDayINT
,Snow   INT
,Holiday INT
));
GO

-- rxDTree

EXEC sp_execute_external_Script
@LANGUAGE = N'R'
,@script = N'
        library(RevoScaleR)
        dr_rent <- InputDataSet
        Formula_supervised =  RentalCount ~ Year + Month + Day  +
WeekDay + Snow + Holiday

        #PREDICT
                rent_dt <- rxDTree(formula = Formula_supervised,
data = dr_rent)
                rent_Pred <- rxPredict(modelObject = rent_dt, data
= dr_rent, extraVarsToWrite=c("RentalCount","Year","Month","Day"),
writeModelVars = TRUE)
        OutputDataSet <- data.frame(rent_Pred)
            '
,@input_data_1 = N'SELECT RentalCount,Year, Month, Day,
WeekDay,Snow,Holiday  FROM rental_data'
WITH RESULT SETS ((
```

```
 RentalCount_Pred     NUMERIC(16,3)
,RentalCount   NUMERIC(16,3)
,YearINT
,MonthINT
,DayINT
,WeekDayINT
,Snow    INT
,Holiday INT
));
GO
```

Both will give you the predicted values based on the inputted dataset, along with the newly predicted values:

	RentalCount_Pred	RentalCount	Year	Month	Day	WeekDay	Snow	Holiday
4	37.083	38.000	2014	3	31	2	0	0
5	25.143	23.000	2014	4	24	5	0	0
6	46.556	42.000	2015	2	11	4	0	0
7	293.571	310.000	2013	4	28	1	0	0
8	321.636	240.000	2014	3	8	7	0	0
9	25.143	22.000	2013	4	5	6	0	0
10	359.133	360.000	2015	3	29	1	0	0
11	27.000	20.000	2015	4	22	4	0	0
12	33.692	36.000	2014	4	1	3	1	0
13	37.150	42.000	2015	3	6	6	0	0

A curious eye will tell you that the predicted values are far-off from the original values. So, the prediction formula in both cases was trying to predict variable RentalCount based on variables: Year, Month, Day, WeekDay, Snow, and Holiday. The formula is set as follows:

```
Formula_supervised =  RentalCount ~ Year + Month + Day  + WeekDay + Snow +
Holiday
```

Comparing the variables RentalCount_Pred and RentalCount will show the difference/offset from the real and predicted values.

In the preceding sample, you can also compare the results of all the three algorithms. If you run comparison with all three datasets, observation by observation, you can see immediately which algorithms performed best:

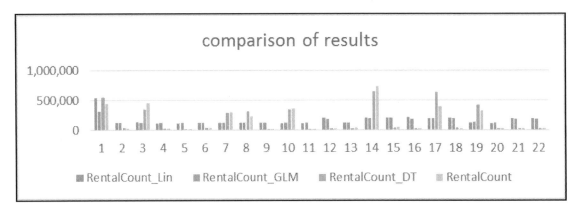

So, the yellow bar represents the original values, and by far the best hit is the decision trees algorithm, given the upper formula and understanding the insights of the data. The graph just represents a randomly taken observation. This can also be achieved by calculating the accuracy or measure that calculates how much deviation had accrued from the original values.

Deploying and using predictive solutions

When developing the in-database solution and creating it for continuous development (and also deployment), several aspects should be taken into consideration. First of all, the environment where data scientists will be working. You might give them a powerful, standalone server or even allocate proper seats in the cloud. They will need it, especially when training the model. This is extremely important, as you don't want to have your highly-paid statisticians and mathematicians wait for the models to compute and generate. So, enabling the route to a highly scalable CPU and RAM powerful computations is a must. Second to this, you have to get the data there. Whether it's on cloud or on premises, getting data there (and later also, back) should not be overlooked, as this might also be the point where you will lose precious time. And, lastly, having the environment set with proper settings, environment variables, packages, and all paths to proprietary software enabled is also of importance.

`RevoScaleR` package comes equipped with a function for easily switching the computational environments. We will now invoke a simple command in R:

```
rxSetComputeContext(local)
rxSetComputeContext(sql)
```

By doing this, you can set the local computational environment (that is, the client's machine) or the server side, where—in this case—a standalone R Server would reside. With a simple function call, the computational context (or simple environment) is switched, as course, keeping in mind that all the data resides on both sides (so that you avoid the unneeded data transferring) and that all the server environment variables are set correctly.

For training the model, several good practices can be chosen. Splitting the data for training, testing or training, and testing and validating are several practices. Also, a very good practice is to test the percentage of training/testing/validating datasets. You might get a 50/50 or 60/40 or 70/30 percentage, but usually you carry out and decide this when mining the data. After that, you should also consider validation of the data; several aspects are available, from **leave one out** (**LOO**) or 10-folds or 5-folds for choosing the validation data for validating the results.

Not going into the topic too deep, and to make this demo simpler, we can decide to do a 70/30 percentage on the spot. Since we have the pleasure of the T-SQL database here, we can select and store the training subset in a table, or create a view, or decide which 70% we want to take.

```
-- We can set 70% of the original data
-- IN SQL Server
SELECT
TOP (70)PERCENT
*
INTO dbo.Train_rental_data
FROM rental_data
ORDER BY ABS (CAST(BINARY_CHECKSUM(RentalCount,NEWID())asint))ASC
-- (318 rows affected)
-- Or we can set by the year; year 2013 and 2014 for training and 2015 for
testing? making it cca 70% for training as well
SELECT COUNT(*),YEAR FROM rental_data GROUP BY YEAR
```

This also heavily depends on your business model. The first approach simply takes 70% of the data from the original dataset, whereas the second select statement takes roughly 70% of the original data, but makes a split based on the year of the rental. This might have a crucial impact on how the model will behave and also how you want the decision to be affected by this, especially the business model.

Once this is cleared and covered, a best practice is to store the trained model in the tables for faster predictions. We will now create a table as follows:

```
-- or in R
EXEC sp_execute_external_Script
        @language = N'R'
        ,@script = N'
                        library(caTools)
                        set.seed(2910)
                        dr_rent <- InputDataSet
                        Split <- .70
                        sample = sample.split(dr_rent$RentalCount,
SplitRatio = Split)
                        train_dr_rent <- subset(dr_rent, sample == TRUE)
                        test_dr_rent  <- subset(dr_rent, sample == FALSE)
                OutputDataSet <- data.frame(train_dr_rent)
                        '
        ,@input_data_1 = N'SELECT * FROM rental_data'
WITH RESULT SETS ((
        [Year] INT
        ,[Month] INT
        ,[Day] INT
        ,[RentalCount] INT
        ,[WeekDay] INT
        ,[Holiday] INT
        ,[Snow] INT
        ,[FHoliday] INT
        ,[FSnow] INT
        ,[FWeekDay] INT
));
GO
```

Since the set.seed is defined, you will always get the same subset, wherever you run this code. If you want to get different results, you should comment it out.

Once the sampling is done again, based on the problem you are predicting, you need to define your prediction formula. In this case, I am using a formula converter to create a proper formula:

```
-- Variables to keep
-- and creating formula
EXEC sp_execute_external_Script
        @language = N'R'
        ,@script = N'
        dr_rent <- InputDataSet
            variables_all <- rxGetVarNames(dr_rent)
            variables_to_remove <- c("FSnow", "FWeekDay", "FHoliday")
```

```
            traning_variables <- variables_all[!(variables_all %in%
c("RentalCount", variables_to_remove))]
            #use as.formula to create an object
        formula <- as.formula(paste("RentalCount ~",
paste(traning_variables, collapse = "+")))
                #formula <- paste("RentalCount ~", paste(traning_variables,
collapse = "+"))
            OutputDataSet <- data.frame(formula)'
,@input_data_1 = N'SELECT * FROM dbo.Train_rental_data'
WITH RESULT SETS ((
        [Formula_supervised] NVARCHAR(1000)
));
GO
```

Creating a formula through a procedure, making it not hard coded, is also a very useful approach, especially in the corporate environment where data scientists will set up the pool of independent variables and later the data engineer would choose which to include, prior to pushing the data to compute the model and deploy it.

The process of bi-variate and multi-variate statistics can also give the data engineers and stewards better insights and understanding of what and how the data is operating and correlating, and that there are no unwanted correlations or variables that just do not function.

With this cleared up, we can set up and build the procedures that will run the model training and have the models stored in the database. Due to the space limits of this chapter, I will only show the creation of one procedure; the rest of the procedures can be found in the accompanying chapter materials:

The procedure for random forest in T-SQL would look like this:

```
-- Random forest

DROP PROCEDURE IF EXISTS dbo.forest_model;
GO


CREATE OR ALTER PROCEDURE dbo.forest_model(
        @trained_model VARBINARY(MAX)OUTPUT
        ,@accuracy FLOATOUTPUT
        )
AS
BEGIN
EXEC sp_execute_external_script
@language = N'R'
,@script = N'
```

```
                    library(RevoScaleR)
                    library(caTools)
            library(MLmetrics)

                    dr_rent <- InputDataSet
                    set.seed(2910)
                    Split <- .70
                    sample = sample.split(dr_rent$RentalCount,
SplitRatio = Split)

                    train_dr_rent <- subset(dr_rent, sample == TRUE)
                    test_dr_rent  <- subset(dr_rent, sample == FALSE)
                    y_train <- train_dr_rent$RentalCount
                    y_test  <- test_dr_rent$RentalCount


            variables_all <- rxGetVarNames(dr_rent)
            variables_to_remove <- c("FSnow", "FWeekDay", "FHoliday")
            traning_variables <- variables_all[!(variables_all %in%
c("RentalCount", variables_to_remove))]
            formula <- as.formula(paste("RentalCount ~",
paste(traning_variables, collapse = "+")))

                    forest_model <- rxDForest(formula = formula,
                      data = train_dr_rent,
                      nTree = 40,
                      minSplit = 10,
                      minBucket = 5,
                      cp = 0.00005,
                      seed = 5)

                    trained_model <- as.raw(serialize(forest_model,
connection=NULL))
                    #calculating accuracy
            y_predicted<- rxPredict(forest_model,test_dr_rent)

            predict_forest <-data.frame(actual=y_test,pred=y_predicted)
            #ConfMat <-
confusionMatrix(table(predict_forest$actual,predict_forest$RentalCount_Pred
))
            #accuracy <- ConfMat$overall[1]
            accu <- LogLoss(y_pred = predict_forest$RentalCount_Pred ,
y_true =predict_forest$actual)
            accuracy <- accu'


        ,@input_data_1 = N'SELECT * FROM dbo.rental_data'
        ,@params = N'@trained_model VARBINARY(MAX) OUTPUT, @accuracy FLOAT
OUTPUT'
```

```
        ,@trained_model = @trained_model OUTPUT
        ,@accuracy = @accuracy OUTPUT;
END;
GO
```

I have added something extra to the procedure, such that every time the model is trained, an extra is added. This is accuracy, which will also give the data engineer and stewards in the later phases a good insight into deciding which model outperforms the others.

You can simply run the procedure as follows:

```
DECLARE @model VARBINARY(MAX);
DECLARE @accur FLOAT;
EXEC dbo.forest_model@model OUTPUT, @accur OUTPUT;
INSERT INTO [dbo].[Rental_data_models](model_name, model, accuracy) VALUES
('Random_forest_V1', @model, @accur);
GO
```

This will populate the destination table where the models are kept. The results should be stored in the table `[dbo].[Rental_data_models]`:

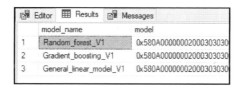

Once this is done, you need to have the evaluation procedure set as well that will help determine which model functions the best. However, this part can be done using Power BI, or reporting services, or simply just R.

This is part of R code that can be included in your visualization tool for easier comprehension:

```
library(RevoScaleR)
library(caTools)
library(MLmetrics)

#evaluate_model function; Source: Microsoft
evaluate_model <- function(observed, predicted_probability, threshold,
model_name) {

  # Given the observed labels and the predicted probability, plot the ROC
curve and determine the AUC.
  data <- data.frame(observed, predicted_probability)
  data$observed <- as.numeric(as.character(data$observed))
```

```
  if(model_name =="RF"){
    rxRocCurve(actualVarName = "observed", predVarNames =
"predicted_probability", data = data, numBreaks = 1000, title = "RF" )
  }else{
    rxRocCurve(actualVarName = "observed", predVarNames =
"predicted_probability", data = data, numBreaks = 1000, title = "GBT" )
  }
  ROC <- rxRoc(actualVarName = "observed", predVarNames =
"predicted_probability", data = data, numBreaks = 1000)
  auc <- rxAuc(ROC)

  # Given the predicted probability and the threshold, determine the binary
prediction.
  predicted <- ifelse(predicted_probability > threshold, 1, 0)
  predicted <- factor(predicted, levels = c(0, 1))

  # Build the corresponding Confusion Matrix, then compute the Accuracy,
Precision, Recall, and F-Score.
  confusion <- table(observed, predicted)
  print(model_name)
  print(confusion)
  tp <- confusion[1, 1]
  fn <- confusion[1, 2]
  fp <- confusion[2, 1]
  tn <- confusion[2, 2]
  accuracy <- (tp + tn) / (tp + fn + fp + tn)
  precision <- tp / (tp + fp)
  recall <- tp / (tp + fn)
  fscore <- 2 * (precision * recall) / (precision + recall)

  # Return the computed metrics.
  metrics <- list("Accuracy" = accuracy,
"Precision" = precision,
"Recall" = recall,
"F-Score" = fscore,
"AUC" = auc)
  return(metrics)
}


RF_Scoring <- rxPredict(forest_model, data = train_dr_rent, overwrite = T,
type = "response",extraVarsToWrite = c("RentalCount"))

Prediction_RF <- rxImport(inData = RF_Scoring, stringsAsFactors = T,
outFile = NULL)
observed <- Prediction_RF$RentalCount

# Compute the performance metrics of the model.
```

```
Metrics_RF <- evaluate_model(observed = observed, predicted_probability =
Prediction_RF$RentalCount_Pred , model_name = "RF", threshold=50)

# Make Predictions, then import them into R. The observed Conversion_Flag
is kept through the argument extraVarsToWrite.
GBT_Scoring <- rxPredict(btree_model,data = train_dr_rent, overwrite = T,
type="prob",extraVarsToWrite = c("RentalCount"))

Prediction_GBT <- rxImport(inData = GBT_Scoring, stringsAsFactors = T,
outFile = NULL)
observed <- Prediction_GBT$RentalCount
```

The observed values should tell you which model is performing best. Once you have done this, you can choose the model and see how the predictions can be done.

Performing predictions with R Services in the SQL Server database

Calling stored procedures is the easiest way to organize your code and start predicting right away.

Again, only a sample will be shown here of how to create a stored procedure to predict new datasets:

```
CREATE OR ALTER PROCEDURE [dbo].[Predicting_rentalCount]
(
                @model VARCHAR(30)
              , @query NVARCHAR(MAX)
)
AS
BEGIN
       DECLARE @nar_model VARBINARY(MAX) = (SELECT model FROM
[dbo].[Rental_data_models] WHERE model_name = @model);

       EXEC sp_execute_external_script
               @language = N'R'
             , @script = N'

                              #input from query
                              new_data <- InputDataSet
                              #model from query
                              model <- unserialize(nar_model)

                              #prediction
```

```
                                    prediction <- rxPredict(model,data =
new_data, overwrite = TRUE, type="response",extraVarsToWrite =
c("RentalCount"))
                                    Prediction_New <- rxImport(inData =
prediction, stringsAsFactors = T, outFile = NULL)

                                    OutputDataSet <- data.frame(Prediction_New)

                                    '
            ,@input_data_1 =  @query
            ,@params = N'@nar_model VARBINARY(MAX)'
            ,@nar_model = @nar_model
    WITH RESULT SETS((
            Prediction_new NVARCHAR(1000)
            , OrigPredictecCount NVARCHAR(1000)
        ))
END;
```

Once this is done, you can start predicting using the following code:

```
-- Example of running predictions against selected model
EXEC [dbo].[Predicting_rentalCount]
        @model = N'Random_forest_V1'
        ,@query = N'SELECT
                                    2014 AS Year
                                    ,5 AS Month
                                    ,12 AS Day
                                    ,1 AS WeekDay
                                    ,0 AS Holiday
                                    ,0 AS Snow
                                    ,0 AS RentalCount'
```

And, as a result, you will get a predicted value for the variables of Year, Month, Day, WeekDay, Holiday, and Snow:

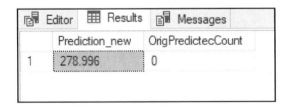

Intentionally, the field `OrigPredictedCount` was set to 0, but the new predicted value is the value of `278.996` and that is based on the input variables. While checking how the model learned, it is best to also check the original value:

```
SELECT
*
FROM Rental_data
WHERE [year] = 2014
AND [day] = 12
```

We see that there is no values in month= 5, so the model must have it learned from other values:

	Year	Month	Day	RentalCount	WeekDay	Holiday	Snow	FHoliday	FSnow	FWeekDay
1	2014	4	12	390	7	0	0	0	0	7
2	2014	2	12	36	4	0	1	0	1	4
3	2014	12	12	40	6	0	1	0	1	6
4	2014	3	12	28	4	0	1	0	1	4
5	2014	1	12	425	1	0	1	0	1	1

Now that we have covered the supervised predictive algorithms, let's quickly jump into the cluster—part of the functions that `RevoScaleR` package supports as the only undirected algorithm.

The following is the example of how to create a simple clustering:

```
library("cluster")
# and remove the Fholidays and Fsnow variables
DF <- DF[c(1,2,3,4,5,6,7)]
XDF <- paste(tempfile(), "xdf", sep=".")
if (file.exists(XDF)) file.remove(XDF)
rxDataStep(inData = DF, outFile = XDF)

# grab 3 random rows for starting
centers <- DF[sample.int(NROW(DF), 3, replace = TRUE),]

Formula =  ~ Year + Month + Day + RentalCount + WeekDay + Holiday + Snow

# Example using an XDF file as a data source
z <- rxKmeans(formula=Formula, data = DF, centers = centers)
clusplot(DF, z$cluster, color=TRUE, shade=TRUE, labels=4, lines=0, plotchar
= TRUE)
```

The following is the output, which is the presentation of the clusters:

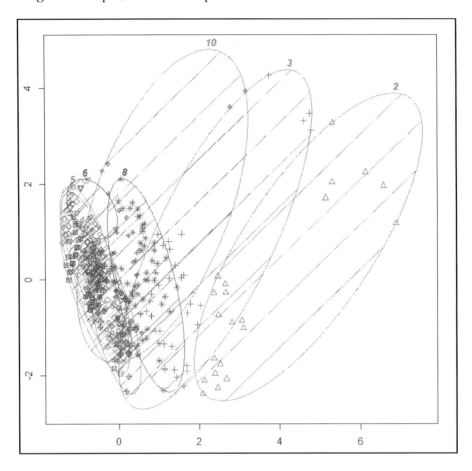

To explore the clustering and play with different number of clusters, one thing for sure would be to use R code directly or to create a report for exploring the characteristics of clusters using Power BI, Excel, or SSRS.

Adding some additional information on cluster centers, statistics as `withinSS`, `betweenSS`, `totSS`, and others will also help us to understand the clusters.

Scree plot is also an additional and very nice presentation of choosing the correct number of clusters. Adding such graphics into a report will also help the user choose the right number of clusters and help them understand what and how clusters are formed.

Scree plot R code is used for determining where elbow is happening and does whether it has the right number of clusters; if so, three clusters would be an optimum number:

```
wss <- (nrow(DF) - 1) * sum(apply(DF, 2, var))
for (i in 2:20)
  wss[i] <- sum(kmeans(DF, centers = i)$withinss)
plot(1:20, wss, type = "b", xlab = "Number of Clusters", ylab = "Within
groups sum of squares")
```

On this plot we can see where the elbow is being created and we can determine that the best solution is three clusters:

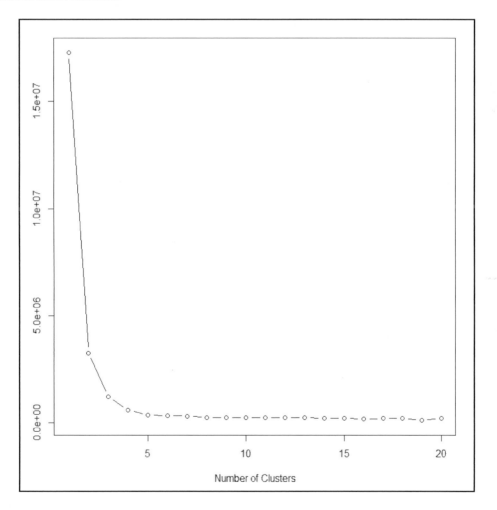

Putting everything together into a report (SSRS report) makes exploring even better:

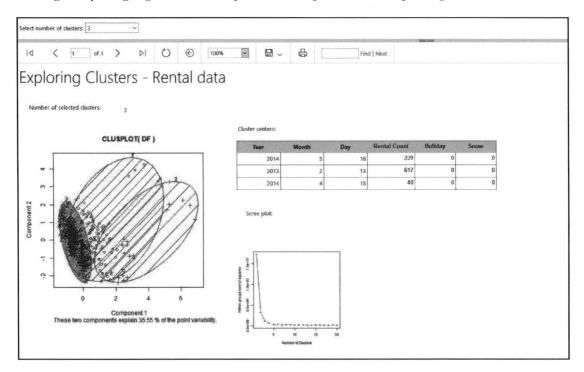

The user can change the number of clusters by selecting the desired number and the report will change accordingly. The report is based on three additional procedures that export the graphs based on the inputted number of clusters:

```
CREATE OR ALTER  PROCEDURE [dbo].[Clustering_rentalCount]
(
                @nof_clusters VARCHAR(2)
)
AS
BEGIN

DECLARE @SQLStat NVARCHAR(4000)
SET @SQLStat = 'SELECT  * FROM rental_data'
DECLARE @RStat NVARCHAR(4000)
SET @RStat = 'library(ggplot2)
                library(RevoScaleR)
library(cluster)
                image_file <- tempfile()
                jpeg(filename = image_file, width = 400, height = 400)
  DF <- data.frame(dr_rent)
```

```
                        DF <- DF[c(1,2,3,4,5,6,7)]
XDF <- paste(tempfile(), "xdf", sep=".")
                    if (file.exists(XDF)) file.remove(XDF)
                    rxDataStep(inData = DF, outFile = XDF)

                    centers <- DF[sample.int(NROW(DF), 3, replace = TRUE),]
Formula =  ~ Year + Month + Day + RentalCount + WeekDay + Holiday + Snow
                    rxKmeans(formula = Formula, data = XDF,
numClusters='+@nof_clusters+')
                    z <- rxKmeans(formula=Formula, data = DF,
numClusters='+@nof_clusters+')
                    clusplot(DF, z$cluster, color=TRUE, shade=TRUE, labels=4,
lines=0, plotchar = TRUE)
dev.off()
                        OutputDataSet <-
data.frame(data=readBin(file(image_file, "rb"), what=raw(), n=1e6))'

EXECUTE sp_execute_external_script
        @language = N'R'
        ,@script = @RStat
        ,@input_data_1 = @SQLStat
        ,@input_data_1_name = N'dr_rent'
WITH RESULT SETS ((plot varbinary(max)))
END;
GO
```

Running this in SSMS will give you a var binary string, but adding the result of this procedure as an image in SSRS or Power BI/Excel will yield a plot derived from R.

Adding a nice visualization to your exploratory project upon building a predictive analytics system is definitely a very nice wrap-up for business and end users, as well as for the data wranglers and engineers.

Summary

In this chapter, we have covered the extensible functionalities of the `RevoScaleR` package to deliver fast and good predictions based on the explored datasets. In the previous chapter *Statistical learning with RevoScaleR package*, we have covered data exploration, preparation and simple and bi-variate statistics. This chapter showed how `RevoScaleR` package was designed to work with large datasets (that overcome the limitations of RAM and single CPU), enabling spill to disk and multi threading. The same procedures can be used as well in database instances of R, for delivering the predictions to your business and data residing in the database. We have covered this aspect as well, exploring different algorithms and comparing the solutions. Once you have your model selected, you may want to use the `PREDICT` clause. which is a new feature in SQL Server 2017 with a slightly altered architecture. Please note that currently (at the time of writing this chapter) the model size can not exceed 100 MB if you want to use `PREDICT` clause. Currently, only `RevoScaleR` and `MicrosoftML` packages are supported to use this clause, and not even all `RevoScaleR` (and MicrosoftML) algorithms are supported—currently supported are `rxLinMod`, `rxLogit`, `rxBTrees`, `rxDtree`, `rxdForest`. However, this real-time scoring with `PREDICT` clause will definitely develop and evolve in the next release of SQL Server.

We need to predict a classification or regression problem. The majority of the problems can be supported using `RevoScaleR` package and many of these algorithms were also empowered by a new set of additional classifiers available in the `MicrosoftML` package. Exploring both packages will give your decision-making a much-needed boost. Also, storing serialized models into the database is an optimal way of storing and calling trained models (functions) that can be retrained by adding a simple logic implementation using SQL Server agents or triggers.

In `Chapter 07`, *Operationalizing R Code*, you will learn how to operationalize your model and solution and explore different ways how to do it and some good practices.

7
Operationalizing R Code

As you learned the essentials of predictive modeling and explored advanced predictive algorithms available in `RevoScaleR` package in the previous chapter, now is a good time to learn how to operationalize it. This chapter discusses how you can operationalize R Prediction models in both SQL Server 2016 and SQL Server 2017.

The idea of marrying SQL Server and machine learning is to keep analytics close to the data and eliminate costs, as well as security risks. In addition, using Microsoft R libraries helps to improve the scale and performance of your R solutions.

This chapter outlines the steps for operationalizing your R prediction models into a powerful workflow integrated in SQL Server. First, we'll discuss the concept of integrating an existing R model into SQL Server using the extensibility framework, native scoring (SQL Server 2017), and real-time scoring. Then, we'll talk about how to manage roles and permissions to run an R model in SQL Server. You will also learn how to use the right tools to operationalize the R model in SQL Server, and how to execute R model as part of workflows, PowerShell, SQL Server Agent jobs, and SSIS.

Integrating an existing R model

This section takes an existing R code that generates the R model and runs against the SQL Server dataset into a workflow, where the model can be refreshed and evaluated on a regular basis, then used for predictive analysis. The following figure shows a typical predictive modeling workflow in an R script:

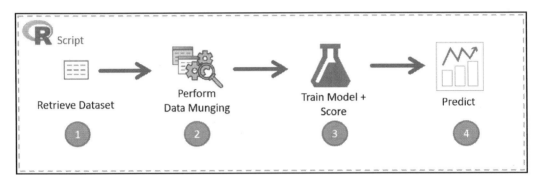

Figure 7.1: Typical predictive modeling workflow

To integrate this script in SQL Server, you'll need to organize the workflow into three steps:

1. Prepare the data for training
2. Train and save the model using T-SQL
3. Operationalize the model

In this section, the last two steps will use sp_execute_external_script, which invokes an R process. These steps are using the SQL Server extensibility framework, described later on.

Prerequisite – prepare the data

We will use the NYC Taxi sample data from the *R: In-Database Analytics for SQL Developers* tutorial, as referred to at https://github.com/Microsoft/sql-server-samples/blob/master/samples/features/r-services/predictive-analytics/scripts/Lab.md.

You can also download the nyctaxi_sample.csv file from the Packt code file repository, and execute the following bcp command:

```
bcp <database name>.dbo.nyctaxi_sample in <file path> -c -t, -T -S<server
name>
```

where:

- <database name> is the name of the database
- <file path> is the location to the nyctaxi_sample.csv file
- <server name> is your server name.

As an example:

```
bcp NYCTaxi.dbo.nyctaxi_sample in c:\nyctaxi_sample.csv -c -t, -T -
SMsSQLGirl
```

In this scenario, the goal is to predict the likelihood of tipping. As part of the process, we will create a logistic regression model, along with the model's **Receiver Operating Characteristic** (**ROC**) curve and its **Area Under Curve** (**AUC**). An ROC is a plot of the true positive rate against the false positive rate for various threshold points of a diagnostic test. The closer the curve comes to the diagonal of the ROC space, the less accurate the test.

The closer the curve comes to the left and top borders, the more accurate it is. AUC provides the test of accuracy in numerical form. Luckily, both the ROC plot and AUC value can be easily calculated in R.

Once we are comfortable that the model is accurate enough, we can then share it and reuse it for predicting if a taxi driver will be tipped, based on the inputs provided.

Here's the table definition of the NYC Taxi dataset that we will use for training:

```
CREATE TABLE [dbo].[nyctaxi_sample](
    [medallion] [varchar](50) NOT NULL,
    [hack_license] [varchar](50) NOT NULL,
    [vendor_id] [char](3) NULL,
    [rate_code] [char](3) NULL,
    [store_and_fwd_flag] [char](3) NULL,
    [pickup_datetime] [datetime] NOT NULL,
    [dropoff_datetime] [datetime] NULL,
    [passenger_count] [int] NULL,
    [trip_time_in_secs] [bigint] NULL,
    [trip_distance] [float] NULL,
    [pickup_longitude] [varchar](30) NULL,
    [pickup_latitude] [varchar](30) NULL,
    [dropoff_longitude] [varchar](30) NULL,
    [dropoff_latitude] [varchar](30) NULL,
    [payment_type] [char](3) NULL,
    [fare_amount] [float] NULL,
    [surcharge] [float] NULL,
    [mta_tax] [float] NULL,
```

```
        [tolls_amount] [float] NULL,
        [total_amount] [float] NULL,
        [tip_amount] [float] NULL,
        [tipped] [int] NULL,
        [tip_class] [int] NULL
    ) ON [PRIMARY]
    GO
```

There are a few variables that we can start using to analyze the likelihood of a taxi driver being tipped. As you learned in the previous chapter, you'll want to try out a few variables and algorithms to determine which one is more accurate. This can involve a few iterative processes, and that's the beauty of data science—you keep experimenting.

To start with, let's use the following variables:

Variable	Type	Column Name
Taxi driver is tipped (yes/no)	Output	`tipped`
Passenger count	Input	`passenger_count`
Trip time in seconds	Input	`trip_time_in_seconds`
Trip distance as per the taxi meter	Input	`trip_distance`

The direct distance based on the longitudes and the latitudes between the two locations	Input	`pickup_longitude`
		`pickup_latitude`
		`dropoff_longitude`
		`dropoff_latitude`

In order to make it easier to calculate the direct distance, let's define the following function:

```
CREATE FUNCTION [dbo].[fnCalculateDistance]
(@Lat1 FLOAT, @Long1 FLOAT, @Lat2 FLOAT, @Long2 FLOAT)
-- User-defined function calculate the direct distance
-- between two geographical coordinates.
RETURNS FLOAT
AS
BEGIN
  DECLARE @distance DECIMAL(28, 10)
  -- Convert to radians
  SET @Lat1 = @Lat1 / 57.2958
  SET @Long1 = @Long1 / 57.2958
  SET @Lat2 = @Lat2 / 57.2958
  SET @Long2 = @Long2 / 57.2958
  -- Calculate distance
  SET @distance = (SIN(@Lat1) * SIN(@Lat2)) + (COS(@Lat1) * COS(@Lat2) *
```

```
COS(@Long2 - @Long1))
   --Convert to miles
   IF @distance <> 0
   BEGIN
      SET @distance = 3958.75 * ATAN(SQRT(1 - POWER(@distance, 2)) /
@distance);
   END
   RETURN @distance
END
```

Here's the table definition of the trained prediction model(s) that we want to store in the database. One of the advantages in storing the trained prediction model(s) in a table is that we can easily reuse it later and can version control our experiments.

Please note that there is a column called `IsRealTimeScoring`. SQL Server 2017 adds a new capability for real-time scoring, which will be discussed in the *Integrating the R model for real-time scoring* section. If you are using SQL Server 2016, ignore this value:

```
CREATE TABLE [dbo].[NYCTaxiModel](
    [Model] VARBINARY(MAX) NOT NULL,
    [AUC] FLOAT NULL,
    [CreatedOn] DATETIME NOT NULL
        CONSTRAINT DF_NYCTaxiModel_CreatedOn DEFAULT (GETDATE()),
    [IsRealTimeScoring] BIT NOT NULL
        CONSTRAINT DF_NYCTaxiModel_IsRealTimeScoring DEFAULT (0)
) ON [PRIMARY]
```

Step 1 – Train and save a model using T-SQL

In this step, you can create a predictive model (and optionally, the score), into a table via a stored procedure. The motive behind this is that instead of creating a new model every time an intelligent application needs to do prediction, we want to save the model for reuse:

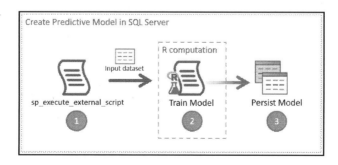

Figure 7.2: Create predictive model and store it in SQL Server

In *Figure 7.2* we assume that the data munging part is already done, and the input dataset is ready for the R computation to consume in order to train and score a model.

Here's an example of a stored procedure that produces the predictive model based on the NYC Taxi sample dataset, and saves it in a table. The model predicts the likelihood of tipping. Both the model and the AUC of the model are saved in the `dbo.nyc_taxi_models_v2` table:

```
CREATE PROCEDURE [dbo].[uspTrainTipPredictionModel]
AS
BEGIN
    DECLARE @auc FLOAT;
    DECLARE @model VARBINARY(MAX);

    -- The data to be used for training
    DECLARE @inquery NVARCHAR(MAX) = N'
        SELECT
                tipped,
                fare_amount,
                passenger_count,
                trip_time_in_secs,
                trip_distance,
                pickup_datetime,
                dropoff_datetime,
                dbo.fnCalculateDistance(pickup_latitude,
                        pickup_longitude,
                        dropoff_latitude,
                        dropoff_longitude) as direct_distance
        FROM dbo.nyctaxi_sample
        TABLESAMPLE (10 PERCENT) REPEATABLE (98052)'

    -- Calculate the model based on the trained data and the AUC.
    EXEC sp_execute_external_script @language = N'R',
                                    @script = N'
        ## Create model
        logitObj <- rxLogit(tipped ~ passenger_count +
                        trip_distance +
                        trip_time_in_secs +
                        direct_distance,
                        data = InputDataSet);
        summary(logitObj)

        ## Serialize model
        model <- serialize(logitObj, NULL);
        predOutput <- rxPredict(modelObject = logitObj,
                    data = InputDataSet, outData = NULL,
                    predVarNames = "Score", type = "response",
```

```
                              writeModelVars = FALSE, overwrite = TRUE);
            library(''ROCR'');
            predOutput <- cbind(InputDataSet, predOutput);
            auc <- rxAuc(rxRoc("tipped", "Score", predOutput));
            print(paste0("AUC of Logistic Regression Model:", auc));
            ',
        @input_data_1 = @inquery,
        @output_data_1_name = N'trained_model',
        @params = N'@auc FLOAT OUTPUT, @model VARBINARY(MAX) OUTPUT',
        @auc = @auc OUTPUT,
        @model = @model OUTPUT;
    -- Store the train model output and its AUC
    INSERT INTO [dbo].[NYCTaxiModel] (Model, AUC)
    SELECT @model, @auc;

END
GO
```

Once you have this stored procedure defined, you can then execute it to generate the model and the AUC. For example:

```
EXEC [dbo].[uspTrainTipPredictionModel]
```

Then, view the content of the NYCTaxiModel table by executing the following statement:

```
SELECT [Model], [AUC], [CreatedOn], [IsRealTimeScoring]
FROM [dbo].[NYCTaxiModel]
```

If the stored procedure executed properly, you should see a record similar to the following:

Step 2 – Operationalize the model

Once the model is created and stored in a table as part of the previous step, we are now ready to create a stored procedure where an intelligent application can call it to predict tipping:

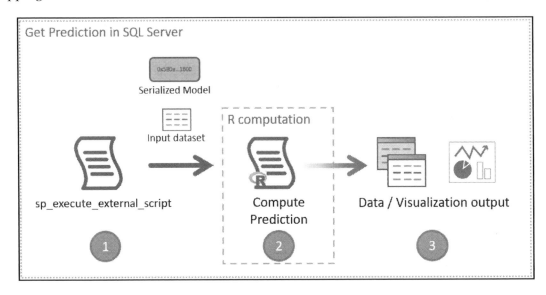

Figure 7.3: Get predictions in the SQL Server

Figure 7.3 illustrates what the workflow of a stored procedure that operationalizes a predictive model looks like.

Here's an example of a stored procedure where we use one of the saved models, and the dataset that we want to predict against. We are using the latest model that has been created:

```
CREATE PROCEDURE [dbo].[uspPredictTipSingleMode]
    @passenger_count int = 0,
    @trip_distance float = 0,
    @trip_time_in_secs int = 0,
    @pickup_latitude float = 0,
    @pickup_longitude float = 0,
    @dropoff_latitude float = 0,
    @dropoff_longitude float = 0
AS
BEGIN

  DECLARE @inquery nvarchar(max) = N'
    SELECT
```

```
                @passenger_count as passenger_count,
                @trip_distance as trip_distance,
                @trip_time_in_secs as trip_time_in_secs,
                [dbo].[fnCalculateDistance] (
                        @pickup_latitude,
                        @pickup_longitude,
                        @dropoff_latitude,
                        @dropoff_longitude) as direct_distance';

    DECLARE @lmodel2 varbinary(max);
    -- Get the latest non-real-time scoring model
    SET @lmodel2 = (SELECT TOP 1
                [Model]
                FROM [dbo].[NYCTaxiModel]
                WHERE IsRealTimeScoring = 0
                ORDER BY [CreatedOn] DESC);

    EXEC sp_execute_external_script @language = N'R',
      @script = N'
            mod <- unserialize(as.raw(model));
            print(summary(mod))
            OutputDataSet<-rxPredict(modelObject = mod,
data = InputDataSet,
                            outData = NULL, predVarNames = "Score",
                            type = "response",
writeModelVars = FALSE,
overwrite = TRUE);
                str(OutputDataSet)
                print(OutputDataSet)',
            @input_data_1 = @inquery,
            @params = N'@model varbinary(max),
@passenger_count int,
@trip_distance float,
                            @trip_time_in_secs INT ,
                            @pickup_latitude FLOAT ,
                            @pickup_longitude FLOAT ,
                            @dropoff_latitude FLOAT ,
                            @dropoff_longitude FLOAT',
```

```
        @model = @lmodel2,
        @passenger_count =@passenger_count ,
        @trip_distance=@trip_distance,
        @trip_time_in_secs=@trip_time_in_secs,
        @pickup_latitude=@pickup_latitude,
        @pickup_longitude=@pickup_longitude,
        @dropoff_latitude=@dropoff_latitude,
        @dropoff_longitude=@dropoff_longitude
    WITH RESULT SETS ((Score FLOAT));

END
GO
```

Once [dbo].[uspPredictTipSingleMode] is created, your application can now use this stored procedure to get the score (probability of tipping); for example:

```
EXEC [dbo].[uspPredictTipSingleMode]
    @passenger_count = 2
  ,@trip_distance    = 10
  ,@trip_time_in_secs      = 1950
  ,@pickup_latitude = 47.643272
  ,@pickup_longitude       = -122.127235
  ,@dropoff_latitude       = 47.620529
  ,@dropoff_longitude      = -122.349297
```

The output should be similar to the following. In this case, the value 0.64 shows the probability of getting tipped—that is, 64%:

```
Score
---------------------
0.640058591034195
```

Fast batch prediction

As seen in the previous section, both the model training step and the prediction step call sp_execute_external_script, which invokes the R process. Real-time scoring and native scoring allow you to do predictions without invoking an R process. Therefore, these scoring methods improve the performance of prediction operations.

In addition, real-time scoring and native scoring let you use a machine learning model without having to install R. As long as you obtain a pretrained model in a compatible format and save it in an SQL Server database, you can call prediction operations easily.

Prerequisites

- There is no prerequisite when using the PREDICT function in SQL Server 2017. More information about PREDICT is covered in the *Native scoring* section later.

- sp_rxPredict requires some additional steps, as outlined in *Enable real-time scoring model* at https://docs.microsoft.com/en-us/sql/advanced-analytics/r/how-to-do-realtime-scoring#bkmk_enableRtScoring.

- Currently, both real-time scoring and native scoring in SQL Server 2016 and SQL Server 2017 only support RevoScaleR and MicrosoftML compatible models. For the most up-to-date list of supported algorithms, see *Real-time scoring* at https://docs.microsoft.com/en-us/sql/advanced-analytics/real-time-scoring.

Real-time scoring

Both SQL Server 2016 and SQL Server 2017 support real-time scoring using sp_rxPredict.

 This stored procedure is a CLR stored procedure using an UNSAFE assembly, and requires you to set the database to TRUSTWORTHY.

Here's an example of calling the PREDICT function as part of the SELECT statement:

```
EXEC dbo.sp_rxPredict @model,
@inputData = @query;
```

In this case:

- @model: Consists of the real-time scoring model that was previously prepared
- @query: The query definition of the data to be scored

Native scoring

SQL Server 2017 introduces a new function, PREDICT, allowing you to get a predicted value using native scoring. Instead of using sp_execute_external_script with R script to do prediction, you can call it as part of the FROM clause of a SELECT statement, making operationalization of prediction analytics much easier. In addition, using PREDICT means that you no longer have to invoke an additional R process every time you want to do prediction.

> This PREDICT function is new to T-SQL and is not to be confused with the existing DMX's PREDICT function.

Here's an example of calling the PREDICT function as part of the SELECT statement:

```
SELECT   d.Input1, d.Input2, p.Output_Pred
FROM PREDICT ( MODEL = @model,   DATA = d)
     WITH (Output_Pred FLOAT) p;
```

In this case:

- d: Data source, such as a table, a view, or a Common Table Expression.
- Input1, Input2: Columns from the data source.
- @model: Consists of the real-time scoring model that has been previously prepared.
- Output_Pred: The output value that is being predicted. Usually, the column name is constructed from the column name of the predicted value followed by a _Pred suffix; for example, Tipped_Pred, where Tipped is the name of the column being predicted.

Integrating the R model for fast batch prediction

Before continuing to the next steps, please follow the *Prerequisite - Prepare the data* section.

Step 1 – Train and save a real-time scoring model using T-SQL

In this step, you can create a predictive model for real-time scoring and native scoring, and optionally for the AUC, into a table via a stored procedure. The goal is to build a model that is reusable. You can skip this step if there is an existing compatible model that was created and stored in a table in SQL Server already.

The following stored procedure uses `rxSerializeModel`, which lets you serialize an R model in raw format. This then allows you to save the model in the VARBINARY format, which can be loaded into SQL Server for real-time scoring. To reverse the serialization for use in R, you could use `rxUnserializeModel`:

```
CREATE PROCEDURE [dbo].[uspTrainTipPredictionModelWithRealTimeScoring]
AS
BEGIN
    DECLARE @auc FLOAT;
    DECLARE @model VARBINARY(MAX);

    -- The data to be used for training
    DECLARE @inquery NVARCHAR(MAX) = N'
        SELECT
                tipped,
                fare_amount,
                passenger_count,
                trip_time_in_secs,
                trip_distance,
                pickup_datetime,
                dropoff_datetime,
                dbo.fnCalculateDistance(pickup_latitude,
                        pickup_longitude,
                        dropoff_latitude,
                        dropoff_longitude) as direct_distance
        FROM dbo.nyctaxi_sample
        TABLESAMPLE (10 PERCENT) REPEATABLE (98052)'

    -- Calculate the model based on the trained data and the AUC.
    EXEC sp_execute_external_script @language = N'R',
                                    @script = N'
        ## Create model
        logitObj <- rxLogit(tipped ~ passenger_count +
                        trip_distance +
                        trip_time_in_secs +
                        direct_distance,
                        data = InputDataSet);
```

```
            summary(logitObj)

            ## Serialize model
            ## model <- serialize(logitObj, NULL);
            model <- rxSerializeModel(logitObj,
realtimeScoringOnly = TRUE);
            predOutput <- rxPredict(modelObject = logitObj,
                        data = InputDataSet, outData = NULL,
                        predVarNames = "Score", type = "response",
                        writeModelVars = FALSE, overwrite = TRUE);
            library(''ROCR'');
            predOutput <- cbind(InputDataSet, predOutput);
            auc <- rxAuc(rxRoc("tipped", "Score", predOutput));
            print(paste0("AUC of Logistic Regression Model:", auc));
            ',
        @input_data_1 = @inquery,
        @output_data_1_name = N'trained_model',
        @params = N'@auc FLOAT OUTPUT, @model VARBINARY(MAX) OUTPUT',
        @auc = @auc OUTPUT,
        @model = @model OUTPUT;
    -- Store the train model output and its AUC
    INSERT INTO [dbo].[NYCTaxiModel] (Model, AUC, IsRealTimeScoring)
    SELECT @model, @auc, 1;

END
GO
```

To store a model created in R in an SQL Server table, you must serialize it first. In R, a serialized model must be unserialized before we can use it for prediction.

Step 2a – Operationalize the model using real-time scoring

The following is a sample script where we use sp_rxPredict with a real-time scoring model to predict the likelihood of tipping:

```
DECLARE @logit_model VARBINARY(MAX) =
    (SELECT TOP 1 [Model]
    FROM [dbo].[NYCTaxiModel]
    WHERE [IsRealTimeScoring] = 1
    ORDER BY [CreatedOn] DESC);
```

```
EXEC dbo.sp_rxPredict @model = @logit_model,
@inputData = N'SELECT
                    2 AS passenger_count,
                    10 AS trip_distance,
                    1950 AS trip_time_in_secs,
                    dbo.fnCalculateDistance(47.643272,
                        -122.127235,
                        47.620529,
                        -122.349297) AS direct_distance';
```

The output should only give you the prediction value for the rows that are pushed through:

```
tipped_Pred
----------------------
0.640058591034195
(1 row affected)
```

Step 2b – Operationalize the model using native scoring

The following is a sample script where we use the PREDICT function with an R real-time scoring model to predict the likelihood of tipping. The PREDICT function in SQL Server 2017 can read the stored serialized model for predictive analysis from the previous step:

```
DECLARE @logit_model VARBINARY(MAX) =
    (SELECT TOP 1 [Model]
    FROM [dbo].[NYCTaxiModel]
    WHERE [IsRealTimeScoring] = 1
    ORDER BY [CreatedOn] DESC);

WITH d AS (
    SELECT      2 AS passenger_count,
                10 AS trip_distance,
                1950 AS trip_time_in_secs,
                dbo.fnCalculateDistance(47.643272,
                    -122.127235,
                    47.620529,
                    -122.349297) AS direct_distance)
SELECT  *
FROM PREDICT( MODEL = @logit_model, DATA = d)
WITH (tipped_Pred FLOAT) p;
```

The output should include any columns that you specify in the SELECT statement, and should look like this:

```
tipped_Pred passenger_count trip_distance trip_time_in_secs direct_distance
----------- --------------- ------------- ----------------- ---------------
0.640058591 2               10            1950              10.4581575644
(1 row affected)
```

Managing roles and permissions for workloads

Operationalizing an R script as part of the extensibility framework workloads, as well as prediction operations using real-time scoring and native scoring, require that a few roles and permissions be set up first.

Extensibility framework workloads

This section outlines the typical security requirements for operationalizing R from SQL Server using sp_execute_external_script. An SQL Server login or Windows user account can be used to run R scripts directly from SQL Server using stored procedures. The following are the steps to set up this account, such that it has sufficient privileges:

1. Allow permission to access the database where the R scripts will be run from.
2. Allow permission to read data from secured objects, such as tables. This includes (but is not limited to) the table where the model might have been stored from and the table/view to be used to train the model or input to the prediction.
3. If the R script needs to write new data to a table, such as a model or a scoring result, allow permission to write the new data.
4. If the R script needs to install R packages during runtime, allow permission to install new packages.

In general, it is easier to create roles to manage sets of permissions, and then assign users to those roles, instead of individually setting user permissions.

The following is an example of how to create a role and assign it to a login called `JulieGuest2`, as per steps 1, 2, and 3:

```
-- Create a new role
CREATE ROLE TutorialDBRUser AUTHORIZATION dbo
GO

-- Assign the role to a new member JulieGuest2 so that the login
-- can connect to the database Tutorial DB.
ALTER ROLE TutorialDBRUser ADD MEMBER JulieGuest2
GO

-- Allow members of TutorialDBRUser to read and write.
ALTER ROLE db_datareader ADD MEMBER TutorialDBRUser
GO

ALTER ROLE db_datareader ADD MEMBER TutorialDBRUser
GO

-- Allow members of TutorialDBRUser to run external script
GRANT EXECUTE ANY EXTERNAL SCRIPT TO [TutorialDBRUser]
GO

-- Allow members of TutorialDBRUser to run a specific
-- stored procedure.
GRANT EXECUTE ON [dbo].[predict_rentals] TO [TutorialDBRUser]
GO
```

Fast batch prediction workloads

Follow the following steps only if you are using real-time scoring or native scoring:

- For real-time scoring using `sp_rxPredict`, you will need to add the user who will execute this stored procedure to `rxpredict_users`
- For native scoring using the new `PREDICT` syntax available in SQL Server 2017, you will need to grant `EXECUTE` permission on the database

The preceding steps assume that the users have read access to the real-time scoring model and the input data set for the prediction operation.

External packages

From SQL Server 2017, you can also add an external library through CREATE EXTERNAL LIBRARY, as long as you have the ALTER ANY EXTERNAL LIBRARY permission:

```
GRANT ALTER ANY EXTERNAL LIBRARY TO [TutorialDBRUser]
GO
```

You'll have to download the package from the source first; for example, ggplot2 from CRAN (https://cran.r-project.org/web/packages/ggplot2/index.html) to a path SQL Server has access to:

```
CREATE EXTERNAL LIBRARY ggplot2pkg
FROM
   (CONTENT = 'C:\Program Files\Microsoft SQL
Server\MSSQL14.MSSQLSERVER\ggplot2.zip')
WITH (LANGUAGE = 'R');
```

If you are using SQL Server 2016, to install a new R package, you'll need to have administrative access on the machine. The installation steps are outside of SQL Server and directly on the R that is associated to the SQL Server R Services. The detailed steps are outlined in Chapter 3, *Managing Machine Learning Services for SQL Server 2017 and R*.

Tools

There are three main options for operationalizing R code embedded in T-SQL. All of these tools are free:

- **SQL Server Management Studio (SSMS)**
- **R Tools for Visual Studio (RTVS)**
- **SQL Server Data Tools (SSDT)**

This section provides an overview of how the tools can help you operationalize R code in SQL Server as part of workflows.

Using SSMS as part of operationalizing R script

SSMS is a powerful tool that allows you to operationalize your prediction analytics from the previous section. SSMS also provides the ability for you to manage various administrative tasks related to operationalizing R code in SQL Server and maintaining it, such as:

- Managing permissions, as described earlier in this chapter.
- Managing R packages (in SQL Server 2017), as described earlier in this chapter.
- Managing stored procedures that integrate R code, as described in an earlier section.
- Managing resources for SQL Server R Services, as described in `Chapter 3`, *Managing Machine Learning Services for SQL Server 2017 and R.*
- Monitoring SQL Server R services using built-in custom reports and via DMVs, as described in *Using custom reports for SQL Server R Services.*
- Creating and managing jobs that execute R Scripts. See *Scheduling training and prediction operations* later in this chapter.

To get the latest version of SSMS to help you develop and manage workflows with SQL Server R services, go to `https://docs.microsoft.com/en-us/sql/ssms/download-sql-server-ma nagement-studio-ssms`.

Using custom reports for SQL Server R Services

There are custom reports for SQL Server R Services available on GitHub: `https://github. com/Microsoft/sql-server-samples/tree/master/samples/features/r-services/ssms- custom-reports`

The following is a list of the custom reports and what they can help you achieve:

Reports	Purpose
`R Services - Configuration.rdl`	View installation settings of R Services and properties of the R runtime. Configure R Services after installation.
`R Services - Packages.rdl`	View R packages installed on the SQL Server instance, as well as their properties, such as name and version.

`R Services – Resource Usage.rdl`	View resource consumption of SQL Server and R scripts execution. View memory setting of external resource pools.
`R Services – Extended Events.rdl`	View the extended events to understand more about R script execution.
`R Services – Execution Statistics.rdl`	View the execution statistics of R Services, including but not limited to the number of R script executions, the number of parallel executions, and `RevoScaleR` functions.

Adding the custom reports for the first time

Once you have downloaded the custom reports from the preceding GitHub location, follow the following steps to add custom reports for the first time:

1. Go to **SSMS | Object Explorer.**
2. Right-click on the SQL Server instance's name in **Object Explorer**, and choose **Reports | Custom Reports...**
3. Add the RDL files from the download location.

    After adding, you might be presented with the following warning dialog box:

Figure 7.4: Run Custom Report warning from SSMS

Clicking **Run** means that you acknowledge that you wish to run these reports.

Figure 7.5 illustrates a successfully imported R Services - Execution Statistics report. It says that there are 24 R script execution errors from 38 executions, and the most popular RevoScaleR function is rxPredict_rxLogit:

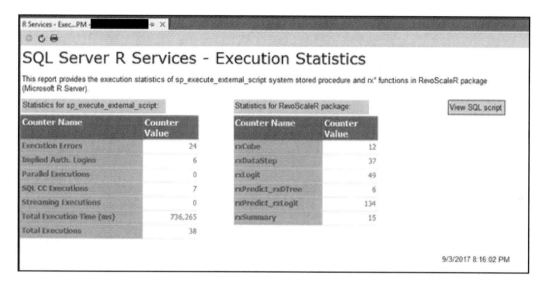

Figure 7.5: SQL Server R Services - Execution Statistics report in SSMS

Viewing an R Services custom report

Once you've added an R Services custom report for the first time, you can revisit it again. Here are the steps:

1. Go to **SSMS | Object Explorer.**
2. Right-click on the SQL Server instance's name.

3. Choose **Reports** | **Custom Reports**. If you have added all the custom reports, you should see something like this:

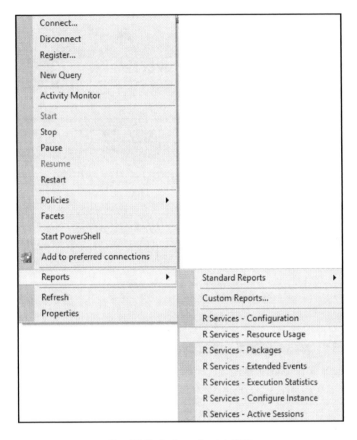

Figure 7.6: Viewing Custom Reports in SSMS

Managing SQL Server Machine Learning Services with DMVs

There are various DMVs that are available to help you monitor the R script that you have operationalized. This section splits the DMVs for SQL Server Machine Learning Services into the following two categories, as specified.

System configuration and system resources

You may be familiar with `sys.dm_exec_sessions` and `sys.dm_os_performance_counter` for understanding active sessions and system performance counters, respectively. The following is a list of DMVs that you should get to know more to track and monitor performance and usage of R script executions in SQL Server:

- `sys.dm_exec_sessions`: View details on user sessions and system sessions, identified as `with session_id >= 51` and `< 51`, respectively.

- `sys.dm_os_performance_counters`: View details on each system performance counter, including those that are related to R script. Here's an example of the script specifically related to SQL Server R Services:

```
SELECT *
FROM sys.dm_os_performance_counters
WHERE object_name LIKE '%External Scripts%'
```

- `sys.dm_external_script_requests`: View active external scripts on the current instance:

```
SELECT
    [external_script_request_id]
  , [language]
  , [degree_of_parallelism]
  , [external_user_name]
FROM sys.dm_external_script_requests;
```

- `sys.dm_external_script_execution_stats`: View the overall usage of the new external script through counters.

Resource governor

In SQL Server 2016, two new DMVs have been added to help monitor external resource pools: `sys.resource_governor_external_resource_pools` and `sys.dm_resource_governor_external_resource_pool_affinity`. If you are familiar with tracking and managing resource governors in general, you are likely to know the other two DMVs that are listed as follows:

- `sys.resource_governor_resource_pools`: View the current resource pool state, the current configuration of resource pools, and their statistics.

- `sys.resource_governor_workload_groups`: View the workload group statistics and the current configuration of the workload group. This DMV has been enhanced with a new column to show the ID of the external pool associated with the workload group.

- `sys.resource_governor_external_resource_pools`: View the current configuration values for external resource pools. At the time of writing, SQL Server 2016/2017 Enterprise Edition allows you to configure additional resource pools, such that resources for R jobs running in SQL Server will be isolated from those that originate from a remote client.

- `sys.dm_resource_governor_external_resource_pool_affinity`: This DMV allows you to see the processors and resources that are affinitized to a particular resource pool.

Operationalizing R code with Visual Studio

Developing R script, or T-SQL that uses R script, is now made easy with **R Tools for Visual Studio (RTVS)**. If you are already using SQL Server Data Tools as your IDE for your SQL Server database projects, you can simply add a new R project in the solution. This integration has improved in Visual Studio 2017.

If you don't have Visual Studio installed, go to `https://www.visualstudio.com/downloads/`.

RTVS is installed as part of the Data science and analytical applications workload.

From the Visual Studio installer, you can add the **Data science and analytics applications** workload to your Visual Studio 2017 installation, as shown in *Figure 7.7*:

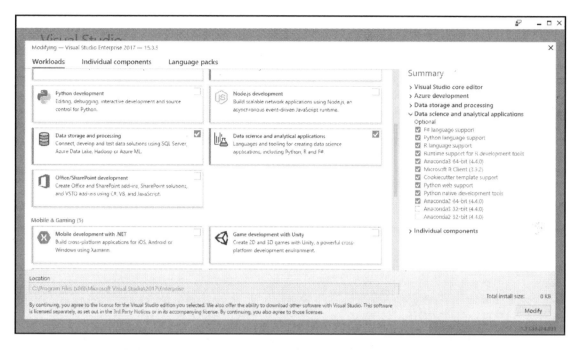

Figure 7.7: Selecting the Data science and analytical applications option in the Visual Studio installer for Visual Studio 2017

The following are additional tips to get started using RTVS:

1. Create a new R project in RTVS by selecting **File | New | Project**. The provided name of the project and file path are similar to the following:

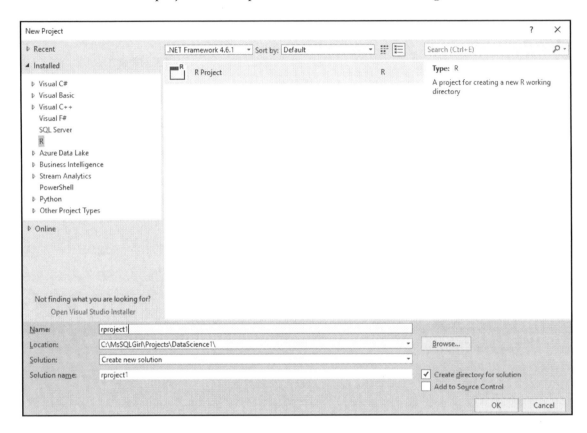

Figure 7.8: Creating a new R project

2. In RTVS, you can choose workspaces that you can run the R script against. If you have already installed SQL Server with R Services as mentioned in `Chapter 4`, *Data Exploration and Data Visualization*, you'll see something like this:

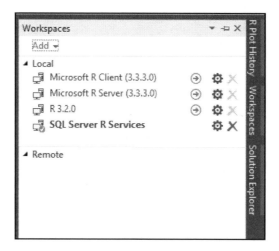

Figure 7.9: Displaying all workspaces available for RTVS to connect to

Go to **R Tools** | **Windows** | **Workspaces** or press *Ctrl + 9* to display the **Workspaces** window.

3. You can run R code from the **R Interactive** window or save R files within the R project. You can refer to `https://docs.microsoft.com/en-us/visualstudio/rtvs/` to learn more about RTVS features.

4. You can also use add an **SQL Query** file within the project by right-clicking on the project and choosing **Add New Item**, then selecting **SQL Query,** shown as follows:

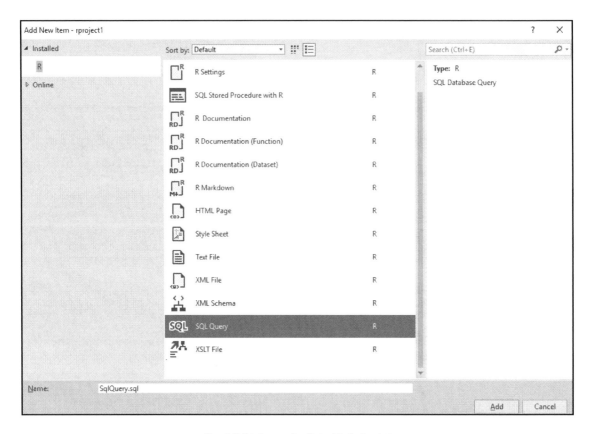

Figure 7.10: Selecting a new item/file to add to the R project

5. RTVS also allows you to develop the R code integration to SQL Server stored procedure via a template. To access this, simply click **Add New Item,** similar to the previous step, and then select **SQL Stored Procedure**. For more information about this, go to `https://docs.microsoft.com/en-us/visualstudio/rtvs/sql-server`.

Integrating R workloads and prediction operations beyond SQL Server

In this section, you will learn how to include R workloads and prediction operations that you have created in the previous sections beyond SQL Server. We will discuss how to run the workloads and operations in PowerShell, SQL Agent Job, and **SQL Server Integration Services** (**SSIS**).

 Please note that you can also execute these workloads/prediction operations using SQLCMD, C# within SSIS, Azure, and also Bash on Linux. This discussion is beyond the scope of this chapter.

Executing SQL Server prediction operations via PowerShell

Assuming that you have already created the stored procedure that executes R script from SQL Server, such as [dbo].[uspTrainTipPredictionModel] from the earlier example, you can execute this command easily as part of your PowerShell workflows.

Here's a simple example of calling the stored procedure from PowerShell:

```
$SqlConnection = New-Object System.Data.SqlClient.SqlConnection
$SqlConnection.ConnectionString = "Server=.;Database=Taxi;Integrated
Security=True"
$SqlCmd = New-Object System.Data.SqlClient.SqlCommand
$SqlCmd.CommandText = "EXEC [dbo].[uspPredictTipSingleMode]
    @passenger_count     = 2
    ,@trip_distance    = 10
    ,@trip_time_in_secs     = 35
    ,@pickup_latitude = 47.643272
    ,@pickup_longitude     = -122.127235
    ,@dropoff_latitude     = 47.620529
    ,@dropoff_longitude     = -122.349297
    "
$SqlCmd.Connection = $SqlConnection
$SqlAdapter = New-Object System.Data.SqlClient.SqlDataAdapter
$SqlAdapter.SelectCommand = $SqlCmd
$DataSet = New-Object System.Data.DataSet
$SqlAdapter.Fill($DataSet)
$SqlConnection.Close()
$DataSet.Tables[0]
```

Scheduling training and prediction operations

In SSMS, you can create a new SQL Server job that allows you to run R code as a one-off or with a specific schedule.

As an example, you can do a scheduled offline predictive analytics workload. To do this, simply create a job through SSMS:

1. To create a job, you'll need to be a member of one of the SQL Server Agent fixed database roles or the sysadmin fixed server role. Only the job owner or a member of the sysadmin role can update the definition of the job.

2. In **Object Explorer** of SSMS, expand the SQL Server instance where you want to create an SQL Server Agent job.

3. Expand **SQL Server Agent** and right-click on the Jobs folder, then select **New Job...**:

Figure 7.11: Creating a new SQL Server Agent job using SSMS

4. Provide details on the **General** page:

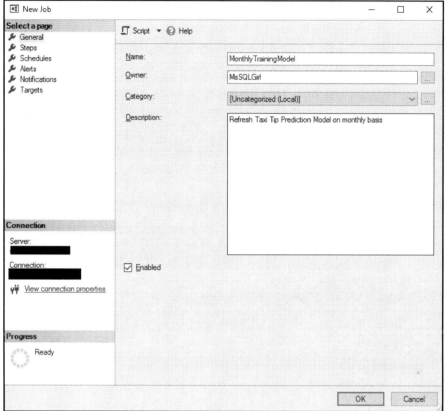

Figure 7.12: Adding more details in the New Job window

5. Click on **Steps** from the left-hand menu of the **New Job** window, then click on **New...** on the bottom of the **New Job** window.

6. Provide the details in the **New Job Step** to execute. In this example, we want to update the NYC Taxi Training Model. Then click **OK**:

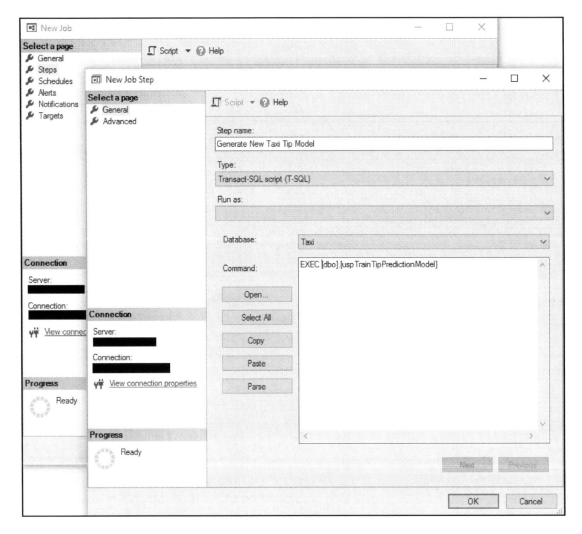

Figure 7.13: Calling an R-integrated stored procedure as a step in an SQL Server Agent job

7. In the **New Job** window, select **Schedules** from the left-hand menu.
8. Click on **New...** from the bottom of the **New Job** window.
9. Provide the details of the schedule that you'd like this job to be subject to.

10. Click on **OK** in the **New Schedule** window, then click on the **New Job** window to save the changes.

Operationalizing R script as part of SSIS

R Script can easily be integrated as part of SSIS workflows. The two main ways are by running as part of Execute Process Task and running as part of Execute SQL Task:

1. Running R code (not as a part of SQL Server R Services) in Execute Process Task can be simply done by calling `Rscript.exe`. If you already have an R file that is ready to be executed, then simply add Execute Process Task in an SSIS package. You can also weave the input/output in Execute Process Task within the SSIS package into the R file:

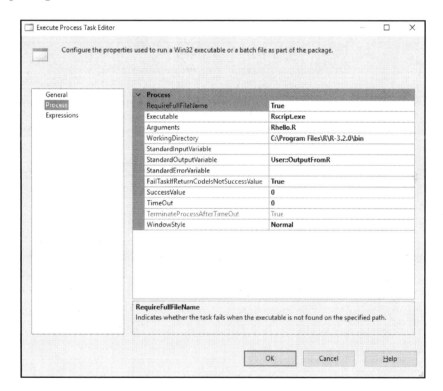

Figure 7.14: Executing R script externally within SSIS Execute Process Task

2. Running prediction operations in SQL Server using Execute SQL Task in SSIS: if you already have a stored procedure that does prediction (or a training model), then simply call this stored procedure from Execute SQL Task in SSIS. It is also possible to weave the input/output in Execute SQL Task with the SSIS package:

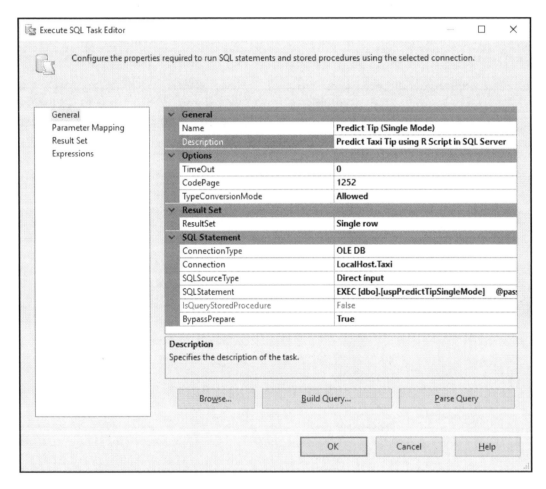

Figure 7.15: Executing an R-integrated stored procedure as an Execute SQL Task step in SSIS

Summary

In this chapter, you learned the steps required to integrate an existing predictive analytics R code into resides outside of SQL Server R with the Extensibility Framework. You have also seen the simplicity and the power of the new PREDICT function in SQL Server 2017, which allows native scoring without having to install R. Managing the security required to run predictive analytics workloads is also important in prediction operations. You have learned how to add SQL queries to R projects using RTVS. Finally, you've discovered the different possibilities for integrating R code and prediction operations into your existing workflows as SQL Server stored procedures, SQL Server Agent jobs, PowerShell scripts, and SSIS projects.

With these new skills, we are ready for the next building block in managing data science solutions as part of database lifecycle: management practices. In the next chapter, you'll learn about managing data science solutions in **Continuous Integration/Continuous Delivery (CI/CD)** and continuous model performance monitoring.

8
Deploying, Managing, and Monitoring Database Solutions containing R Code

Operationalizing R code in a SQL Server database means that data scientists/database developers can also leverage productionizing data science solutions as part of **Database Lifecycle Management** (**DLM**). This includes the following:

- Checking in R code as part of a SQL Server database project into a version control
- Adding the stored procedures for the data science solution as part of SQL Server unit tests
- Integrating the data science solution into the **Continuous Integration/Continuous Delivery** (**CI/CD**) process
- Monitoring performance of the data science solution in the production on a regular basis

In this chapter, we will be using **SQL Server Data Tools** (**SSDT**) in Visual Studio 2017 and Visual Studio Team Services to perform this DLM workflow. However, the underlying concept can be applied to any other CI/CD platform that you or your team might already be using.

Integrating R into the SQL Server Database lifecycle workflow

Earlier in `Chapter 7`, *Operationalizing R Prediction Models*, we discussed how to create an R project in Visual Studio 2017. We also talked about integrating R code as part of `sp_execute_external_script` in SQL Server. Here, we will revisit Visual Studio 2017, specifically in the context of integrating R code in `sp_execute_external_script` as part of a SQL Server Database Project, and holistically as part of the database lifecycle workflow.

Preparing your environment for the database lifecycle workflow

In this section, we will discuss the stages of the database lifecycle workflow and the tools that we will be using. For each of the stages in the workflow, there will also be some suggested alternatives for you to explore.

1. **Coding and managing SQL Server database projects/solutions**: There are a few different ways to manage your SQL Server DML/DDL scripts that form a SQL Server database project. SQL SSDT in Visual Studio 2017 (VS2017) is a mature product that formalizes the creation and modification of Database Schema and Objects. In this section, we will use SSDT in VS2017.

   You can use VS2017 Community, Professional, or Enterprise editions. Please check `https://www.visualstudio.com/vs/compare/` for more up-to-date information on how these editions compare. In the walkthroughs and examples in this section, we will be using Visual Studio Enterprise Edition, but you can use any of the editions. You can download these from: `https://www.visualstudio.com/vs/`.

   Other following alternatives worth trying are:

   - **SQL Server Management Studio**: There are a few plugins developed by RedGate that can enrich DevOps/Database Lifecycle Management
   - **SQL Operations Studio** (in Preview): This tool is built based on VS Code, which means that it has high potential of meeting DevOps workflows too, including source control

2. **Unit testing**: Just like application development, database development would benefit from a unit testing framework, especially if it can be automated. There are two well-known unit testing frameworks that are available for SQL Server databases, tSQLt, and SQL Server Unit Test integrated in Visual Studio. Here are the links:

- **tSQLt**: `http://tsqlt.org/`
- **SQL Server Unit Test in Visual Studio**: `https://msdn.microsoft.com/en-us/library/jj851200(v=vs.103).aspx`

In this section, we will use SQL Server Unit Test in VS2017.

Another tool worth trying is:

- RedGate SQL Test that is based on the tSQLt framework, an extension of SSMS

3. **Version Control**: There are a number of popular choices for Version Control systems out there, for example, Git and **Team Foundation Version Control (TFVC)**. In this section, we will use TFVC hosted in **Visual Studio Team Services (VSTS)**. VS2017 can connect to a VSTS repository. You can sign up for a VSTS account online at: `https://www.visualstudio.com/team-services/`.

Other alternatives worth trying are:

Using Visual Studio, you can connect to online version control hosts, such as GitHub and VSTS, as well as a private on-premises version control servers, such as **Team Foundation Server (TFS)**:

- **GitHub Extension for Visual Studio**: `https://visualstudio.github.com/`
- **Team Foundation Server**: `https://www.visualstudio.com/tfs/`

4. **CI/CD**: VSTS supports both hosted agent and private agent. Hosted agent is a cloud-based agent that performs continuous integration and continuous delivery. Private agent is an on-premises-based agent version, available in Visual Studio 2017. Having CI in place means that as the script is checked in, the agent will automatically build and optionally perform a number of tests. Having CD in place allows us to test the code release and/or the schema changes only against the baseline. In this chapter, we will use VSTS with a private agent to deploy against an on-premises SQL Server database.

Other alternatives worth trying are:

- VSTS supports the hosted agent, which allows you to deploy automatically to Azure VM
- VSTS supports the hosted agent, which allows you to deploy to the Azure SQL Database, which since October 2017, also supports R

Figure 8.1 shows a CI/CD workflow using VSTS, which we will use in this chapter for our sample SQL Server R Services solution:

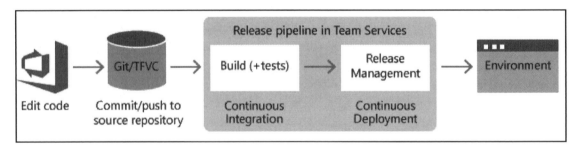

Figure 8.1 CI/CD process using VSTS

Source: `https://docs.microsoft.com/en-us/vsts/build-release/actions/ci-cd-part-1`

Prerequisites for this chapter

Tools	URL	Notes
Visual Studio 2017	To download: `https://www.visualstudio.com/downloads/`	The Community Edition is free.
VSTS	Sign up/sign in: `https://www.visualstudio.com/team-services/`	Sign up for the personal account for free.

Power Shell v2.0 or above	Download PowerShell: `https://www.microsoft.com/en-us/download/details.aspx?id=42554`	You will need this for setting up the Private Agent locally.

Creating the SQL Server database project

In this section, we will walk you through how to create a database project in VS2017.

1. In VS2017, click on **File** | **New Project**.
2. Choose **SQL Server** from Installed on the left pane and click on the **SQL Server Database Project** template.
3. Type Ch08 in the **Name:** field and SQL Server R Services Book in the **Solution name:** file, as shown in the following screenshot:

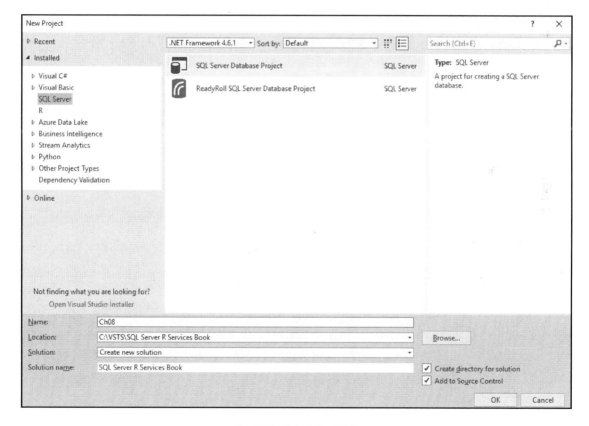

Figure 8.2 New Project in Visual Studio

4. Choose the **Location** to save the solution.

> If you already have a local folder for your version control, you can specify
> the path here.

In this example, my VSTS project is named **SQL Server R Services Book**, which is
associated to my local folder named `C:\VSTS\SQL Server R Services Book`.

5. Ensure that both Create directory for solution and Add to Source Control are
checked.
6. Click on **OK** in the **New Project** dialog box. The **Solution Explorer** window
should show something similar to the following screenshot:

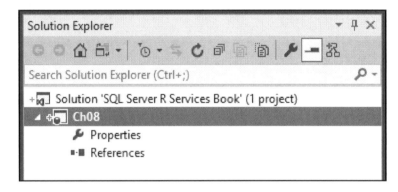

Figure 8.3 Database Project in Solution Explorer

From here, you can add new objects such as a table, a stored procedure, and many
other objects.

Importing an existing database into the project

Now that we have a blank database, we can import an existing database that you have created from Chapter 7, *Operationalizing R Prediction Models*:

1. On **Ch08**, right-click and choose **Import | Database**:

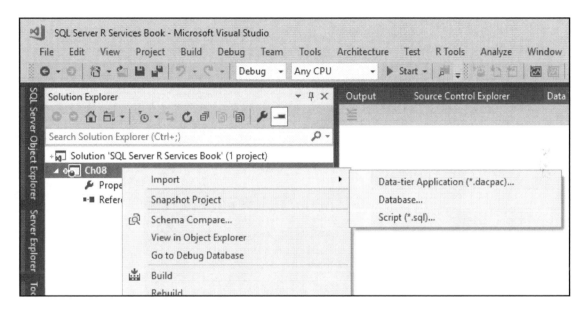

Figure 8.4 Import database into a database project

2. In the **Import Database** dialog box, click on **Select Connection**. Then, specify the database connection to the database that you previously created in Chapter 7, *Operationalizing R Prediction Models*.

3. The **Import Database** dialog box should look like the following. Click on **Start**:

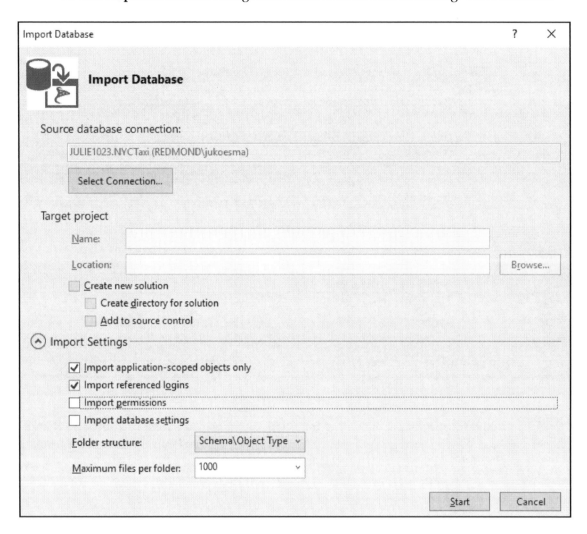

Figure 8.5 Import Database dialog box

4. The **Import Database** dialog box then shows **Summary** of the import progress:

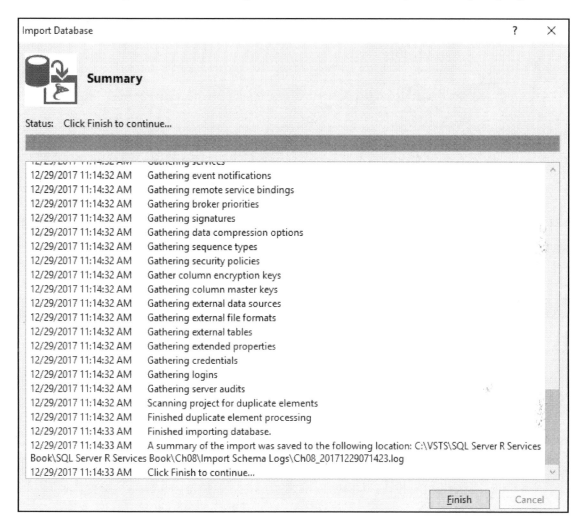

Figure 8.6 Summary of database project import

5. The solution should look something as follows:

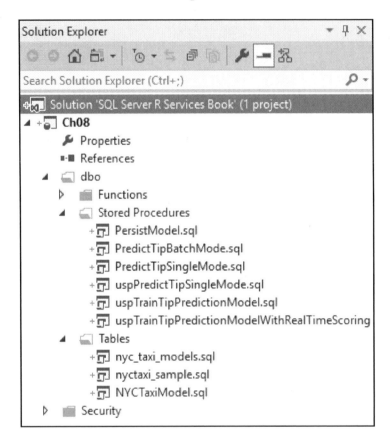

Figure 8.7 Solution Explorer displaying a database project after the database is imported

6. Before we make any more changes, let's build the solution by right-clicking on the root **Solution** node and choose **Build Solution**, or you can also click on *Ctrl + Shift + B*.

Note that the output should contain a number of warnings for each stored procedure referring to the `sp_execute_external` script similar to the following:

```
C:\VSTS\SQL Server R Services Book\SQL Server R Services
Book\Ch08\dbo\Stored
Procedures\uspTrainTipPredictionModelWithRealTimeScoring.sql(27,8):
Warning:  SQL71502: Procedure:
[dbo].[uspTrainTipPredictionModelWithRealTimeScoring] has an
unresolved reference to object [dbo].[sp_execute_external_script].
```

Adding a new stored procedure object

Here's an example of how to add a new object to an existing database project:

1. To create a new procedure, you can right-click on the `Stored Procedures` folder, then click on **Add | Stored Procedure...**
2. Type `uspTrainTipPredictionModelWithRealTimeScoringDTree` in the **Name** field as the new stored procedure:

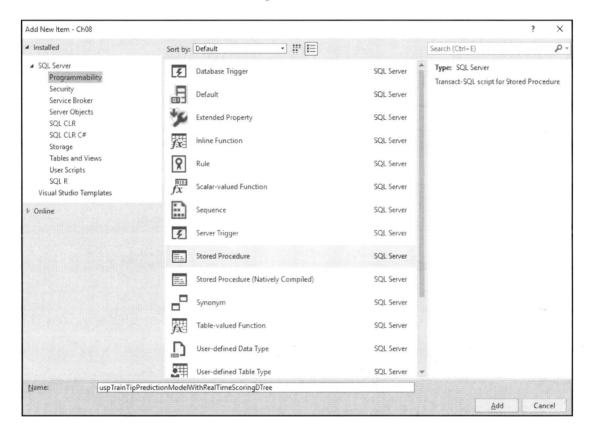

Figure 8.8 Adding a new item to a Database Project

3. Add the following script to the stored procedure:

```
CREATE PROCEDURE
[dbo].[uspTrainTipPredictionModelWithRealTimeScoringDTree]
AS
BEGIN
    DECLARE @auc FLOAT;
    DECLARE @model VARBINARY(MAX);

    -- The data to be used for training
    DECLARE @inquery NVARCHAR(MAX)= N'
        SELECT
            tipped,
            fare_amount,
            passenger_count,
            trip_time_in_secs,
            trip_distance,
            pickup_datetime,
            dropoff_datetime,
            dbo.fnCalculateDistance(pickup_latitude,
                pickup_longitude,
                dropoff_latitude,
                dropoff_longitude) as direct_distance
        FROM dbo.nyctaxi_sample
        TABLESAMPLE (10 PERCENT) REPEATABLE (98052)'

-- Calculate the model based on the trained data and the AUC.
EXEC sys.sp_execute_external_script @language = N'R',
                                    @script = N'
        ## Create model
        dTreeObj<- rxDTree(tipped ~ passenger_count +
trip_distance +
trip_time_in_secs +
direct_distance,
                    data = InputDataSet);

treeCp <- rxDTreeBestCp(dTreeObj);
        dTreeObjChosen<- prune.rxDTree(dTreeObj, cp = treeCp);

        ## Serialize model
        model <- serialize(dTreeObjChosen, NULL);

        predictTree <- rxPredict(dTreeObjChosen, data =
InputDataSet, overwrite = TRUE)
        library('ROCR');
predOutput <- cbind(InputDataSet, predictTree);
```

```
auc <- rxAuc(rxRoc("tipped", "tipped_Pred", predOutput));
print(paste0("AUC of Classification Model:", auc));
        ',
    @input_data_1 = @inquery,
    @output_data_1_name = N'trained_model',
    @params= N'@auc FLOAT OUTPUT, @model VARBINARY(MAX) OUTPUT',
    @auc= @auc OUTPUT,
    @model = @model OUTPUT;
-- Store the train model output and its AUC
INSERT INTO [dbo].[NYCTaxiModel] (Model, AUC,IsRealTimeScoring)
SELECT @model, @auc, 1;

END
```

4. Press *Ctrl + S* to save the file.
5. You can now rebuild the solution using *Ctrl + Shift + B*.

Publishing schema changes

There are two options of publishing changes to an environment:

- Existing database
- New database

In this example, NYCTaxi already exists in the database. You can identify the schema changes and create an update script:

1. Right-click on **Ch08** and choose **Schema Compare.**
2. Ensure that the source on the left is pointing to the database project path.
3. On the **Select Target** drop-down list, click on it to set the target database.
4. Choose **Database** and click on **Select Connection**. Here, you can provide connection to the existing NYCTaxi database.

5. Click on **Compare**, which should only show one file:

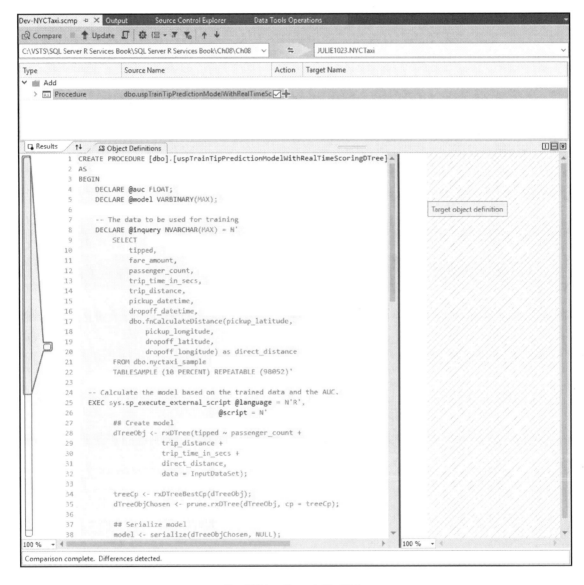

Figure 8.9 Schema Compare in Visual Studio

6. Here, you can click on **Update** to make the changes directly to the database or click on the **Generate Script** icon to generate the script for the changes.

As a best practice, especially if you have a formal production change management process, you would choose generate script and include it in the change management request.

Adding a unit test against a stored procedure

Adding a unit test against programmability objects, such as stored procedures or functions, is part of good practice of programming:

1. Create a unit test suite by right-clicking on one of the stored procedures or functions, such as `Ch08 | dbo | Stored Procedures | uspTrainTipPredictionModel`. Then, choose **Create Unit Tests...**:

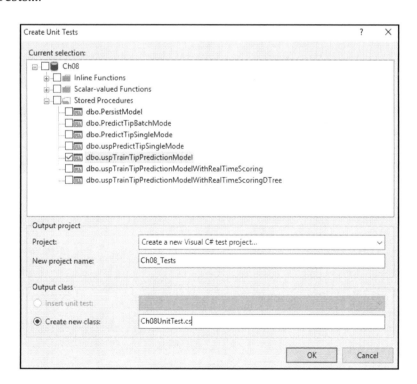

Figure 8.10 Creating unit test in Visual Studio

2. Choose the connection:

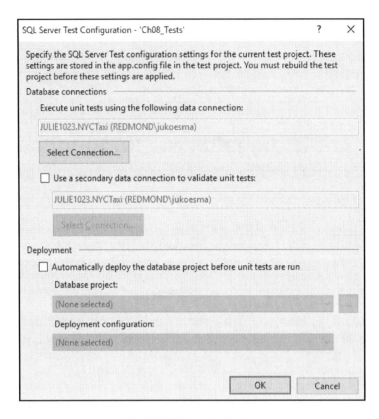

Figure 8.11 SQL Server test configuration

3. Once you click on **OK**, you will see a new unit test project created and an example of a unit test template created:

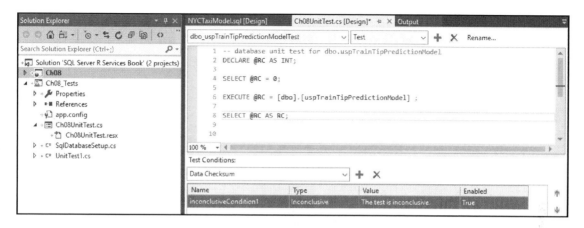

Figure 8.12 SQL Server unit test template

On the top-right pane, you can curate your unit test cases. As `dbo.uspTrianTipPredictionModel` trains sample data and stores the model as well as the AUC into `dbo.NYCTaxiModel`, we are going to create a unit test to ensure that:

- The new record is inserted, and
- The AUC created meets a certain threshold

4. Copy the following code:

```
-- database unit test for dbo.uspTrainTipPredictionModel
DECLARE @RC AS INT;
DECLARE @RowCountBefore AS INT;
DECLARE @RowCountAfter AS INT;
DECLARE @AUC FLOAT;
SELECT @RC = 0;
```

```
SELECT @RowCountBefore = IS NULL((SELECT COUNT(1) ROWCOUNT
FROM [dbo].[NYCTaxiModel]
WHERE [AUC] ISNOTNULL), 0);
EXECUTE @RC = [dbo].[uspTrainTipPredictionModel];
-- Expected value: there should be a new record added to
NYCTaxiModel
-- where AUC is known.
SELECT @RowCountAfter = ISNULL((SELECTCOUNT(1)ROWCOUNT
FROM [dbo].[NYCTaxiModel]
WHERE [AUC] ISNOTNULL), 0);
SELECT @AUC = (SELECTTOP 1 [AUC]
FROM [dbo].[NYCTaxiModel]
ORDER BY [CreatedOn] DESC);
SELECT
@RowCountAfter - @RowCountBeforeRowCountAdded,
IIF(@AUC > 0.5, 1, 0) AUCOfModel;
```

5. In the **Test Conditions** pane, click on **inconclusiveCondition1** and click on the red cross to delete it.

6. Now, choose **Scalar Value** from **Test Conditions** and click on the plus button.

7. Then, right-click on the **scalarValueCondition1** and click on **Properties**.

8. Update the following values in the **Properties** window:
    1. **Name:** TestNYCTaxiModelAdded
    2. **Expected value:** 1
    3. **Null Expected:** False

9. Repeat steps 6 to 8 and change the following values in the **Properties** window:
    1. **Name:** TestNYCTaxiModelAdded
    2. **Expected value:** 1
    3. **Null Expected:** False

Once you have set things up, your Visual Studio should look something like this now:

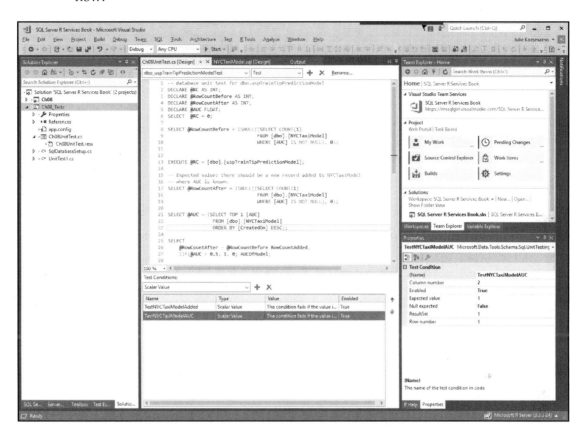

Figure 8.13 SQL Server unit test for dbo.uspTrainTipPredictionModel

10. Remove `UnitTest.cs`.
11. Then, right-click on the **Ch08_Test** project and click on **Build**.
12. Navigate to **Test Explorer** and click on **Run All**.
13. In a few seconds, `dbo_uspTrainTipPredictionModelTest` appears under **Passed Test**. Click on it to see a summary of the execution.

14. Click on **Output** to see more details, for example:

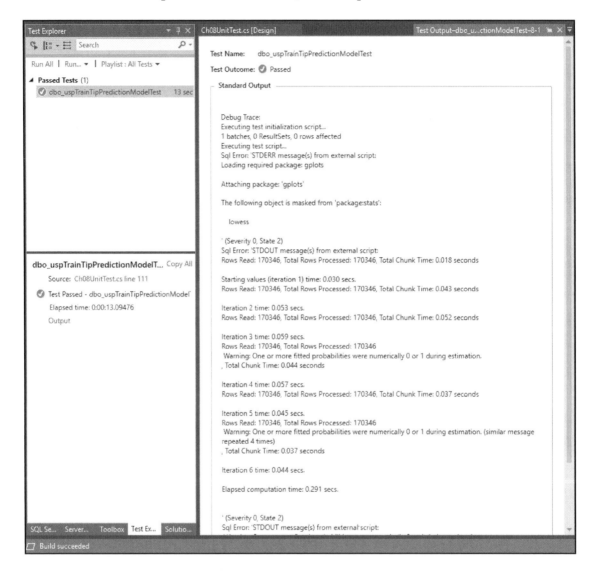

Figure 8.14 Test execution results

You have now learned how to create a unit test against a stored procedure, executed against an existing stored procedure on an existing NYC Taxi Model. Ideally, the unit test is run against a recently published SQL Server.

Using version control

From Visual Studio, we can check in the solution and manage changes in version control. In this specific instance, we are using VSTS to check in. It is assumed that you have created a project in VSTS.

Here are the prerequisites for the rest of this section:

1. **A VSTS project**: To set up a new VSTS project, simply go to: `https://www.visualstudio.com/team-services/`.

   The URL for a VSTS project should follow this format:
   `https://<your account>.visualstudio.com/<VSTS Project>`

   The VSTS project referred to in this chapter is named `SQL Server R Services Book`. So, the URL in my case is
   `https://mssqlgirl.visualstudio.com/SQL%20Server%20R%20Services%20Book`

2. The VSTS project is mapped to a local folder.

   The local folder here mapped to the project is `C:\VSTS\SQL Server R Services Book`. Earlier in this chapter, we created the SQL Server database solution in this path.

Follow these steps to check in your solution from Visual Studio:

1. On the **Solution** root node, right-click and choose **Check In**.
2. In the **Team Explorer** window, under the **Pending Changes**, type `Initial check-in` in the **Comment** text box.

3. Review **Related Work Items**, **Included Changes**, and **Excluded Changes** before you click on **Check In**:

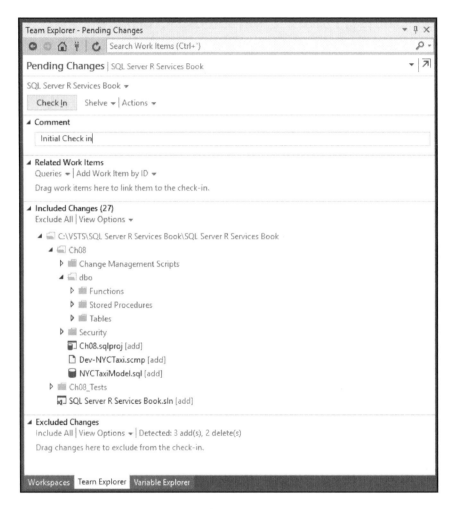

Figure 8.15 Checking in Pending Changes

4. On the **Check-in Confirmation** dialog box, click on **Yes**.

Once all the files are checked in successfully, you can also view them on the VSTS site. As an example:

```
https://mssqlgirl.visualstudio.com/SQL%20Server%20R%20Services%20Book/_
versionControl
```

Setting up continuous integration

The main idea of **continuous integration** (CI) is to perform builds that are automated based on one or more triggers. One of the triggers to perform a build is a check-in event. Another one could be a scheduled build. Choosing which trigger is appropriate depends on various factors, such as the complexity of the project and the culture of the team. In this section, because the project is small, we are going to automate the build triggered by check-ins. We will also add tests as part of the build.

VSTS is a good platform to automate builds, deployments for testing, and monitoring. In this section, we will configure a build definition and schedule a continuous integration in VSTS.

> Ensure that the Visual Studio solution, including the SQL Server database project and the SQL Server Unit Test project, are built successfully.

Figure 8.16 shows the SQL Server R Services Book team in VSTS online. In these next few sections, we will be using VSTS on your browser to configure CI:

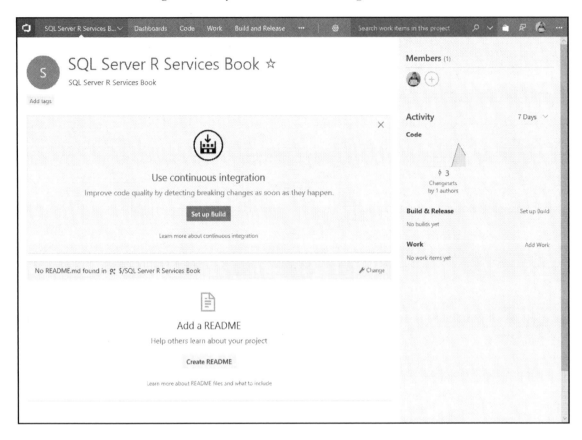

Figure 8.16 Checking in Pending Changes

Here is a prerequisite for the rest of this section:

- To be able to deploy a SQL Server database project to an on-premises SQL Server instance, you will need to create a private agent hosted locally that is registered with VSTS. This is only available in Visual Studio 2017. To set this up, follow the documentation at: `https://docs.microsoft.com/en-us/vsts/build-release/ actions/agents/v2-windows`.

Creating a build definition in VSTS

Follow these steps to create a build definition in VSTS:

1. On the VSTS project site, click on **Build and Release** from the top menu, then choose **Builds**. Choose **New Definition**.
2. Start with Empty Process.
3. Under **Tasks**, go to **Process** and choose the private agent from the **Agent queue** drop-down list. In the mssqlgirl account, the private agent is named **Default**:

Figure 8.17 Selecting Private Agent (Default) for the tasks in the build

4. Review the selections in **Get sources**.

The local path under $(build.sourcesdirectory) is referring to the private agent's workspace to do builds and perform additional tasks.

5. Click on **Phase 1** and replace the **Display name** value with **Build Phase**.
6. On the top menu, choose **Save** from the **Save & Queue** drop-down list.
7. Review **Save build definition** and place a comment.

8. Add a task to **Build Phase** by clicking on the plus sign.

9. In **Add tasks**, search for **MS Build**, then click on **Add**.

10. Change **Project** to $/SQL Server R Services Book/SQL Server R Services Book/SQL Server R Services Book.sln.

The default value is **/*.sln, which refers to all solution files in the VSTS project.

11. On **Build Phase**, add another task, named **Publish Build Artifacts**. This allows us to get the files that can be important later, such as the DACPAC file.

12. On the **Publish Build Artifacts** task, specify the following details:

    1. **Path to publish**: $(Build.Repository.LocalPath)\SQL Server R Services Book\Ch08\bin\Debug

    2. **Artifact name**: DACPAC

    3. **Artifact publish location**: Visual Studio Team Services/TFS

In this step, we are only publishing the DACPAC file. Publishing this specific file in the Visual Studio Team Services area allows us to later refer to this DACPAC in the Release process (a Continuous Delivery step).

13. Click on **Save & Queue** to test the build definition.

14. Review the options in queue build for SQL Server R Services Book-CI and click on **Queue**.

15. The page will then show that a build is being queued, similar to the following:

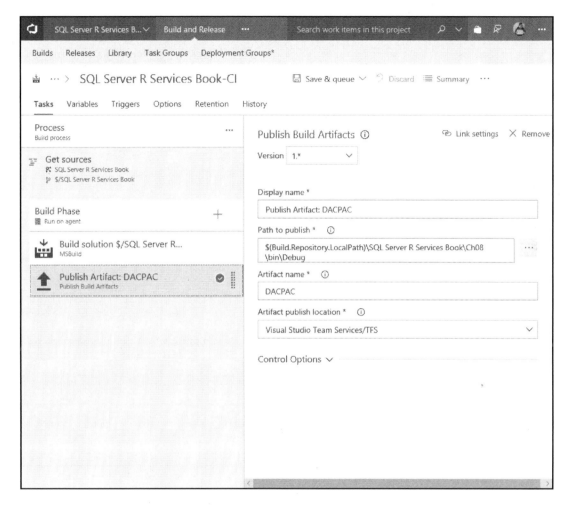

Figure 8.18 Adding publish artifact task

If the build is successful, you will see something similar to the following. Now would be a good time to get familiar with the Summary page of the build and the artifacts page:

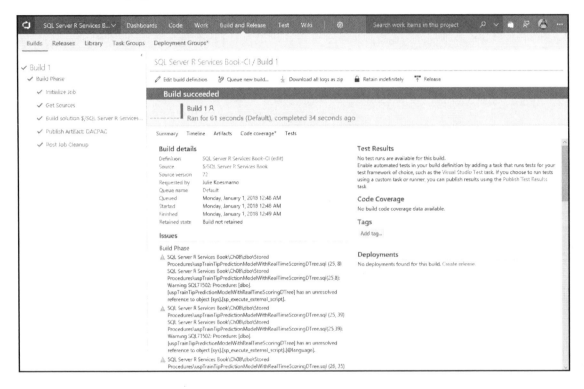

Figure 8.19 Viewing build results

When you navigate to the **Artifacts** tab, you should be able to see the DACPAC folder. By clicking on **Explore**, you can see the files inside the solution including the build output similar to what a local build via Visual Studio would do:

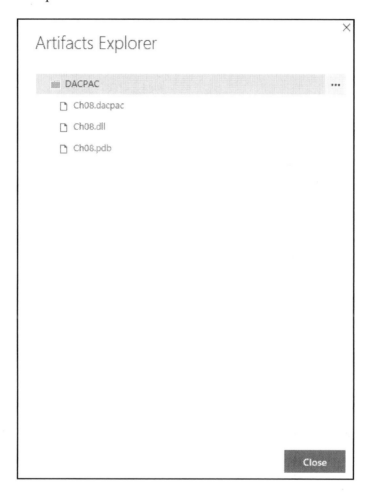

Figure 8.20 Exploring Artifacts published from the previous successful build

Deploying the build to a local SQL Server instance

Now that the build via VSTS on the private agent is successful, let's try deploying the database to an SQL Server instance. The prerequisite for this is that the private agent must be able to access the SQL Server instance. *Figure 8.21* shows how VSTS with on-premises (Private) agent(s) can be used for deploying to multiple on-premises servers/environments:

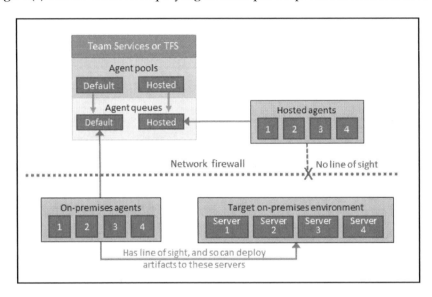

Figure 8.21 High level layout of VSTS and On-prem agents/environment

Source:
https://docs.microsoft.com/en-us/vsts/build-release/concepts/agents/agents

When a SQL Server database project is built, it will produce a DACPAC file that can be used to create a new database. So, in the **Build Phase** of the **SQL Server R Services Book-CI** build definition, we will add a new task:

1. Navigate to the **SQL Server R Services Book-CI** build definition.
2. Click on **Build Phase** and add a new task.
3. Search for WinRM - SQL Server DB Deployment. Then, click on **Add**.

If it doesn't exist, click on **Check out our Marketplace**. Search for `IIS Web App Deployment using WinRM` and install it against your VSTS account.

4. In **Deploy** using : DACPAC, type the following details:
   1. **Machines**: `$(UATMachine)`
   2. **Admin Login**: `$(UATAdminUser)`
   3. **Password**: `$(UATAdminPwd)`
   4. **DACPAC file**: `$(Build.Repository.LocalPath)\SQL Server R Services Book\Ch08\bin\Debug\Ch08.dacpac`
   5. **Specify SQL Using**: `Publish Profile`
   6. **Publish Profile**:
      `$(System.DefaultWorkingDirectory)$(UATPublishProfilePath)`

5. Add the following new variables:

Name	Value	Secret
`UATMachine`	{Enter your machine name in FQDN or IP address, for example: `uatpc.mssqlgirl.com`}	No
`UATAdminUser`	{Enter the admin user that can log in to the UAT Machine}	No
`UATAdminPwd`	{Enter the admin password for the admin}	Yes
`UATPublisProfilePath`	`\SQL Server R Services Book\Ch08\Ch08-UAT.publish.xml`	No

6. Click on Save and Queue to test the build.

Adding the test phase to the build definition

In this section, you will learn how to add a test phase to the **SQL Server R Services Book-CI** build definition. This test phase will perform the unit testing that we have done earlier.

Before we can start unit testing, we need to prepare for the test. This includes populating the `dbo.nyctaxisample` table:

1. To add a new Test Phase, go to **Process,** click on **...,** and choose **Add agent phase.**
2. In Agent phase, type `Test Phase` in **Display name.**
3. On **Test Phase**, add a new task.
4. Search for `Command Line`. Then, click on `Add`.
5. In the Command Line task, type the following details:
   1. **Tool:** `bcp`
   2. **Arguments:** `Ch08.dbo.nyctaxi_sample in "$(System.DefaultWorkingDirectory)$(UATSampleFilePath)" -c -t , -r \n -U $(UATDBUser) -P $(UATDBPwd)`
6. Click on **Save.**

Now, we can add the step that creates and executes the unit testing:

1. On **Test Phase**, add a new task.
2. Search for `Visual Studio Test`. Then, click on **Add.**
3. In `Visual Studio Test`, type the following details:
   1. **Display name:** `Unit Test`
   2. **Select tests using:** `Test assemblies`
   3. **Test assemblies:** `**\Ch08_test*.dll`
   4. **Search folder:** `$(System.DefaultWorkingDirectory)`
   5. **Test platform station:** `Visual Studio 2017`
   6. Test run title: `Ch08 SQL Server Testing`
4. Click on **Save & Queue.**

5. When you view the build, you should be able to see something like the following:

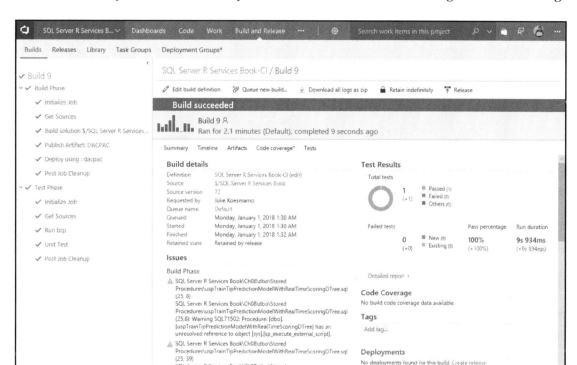

Figure 8.22 Successful automated testing

Automating the build for CI

Now that we have defined the SQL Server R Services Book-CI with Build Phase and Test Phase, we are ready to automate it:

1. In VSTS, edit SQL Server R Services Book-CI.
2. Click on the **Triggers** tab.
3. Ensure that **Enable continuous integration** is checked.

4. Optionally, click on **+ Add** for **Scheduled**:

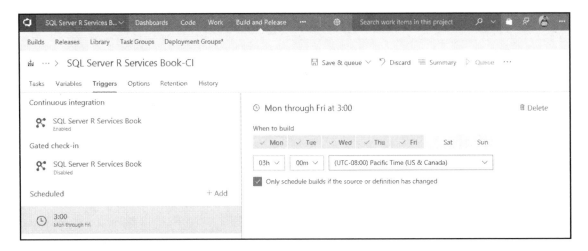

Figure 8.23 Configuring build for CI and specific schedule

5. Click on the **Options** tab.

6. In **Build Properties | Build number format**, type
   `Build_$(Date:yyyyMMdd)$(Rev:.r)`.

7. Click on **Save**.

Now, to test if the automation works, let's make a change to the solution, for example:

1. In Visual Studio, open the **SQL Server R Services Book** solution.

2. Remove the following files from the **Ch08** project:

   1. `nyc_taxi_models.sql`

   2. `PersistModel.sql`

   3. `PredictTipBatchMode.sql`

   4. `PredictTipSingleMode.sql`

3. Let's check in the pending changes now. Right-click on the **Solution** node and choose **Check In**.

4. Optionally, add a comment before clicking on the **Check In** button.

After a successful check-in, you should be able to see the **Changeset** number:

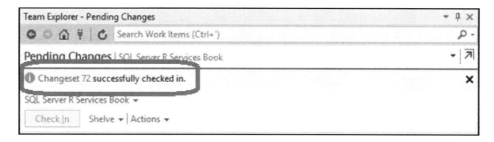

Figure 8.24 Checking Changeset information for Visual Studio

In VSTS, you should be able to go to the latest build and see the matching **Source version**, as shown here:

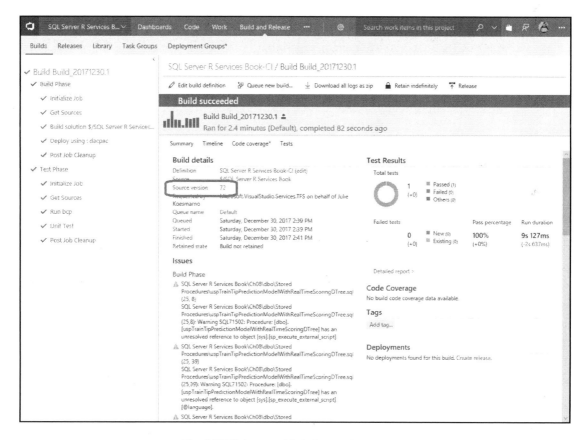

Figure 8.25 Validating automated CI via Changeset information in VSTS

Setting up continuous delivery

Continuous delivery aims to ensure that we can deploy good builds to the desired environment. This could mean the UAT environment or the Production environment. In this section, we will use VSTS to implement continuous delivery:

1. In VSTS, go to the **SQL Server R Services Book** project.
2. Navigate to **Build and Release** | **Release** from the top menu.
3. Click on + | **New Definition**.
4. Review the **Select Template** pane. From here, you can choose from many options, including **Run Automated Tests from Test Manager**. This option is highly recommended for regularly checking the accuracy of your existing model, which will be discussed in the next step of what the manual process entails. For now, let's choose **Empty** and click on **Add**.
5. On the top title where it says **All definitions** | **New Release Definition**, click on the pencil icon to edit the name to UAT Release.
6. Let's continue with the **Pipeline** tab. There are two boxes: Artifacts and **Environments**.
7. In the **Artifacts** box, click on **Add artifact**.
8. Provide the following details and click on **Add**:
    1. **Project**: SQL Server R Services Book
    2. **Source** (build definition): SQL Server R Services Book-CI
9. In the **Environments** box, click on **1 phase, 0 task** in **Environment 1**.
10. In the **Tasks** tab, click on the first line that says **Environment 1**. Change the **Environment name** to UAT.
11. In the **Tasks** tab, click on the **Agent** phase and provide the following details:
    1. **Display name: Deploy to UAT**
    2. **Agent queue: Default**

12. Now, add a new task for **Deploy to UAT**.
13. Search for `WinRM - SQL Server DB Deployment` and click on **Add**.
14. In **Deploy** using : Dacpac, fill in the following details:
    1. **Machines**: `$(UATMachine)`
    2. **Admin Login**: `$(UATAdminUser)`
    3. **Password**: `$(UATAdminPwd)`
    4. **DACPAC File**:
       `$(System.ArtifactsDirectory)\$(Build.DefinitionName)\DA`
       `CPAC\Ch08.dacpac`
    5. **Sever Name**: `{specify the server name, for example: localhost}`
    6. **Database Name**: `NYCTaxiUAT`
15. Go to the **Variables** tab and add the following variables:

Name	Value	Secret
UATMachine	{Enter your machine name in FQDN or IP address, for example: uatpc.mssqlgirl.com}	No
UATAdminUser	{Enter the admin user that can log in to the UAT Machine}	No
UATAdminPwd	{Enter the admin password for the admin}	Yes

16. Then, click on **Save** and accept the default values.
17. To test this release definition, under **New Release Definition**, click on **+ Release** and choose **Create Release**, then choose ....

18. On the **Create new release for New Release Definition**, type `Test UAT deployment` in **Release Description**. Then, click on **Create**, as shown here:

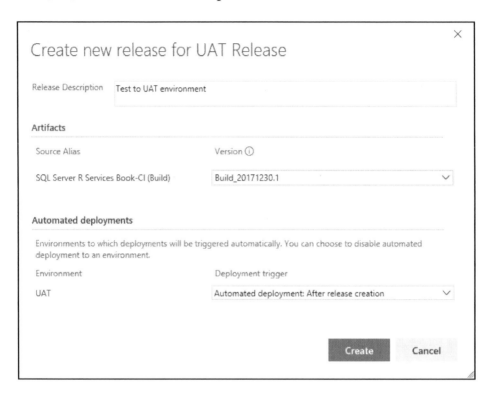

Figure 8.26 Creating a new release for the UAT environment based on the latest successful build

 It is possible to deploy to multiple environments with different database connection settings. An extension that will help you achieve this is XDT Transform:
`https://marketplace.visualstudio.com/items?itemName=qetza.xdttransform`

Once the release is completed, it will look as follows:

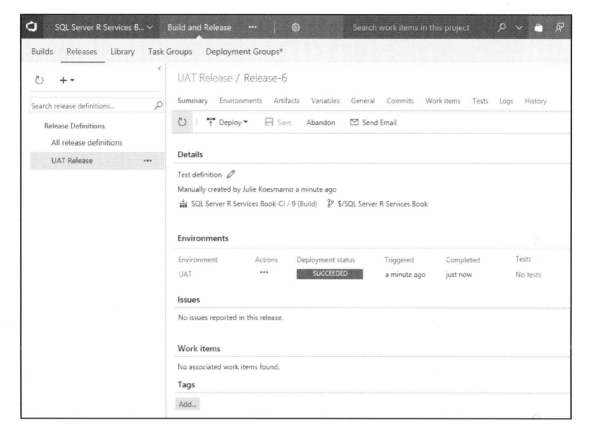

Figure 8.27 Results of a successful release

To enable Continuous Deliverable on the release, you'll have to edit the definition:

1. Go to the Releases view, click on **...** of **UAT Release**, then choose **Edit**.
2. On the **Pipeline** view, go to **SQL Server R Services Book-CI** inside the Artifacts box.

3. Click on the **Continuous deployment trigger**, as shown here:

Figure 8.28 Changing the Continuous Deployment Trigger

4. In the **Continuous deployment trigger** window, ensure that the **Enabled** slider is on.
5. Click on **Save**.

To test the UAT Release's Continuous deliverable setup, you can invoke a new build on **SQL Server R Services Book-CI**. The view should look like this:

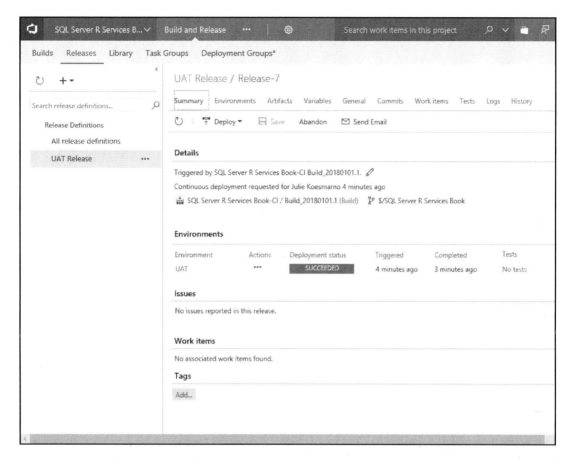

Figure 8.29 Results of a successful release through Continuous Development

In the summary, the **Details** should say that the release is **Triggered by SQL Server R Services Book-CI Build_20180101.1**. Therefore, we successfully created a basic Continuous Delivery process. Advanced steps like setting up integration testing and load testing can now be added to the release using similar steps to the ones shown earlier. For more information about setting this up in VSTS, please refer to the following tutorial from Microsoft: `https://docs.microsoft.com/en-us/vsts/build-release/test/example-continuous-testing#configure-cd`.

Monitoring the accuracy of the productionized model

In Chapter 6, *Predictive Modeling*, we discussed a number of predictive modeling examples. The model(s) created is/are based on trained data. In a real-world scenario, new data keeps coming in, for example, online transactions, taxi cab transactions (remember the earlier NYC taxi example), and air flight delay predictions. Therefore, the data model should be checked regularly to ensure that it is still satisfactory and that there is no other better model that could be generated for it. With the latter, a good data scientist would continuously be asking at least four of these questions:

1. Is there a different algorithm to consider due to changes of the data?

   For example, if the current model is using logistic regression (rxLogit), would the decision tree algorithm more accurate (rxDTree) either due to the size or due to changes in the expected outcome?

2. Are there other features from newer transactions that are becoming more significant?

   Consider the following scenario: Currently, tipping prediction on taxi rides are using passenger count, trip distance, trip time, and direct distance. Perhaps regularly checking whether other features, such as hour of day, day of week, pick-up zip code and/or drop-off zip code, holiday season, cleanliness of the taxi, or customer rating, would contribute more to the tipping prediction.

3. Has there been changes in the requirements that can yield to actions to improve the business or customer?

   In the taxi ride tipping prediction, the current prediction is a binary value, that is, true or false. The business might be interested in understanding more about how cleanliness of the taxi or the customer rating can be correlated to no tips, small tips, medium tips, or large tips. Cleanliness of the taxi cab is an action that the driver can use to drive better improvement.

4. Is performance slow down caused by the model execution or input data bottleneck?

It is possible that as the input dataset/data source grows and is not optimized, the end-to-end predictive modeling would also slow down.

To capture the performance of the model, one should log the performance of the actual prediction or the reasonable representation of actual data. Here is an example of what the log table should look like:

Value	Data Type	Comments
LogID	INT	Sequential ID for execution.
Created On	DATETIME	Date the model was generated and tested.
ModelID	INT	Unique ID for each model.
Model	VARBINARY(MAX)	This is the serialized representation of the model.
RxFunction	VARCHAR(50)	This is the rx function used in the model.
Formula	VARCHAR(1000)	The formula for the prediction model.
Training Input Query	VARCHAR(MAX)	The training dataset that is reproducible
AUC	FLOAT	The AUC representation of the model. This can be any other metric that you can use to compare quality of the model.
Training Row Count	INT	The number of row counts.
CPU Time	INT	The number of seconds to generate the model.

Once you capture the execution, you can analyze the AUC value and the CPU time, as shown in *Figure 8.30*:

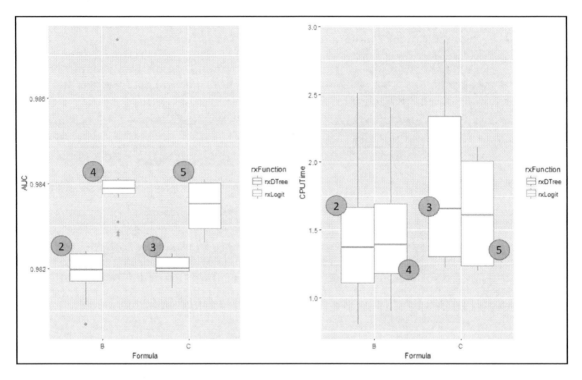

Figure 8.30 Monitoring Model comparisons on AUC and CPU Time

These diagrams compare the performance of the following models:

	Formula B	Formula C
rxDTree	Model ID 2	Model ID 3
rxLogit	Model ID 4	Model ID 5

The description is as follows:

- Formula B is *tipped ~ passenger_count + trip_distance + trip_time_in_secs + direct_distance + payment_type*
- Formula C is *tipped ~ passenger_count + trip_distance + trip_time_in_secs + payment_type*

And each of the models is run against:

- Last 2 months of data
- Random top 5 percent of data

Based on the previously mentioned comparisons, we can see that Model ID 4, which is `rxLogit` with Formula B, has the highest AUC range and lowest CPU time. So, this model is the best out of the two. Next is to decide if this model should replace the ones in production.

Now that you have learned the technique of comparing models and some of the metrics that are important in prediction modeling, you can schedule this performance testing similar to the one shown earlier. The scheduling can be a SQL Agent job, as shown in `Chapter 7`, *Operationalizing R Code*, where you can get alerted should new results fall below a certain threshold. Or, you can issue this as part of a separate SQL Server database unit project deployed in VSTS to check against the database with the latest transactions data.

Useful references

- Integrate SQL Server 2017 into your DevOps pipeline: `https://www.microsoft.com/en-us/sql-server/developer-get-started/sql-devops/`
- Visual Studio Team Services (VSTS): `https://www.visualstudio.com/team-services/`
- Compare Visual Studio 2017 IDEs: `https://www.visualstudio.com/vs/compare/`
- Configure Hosted Agent in VS 2017: `https://docs.microsoft.com/en-us/vsts/build-release/actions/agents/v2-windows`
- Continuous Delivery: `https://www.visualstudio.com/learn/what-is-continuous-delivery/`

Summary

Visual Studio 2017 is a powerful IDE for data scientists/developers to manage their code, unit testing, and version control. Combined with Visual Studio Team Services, they form a complete toolkit to execute Database Lifecycle Management, which can also be easily adapted to DevOps practices. This chapter describes in detail how you can integrate SQL Server Machine Learning Services with R in SQL Server Database projects, DevOps practices, and CI/CD workflows. Finally, you have also learned how to monitor a Prediction Model accuracy over time.

In the next chapter, we'll discuss how DBAs can also take advantage of Machine Learning Services with R.

Machine Learning Services with R for DBAs

9

R integration (along with Python integration in SQL Server 2017) offered a wide range of possibilities that one can use. And the targeted group of people has just increased in terms of people (job roles or departments) using R Services. DBAs (and also SysAdmins) will for sure gain a lot from this. Not only do R and statistics give them some additional impetus for discovering and gaining insights on their captured data, but also they might help them to find some hidden nuggets that they might have missed before. The mixture of different languages-and I am not solely talking about R, but also other languages-for sure bring new abilities to track, capture, and analyze captured data.

One thing is clear, if you have R (any Python) so close to the database, several people can switch from monitoring tasks to predicting tasks. This literally means that instead of taking actions when something has already happened, people can now diagnose and predict what might happen. I'm not saying this is an easy task, since we all know that the complexity, for example, of one query all of a sudden running slow, can have one or more hidden reasons, that might not be seen immediately, R in-database will for sure help find this hidden reason in near real time. Contrary to data-mining in SSAS, which in my personal opinion is still a very strong and good tool, there might be more latency in comparison to sending and analyzing data through R Engine.

This chapter will capture the important steps on how to help DBAs (or other roles to tackle similar issues) to get the advantages of R:

- Gathering data relevant for DBAs
- Exploring and analyzing data
- Creating predictions with R Services
- Improving monitoring with predictions

Gathering relevant data

Gathering data - simple as it might be - is a task that needs to be well crafted. There are a few reasons for that. The first and most important is that we want to gather data in a way that will have minimum or zero impact on the production environment. This means that the process of collecting and storing data should not disturb any on-going process. The second important thing is storage. Where and how do you want to store the data and the retention policy of the stored data? At the beginning, this might seem a very trivial case, but over time, storage itself will play an important role. The third and also utterly important thing is which data you want to gather. Of course, we all want to have smart data present, that is, having all the data relevant for solving or improving our business processes. But in reality, gathering smart is neither that difficult nor that easy. First of all, one must understand the concept of the database feature and furthermore, how to capture the relevant indicators and how this particular feature will work.

Let's see where and how one can see performance improvements, if you know where and how to look for them.

For example, delayed durability is a feature that has been in SQL Server since SQL Server 2014, but can in some scenarios help improve performance for compromising the durability (durability is part of the ACID acronym-atomic, consistent, isolation, and durability-and prevents, in the case of a failure or system restart, committed data from not being saved or saved in an incorrect state). **Write-ahead log (WAL)** is a system that SQL Server uses, which means that all the changes are written to the log first, before they are allowed to be committed to the database table.

For this quick demo, we will create an empty database with DELAYED_DURABILITY set to allowed with NO_WAIT. An additional and important step to this test is to set the backup of the database to NUL, which is similar to the command with truncate_only. This statement discards any inactive logs (when the database is in full or bulk-logged recovery mode; for simple recovery mode, this does not hold water) and from the point when a full backup of the database is done, any inactive log records get discarded (deleted). This could be simulated. When a checkpoint runs, the attempt to back up the log will result in an error message. In other words, a database could be running in simple recovery mode. Essentially, the NUL command simply stores and discards the log:

```
USE [master];
GO
CREATE DATABASE [DelayedDurability];
GO
ALTER DATABASE [DelayedDurability] SET DELAYED_DURABILITY = ALLOWED
WITH NO_WAIT;
```

```
GO
BACKUP DATABASE [DelayedDurability] TO DISK = N'nul'
GO
```

I will create a sample table to do the inserts:

```
USE [DelayedDurability];
GO
DROP TABLE IF EXISTS TestDDTable;
GO
CREATE TABLE TestDDTable
(ID INT IDENTITY(1,1) PRIMARY KEY
,R_num INT
,Class CHAR(10)
,InsertTime DATETIME DEFAULT(GETDATE())
);
GO
```

Having created a table, we can now test two types of insert, with and without delayed durability:

```
EXECUTE sys.sp_flush_log;
GO
DECLARE @count INT = 0
DECLARE @start1 DATETIME = GETDATE()
WHILE (@count <= 250000)
        BEGIN
            BEGIN TRAN
                INSERT INTO TestDDTable(R_num, class) VALUES(@count,
'WITHOUT_DD')
                SET @count += 1
            COMMIT
        END
SET @count = 0
DECLARE @start2 DATETIME = GETDATE()
WHILE (@count <= 250000)
        BEGIN
            BEGIN TRAN
                INSERT INTO TestDDTable(R_num, class) VALUES(@count,
'WITH_DD')
                SET @count += 1
            COMMIT WITH (DELAYED_DURABILITY = ON)
        END
SELECT
DATEDIFF(SECOND, @start1, GETDATE()) AS With_DD_OFF
,DATEDIFF(SECOND, @start2, GETDATE()) AS With_DD_ON
```

And the result is obvious: with the delayed durability set to on, one can gain in performance when doing so many inserts:

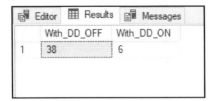

I could have also used the query stress to simulate several threads, each doing the same number of inserts:

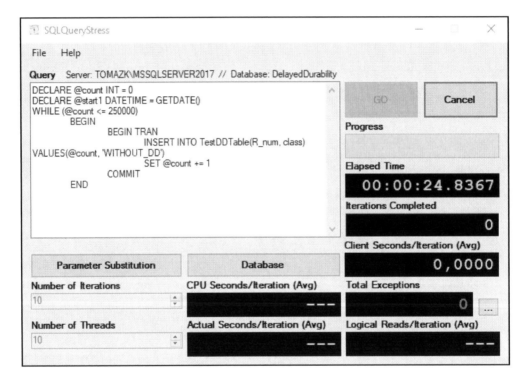

And with such heavy stress tool testing, the question is, How can we monitor and track the behavior of the delayed durability? One can test the performance with the performance monitor:

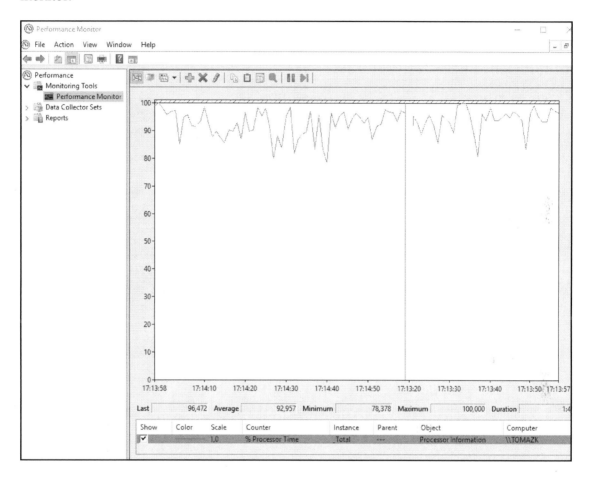

Alternatively, you can test the performance with the activity monitor:

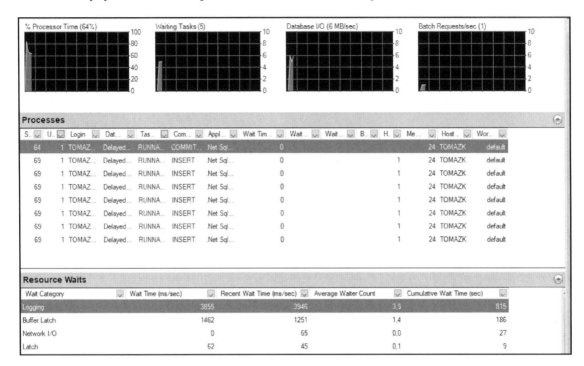

But soon you will realize that either you need to store this information for later analysis or you need to get some additional know-how as to, which performance pointers or extended events are worth monitoring in this case.

So, in this case, you will need to check the wait resources on logging in:

```
SELECT * FROM sys.dm_os_wait_stats
WHERE wait_type IN ('WRITELOG');
GO
```

You will also need to either add some mechanism to capture those wait statistics in a table for later analysis or capture the performance monitor or use profiler, XE, and others. Querying data in runtime and capturing statistics is rather tedious job; imagine merging statistics from `sys.dm_os_wait_stats` and combining them with `sys.dm_io_virtual_file_stats`. All in all the, more data you try to gather, the more complicated querying these statistics might becomes.

Capturing with performance monitor of both queries from earlier, the picture looks as shown in the following screenshot:

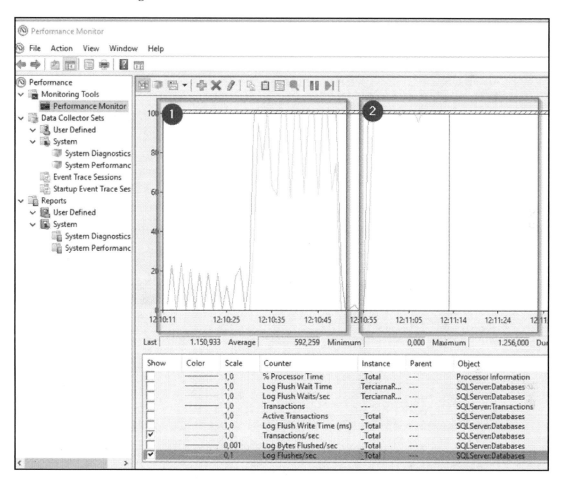

The above screenshot shows, on the left-hand side (1), how delayed durability is working and how log flushing is happening in a sequential period of time. Comparing this to the right-hand side (2), we can see how delayed durability is turned off and log flushing is not active.

Extracting raw data from the performance monitor may not be the right approach, but storing the same set of data through extended events will be much more lightweight on the system, as well as the users, for later analysis.

Setting up the extended event you will need for your analysis can be done fast and easily. But rather than choosing too many events, focus on the ones that are really needed, because, the log file might get big very quickly:

```
-- creating extended event
IF EXISTS(SELECT * FROM sys.server_event_sessions WHERE
name='DelayDurab_Log_flush')
DROP EVENT session DelayDurab_Log_flush ON SERVER;
-- Get DelayedDurability database ID
SELECT db_id()

CREATE EVENT SESSION DelayDurab_Log_flush ON SERVER
ADD EVENT sqlserver.log_flush_start
        (WHERE   (database_id=40)),
ADD EVENT sqlserver.databases_log_flush
        (WHERE (database_id =40)),
ADD EVENT sqlserver.transaction_log
        (WHERE (database_id =40))
-- maybe add batchrequests/second
 ADD TARGET package0.event_file
 (
      SET filename      ='C:\CH09\MonitorDelayDurability.xel'
            ,metadatafile ='C:\CH09\MonitorDelayDurability.xem'
 )
WITH (MAX_MEMORY=4096KB
              ,EVENT_RETENTION_MODE=ALLOW_SINGLE_EVENT_LOSS
              ,MAX_DISPATCH_LATENCY=30 SECONDS
              ,MEMORY_PARTITION_MODE=NONE
              ,STARTUP_STATE=ON);
GO
```

After starting the event, read the content of the file by breaking down the XML structure:

```
SELECT
        CAST(event_data AS XML) AS event_data
FROM sys.fn_xe_file_target_read_file('C:\CH09\MonitorDelayDurability*.xel',
'C:\CH09\MonitorDelayDurability*.xem', null, null)
```

Also, getting the information out of XML is another important task to tackle extended events correctly:

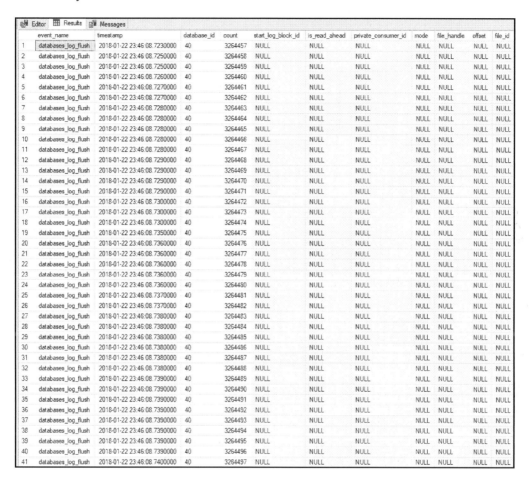

Coming back to the starting point, gathering data for DBAs and further analysis is of the utmost importance. One thing can also be seen from this example: if we also add to log file growth, one of the logs needs to grow additionally by adding new VLF files. Adding delayed durability gives faster inserts as compared to transactions with delayed durability turned off. Sometimes adding new XE or measures can dramatically increase the logging file, where the data is being gathered. Using statistical analysis, we can optimize measure selection or later find that they give us additional insight information. Working on exploring and later analyzing data can give you a huge pay-off, in terms of workloads and in terms of different data gathered.

Exploring and analyzing data

In a similar way, gathering data using event features can give you a rich way to a lot of system information data. Deriving from the previous sample, with the following demo, we will see how measures of a server can be used for advanced statistical analyses and how to help reduce the amount of different information, and pin-point the relevant measures. A specific database and a stage table will be created:

```
CREATE DATABASE ServerInfo;
GO
USE [ServerInfo]
GO
DROP TABLE IF EXISTS server_info;
GO
CREATE TABLE [dbo].[server_info]([XE01] [tinyint] NULL, [XE02] [tinyint]
NULL,
       [XE03] [tinyint] NULL, [XE04] [tinyint] NULL, [XE05] [tinyint] NULL,
       [XE06] [tinyint] NULL, [XE07] [tinyint] NULL, [XE08] [tinyint] NULL,
       [XE09] [tinyint] NULL, [XE10] [tinyint] NULL, [XE11] [tinyint] NULL,
       [XE12] [tinyint] NULL, [XE13] [tinyint] NULL, [XE14] [tinyint] NULL,
       [XE15] [tinyint] NULL, [XE16] [tinyint] NULL, [XE17] [tinyint] NULL,
       [XE18] [tinyint] NULL, [XE19] [tinyint] NULL, [XE20] [tinyint] NULL,
       [XE21] [tinyint] NULL, [XE22] [tinyint] NULL, [XE23] [tinyint] NULL,
       [XE24] [tinyint] NULL, [XE25] [tinyint] NULL, [XE26] [tinyint] NULL,
       [XE27] [tinyint] NULL, [XE28] [tinyint] NULL, [XE29] [tinyint] NULL,
       [XE30] [tinyint] NULL, [XE31] [tinyint] NULL, [XE32] [tinyint] NULL
) ON [PRIMARY];
GO
```

Then, import the measure that can be found in the accompanying code file. There are 433 measuring points from 32 different extended events for the purpose of understanding the server and its environment settings.

After the initial load, the table will be populated with measures of different extended events that have also been discretized and cleaned for further data analysis:

	XE01	XE02	XE03	XE04	XE05	XE06	XE07	XE08	XE09	XE10	XE11	XE12	XE13
1	15	8	15	4	8	9	12	2	4	9	6	20	20
2	3	2	15	8	2	6	20	2	10	3	15	15	20
3	12	2	15	12	6	12	20	6	2	12	6	5	20
4	12	4	15	4	8	9	16	8	8	15	12	5	16
5	6	6	15	4	4	12	20	4	6	9	12	10	20
6	3	2	15	16	6	12	16	4	2	12	9	15	20
7	9	4	15	4	4	3	4	4	10	12	12	5	20
8	15	4	12	8	8	3	16	6	6	15	12	5	16
9	15	2	12	12	4	3	16	8	4	9	12	5	16
10	12	2	15	4	8	9	16	2	10	12	15	5	20
11	15	6	15	4	6	3	16	4	8	15	9	5	12
12	12	8	12	20	4	9	20	10	4	12	6	20	16
13	12	10	15	12	6	12	16	2	6	12	12	5	20
14	15	10	15	16	8	6	16	8	10	12	12	5	20
15	12	8	15	8	8	12	16	2	4	12	12	20	20
16	12	4	6	12	6	12	16	4	2	6	6	5	20

The `boxplot` function enables users to explore the distribution of each of the measures and find potential outliers. Use only R code to explore the data:

```
dbConn <- odbcDriverConnect('driver={SQL
Server};server=TOMAZK\\MSSQLSERVER2017;database=ServerInfo;trusted_connecti
on=true')
server.feature <- sqlQuery(dbConn, 'SELECT * FROM Server_info')
close(dbConn)
boxplot(server.feature)
```

The following graph gives a quick overview:

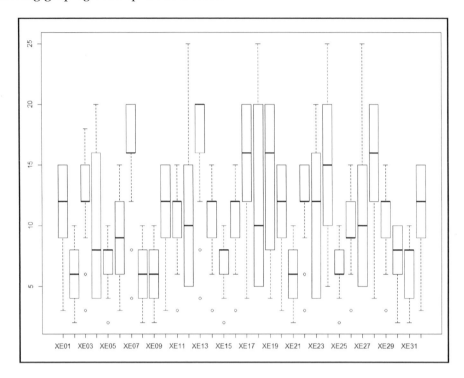

Boxplot shows that there are four events, where the value is vastly exceeding the average and third quartile. Cleaning these outliers will make the data easier to read and not result in abnormal distribution and skewed results. Note that there are particular analyses that deal with outliers and searching for such values. For this demo, we will recode these values into N/A.

After cleaning, adding summary statistics and a correlation is a relevant way to see how all of the events are correlating with one another:

```
# replace value 25 with N/A
server.feature$XE12[server.feature$XE12=="25"]<-NA
server.feature$XE18[server.feature$XE18=="25"]<-NA
server.feature$XE24[server.feature$XE24=="25"]<-NA
server.feature$XE27[server.feature$XE27=="25"]<-NA
cor.plot(server.feature,numbers=TRUE,main="Server Features")
```

A correlation matrix of server features is a nice way to represent which events are correlating and which are not, and how:

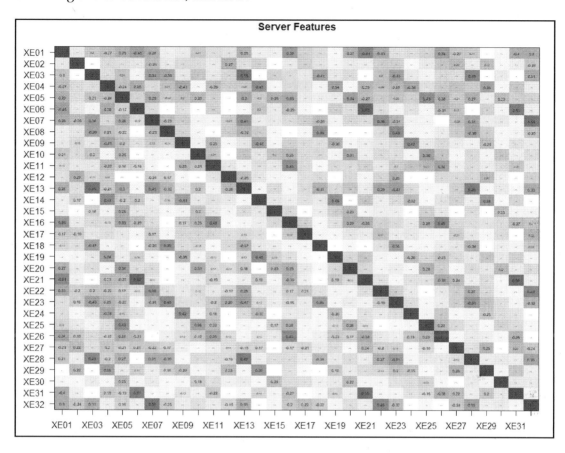

Going a step further, let's reduce these extended event measures, because it is obvious that not all are playing an important role and some might be just overhead. From the preceding heat map, it is hard to see which correlations for certain measures are not working out; therefore, we will use factor analysis. This observes correlations among the variables in such a way that it reflects the lower number of underlying variables. A factor is an underlying variable, that is, a latent variable that gets structured based on the observed and correlated variables. Structure is created by each of the factors being loaded with the response of correlated variable. This means that factor 1 can be, for example, loaded 25% with variable A, 65% with variable B, and 10% with variable C. So factor 1 will take the majority (65%) of the features from variable A and so on.

In this manner, factor analysis will try to reduce the number of original correlated variables (our measures of extended events) and try to create new structured variables.

Exploring data with R code, a simple exploratory factor analysis can reveal a number of factors:

```
fa.parallel(server.feature, fa="fa")
```

The following screen plot reveals that there are seven factors available for extraction:

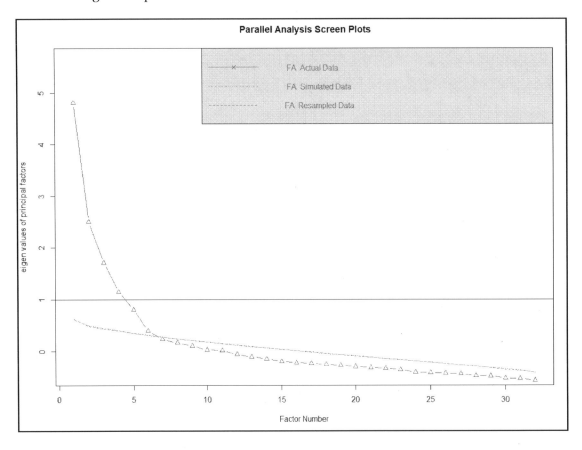

In the following way, this will also reveal the loadings for the factors themselves; simply call the R function:

```
fa.model <- fa(server.feature,7,n.obs = 459,fm="pa",scores="regression",
use="pairwise",rotate="varimax") #can use WLS - weighted least squares
fa.model.r <- target.rot(fa.model)
fa.diagram(fa.model.r)
```

The following diagram shows how loading construct each of the factor.:

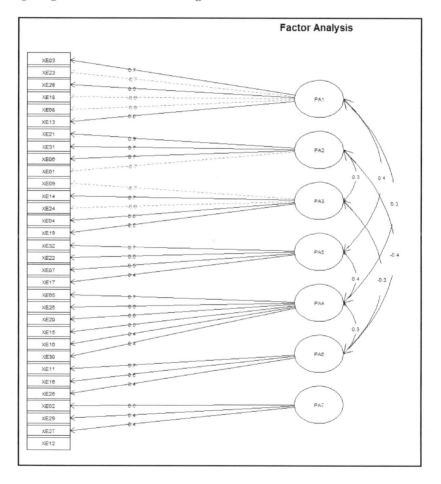

Storing loadings back into the database for further analysis and factor naming are a common practice and given the ability to incorporate factors into any further analysis (for example: classification or clustering methods) . Now that we know the number of factors, we can store the loadings into the database:

```
-- Factor Analysis
-- extract factor loadings
DECLARE @Rcode NVARCHAR(MAX)
SET @Rcode = N'
        ## with actual FA funcitons
        library(psych)
        library(Hmisc)
        ## for data munching and visualization
        library(ggplot2)
        library(plyr)
        library(pastecs)
        server.feature <- InputDataSet
        server.feature$XE12[server.feature$XE12=="25"]<-NA
        server.feature$XE18[server.feature$XE18=="25"]<-NA
        server.feature$XE24[server.feature$XE24=="25"]<-NA
        server.feature$XE27[server.feature$XE27=="25"]<-NA
        fa.model <- fa(server.feature
                ,7
                ,fm="pa"
                ,scores="regression"
                ,use="pairwise"
                ,rotate="varimax") #can use WLS - weighted least squares
        fa.loadings <- as.list.data.frame(fa.model$loadings)
        OutputDataSet <- data.frame(fa.loadings)'
  EXEC sp_execute_external_script
        @language = N'R'
        ,@script = @Rcode
        ,@input_data_1 = N'SELECT * FROM server_info'
WITH RESULT SETS
((
        PA1 NUMERIC(16,3)
        ,PA2 NUMERIC(16,3)
        ,PA3 NUMERIC(16,3)
        ,PA4 NUMERIC(16,3)
        ,PA5 NUMERIC(16,3)
        ,PA6 NUMERIC(16,3)
        ,PA7 NUMERIC(16,3)
  ))
```

The results can be interpreted as: the higher the value (positive or negative), the more loaded is a particular measure is with the accompanying factor:

	PA1	PA2	PA3	PA4	PA5	PA6	PA7
1	0.156	-0.674	-0.045	0.322	0.138	0.066	0.344
2	0.028	-0.097	0.145	-0.479	0.035	0.192	0.354
3	0.680	0.010	0.005	0.154	0.142	0.037	0.122
4	-0.168	0.185	0.608	-0.161	-0.031	-0.091	0.027
5	0.204	-0.253	-0.193	0.117	0.631	-0.040	-0.108
6	0.055	0.679	0.153	-0.110	0.036	-0.079	0.060
7	0.352	-0.115	-0.003	0.538	0.103	-0.067	-0.029
8	-0.581	0.026	0.122	-0.057	-0.031	0.060	0.179
9	0.068	0.013	-0.662	0.105	0.076	0.104	-0.005
10	0.113	-0.043	0.028	0.061	0.468	0.199	0.176
11	0.051	-0.123	-0.225	0.014	0.183	0.581	-0.001
12	-0.150	-0.069	0.079	-0.376	-0.019	0.066	0.129
13	0.640	-0.061	-0.035	0.291	0.178	-0.141	0.144
14	-0.052	0.120	0.692	-0.065	-0.005	0.076	0.153
15	0.122	0.093	0.081	-0.043	0.450	0.025	-0.080
16	0.009	-0.331	-0.076	0.164	0.328	0.553	0.007
17	-0.003	-0.021	-0.097	0.376	0.083	0.077	0.026
18	-0.578	0.000	0.037	-0.013	-0.037	-0.051	-0.084
19	0.107	0.134	0.547	0.059	0.066	-0.106	0.066
20	0.042	-0.146	0.060	0.091	0.532	0.048	0.127

Factor 1, `PA1`, is mostly loaded with XE03 (`0.680`), XE13 (`0.640`), XE18 (`-0.578`), and XE28 (`0.652`). All four are measuring the transactions of query and are as shown in the following screenshot:

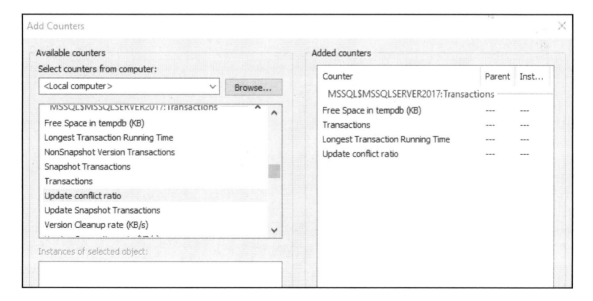

Here, the negative value is the free space in **tempdb (KB)** that is negatively loaded and it only means the relationship to the factor. But having the ability to reduce the number of extended events, and to have them combined through the advanced statistical analysis, is a very neat approach to a potentially complex problem.

With loadings in the database, I can additionally represent how these factors are being dispersed on a scatterplot. I have exported the results of the preceding query to Power BI and used the clustering visual. Furthermore, you can see clusters of these factor loadings and the ones that are similar. The red group (to the left) is again something that DBAs and data scientists should look at together for further examination:

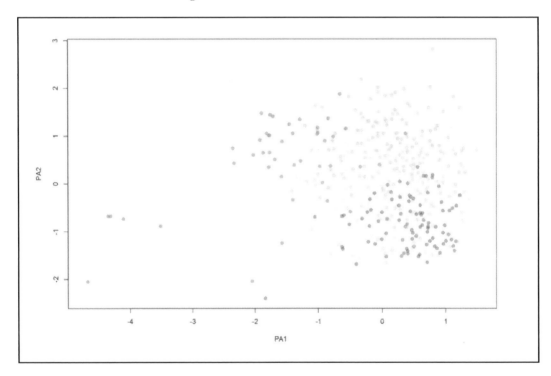

Creating a baseline and workloads, and replaying

Given the ability to reduce and create new measures that are tailored and adapted to your particular server or environment, now we want to understand how the system is behaving with all the other parameters unchanged (in Latin, *ceteris paribus*). This is the baseline. And with the baseline, we establish what is normal, or in other words, what the performance is under normal conditions. A baseline is used for comparing what might be or seem abnormal or out of the ordinary. It can also serve as a control group for any future tests (this works well especially when new patches are rolled out an upgrade of a particular environment/server needs to be performed).

A typical corporate baseline would be described as follows over a period of one day (24 hours) in the form of the number of database requests from users or machines:

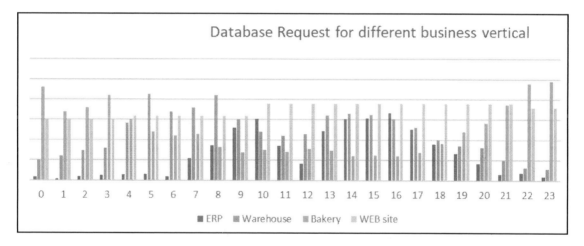

When all requests are represented as a breakdown for each of the corporate processes, immediate patterns can be seen.

The ERP system usually peak when people are at their workplace-on a normal day between 8.00 AM and 5.00 PM with two distinct peaks and a very obvious lunch break from 11.00 AM until 1.00 PM:

Adding ETL jobs for daily ERP system maintenance, it is obvious where and when DBAs and SysAdmins usually try to squeeze these important jobs and how this is also limited and narrated by daily ERP workloads:

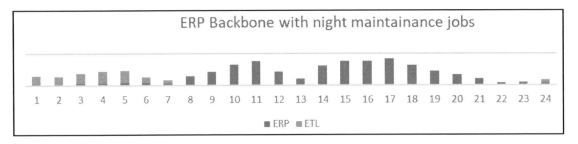

A warehouse has a completely different behavior pattern, which means that it is usually the highest request in the morning hours 4.00 AM and 5.00 AM and somehow steady until evening hours:

A bakery, on the contrary, has a reverse request to the database, since the majority of their activities are done starting from 9.00 PM until 3.00 AM, so that customers get fresh bread in the morning:

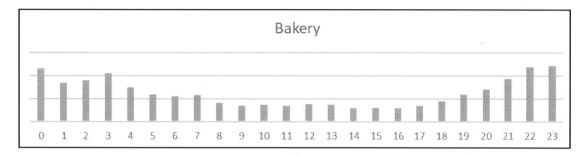

Lastly, websites can be understood as a constant database request resource with relatively slight daily changes:

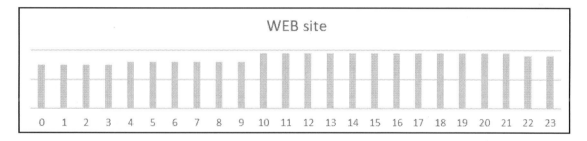

All these can be understood as a daily baseline and of course, things get even more complicated when this is projected on a monthly basis. Also, patterns emerge immediately. During the weekends (day 7, 14, and 21) the requests are diminished and toward the end of the month, the financial cycle needs to be closed; hence, there is additional load on the database:

Showing all these is crucial to understand how the baseline of the system (or environment) must be understood. This data can be collected using performance counters, many of the DMV, using the query store, and other tools. What we usually gather is what we will be later monitoring and predicting. So choosing wisely is the most important task, since through these measures, counters, and values you will be defining when your system is healthy and when it is not. But usually general information on the system and database is crucial. Also, SQL Server information, and many configurable parameters, query-related information, and database-I/O, and RAM-related information need to be stored as well.

After having a baseline, we need to have the workload created. Usually, the workload is captured against the baseline in the production server, and a restore of capture statistics is replayed on the test server/environment. Database tuning or changes in configuration can be alternated by replaying the captured workload from production on the test environment, by alternatively changing the values of a particular parameter. The next demo is a representation of the workload expressed through two parameters that have been changed when the same workload has been replied:

```
USE [master];
GO
CREATE DATABASE Workloads;
GO
USE Workloads;
GO
```

Querying the table [dbo].[WLD] is essentially just repeating the same workloads with changes on one or another parameter:

	WL_ID	Param1	Param2
1	WL1	39	43
2	WL1	28	36
3	WL1	26	31
4	WL1	16	18
5	WL1	23	29
6	WL1	40	37
7	WL1	38	38
8	WL1	42	46
9	WL1	23	28
10	WL1	22	21
11	WL1	38	35
12	WL1	31	26

First, we need to have the outlier analysis against the workload each time something has changed. T-SQL code with R can deliver a *Mahalanobis* graph, which clearly shows where the outliers are:

```
EXEC sp_execute_external_script
 @language = N'R'
,@script = N'
                library(car)
                library(ggplot2)
                dataset <- InputDataSet
                dataset$WL_ID <- as.numeric(recode(dataset$WL_ID,
"''WL1''=1; ''WL2''=2;''WL3''=3"))
                dataset$Param1 <- as.numeric(dataset$Param1)
                dataset$Param2 <- as.numeric(dataset$Param2)

                m.dist <- mahalanobis(dataset, colMeans(dataset),
cov(dataset))
                dataset$maha_dist <- round(m.dist)

                # Mahalanobis Outliers - Threshold set to 7
                dataset$outlier_mah <- "No"
                dataset$outlier_mah[dataset$maha_dist > 7] <- "Yes"

                 image_file = tempfile();
                jpeg(filename = image_file);

                # Scatterplot for checking outliers using Mahalanobis
                ggplot(dataset, aes(x = Param1, y = Param2, color =
outlier_mah)) +
                    geom_point(size = 5, alpha = 0.6) +
                    labs(title = "Mahalanobis distances for multivariate
regression outliers",
                        subtitle = "Comparison on 1 parameter for three
synthetic Workloads") +
                    xlab("Parameter 1") +
                    ylab("Parameter 2") +
                    scale_x_continuous(breaks = seq(5, 55, 5)) +
                    scale_y_continuous(breaks = seq(0, 70, 5))    +
geom_abline(aes(intercept = 12.5607 , slope = 0.5727))

                    dev.off();
                OutputDataSet <- data.frame(data=readBin(file(image_file,
"rb"), what=raw(), n=1e6))'
,@input_data_1 = N'SELECT * FROM WLD'
```

The graph was inserted into Power BI, where the workloads can be changed against both of the parameters. So DBAs cannot only change the workloads, they can also see which outliers have caused and needed extra attention when performing a replay on the restored workload:

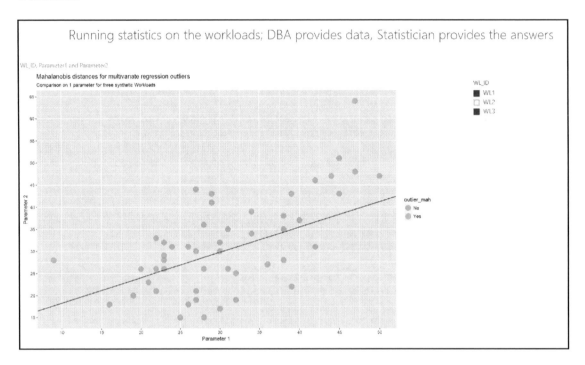

ANOVA or MANOVA can also be performed to see specific changes among the workloads. R code can do just that:

```
dataset$Param1 <- as.numeric(dataset$Param1)
dataset$Param2 <- as.numeric(dataset$Param2)
dataset$WL_ID <- as.numeric(recode(dataset$WL_ID, "'WL1'=1;
'WL2'=2;'WL3'=3"))
LM.man <- Anova(lm(cbind(Param1, Param2) ~ WL_ID, data=dataset))
summary(LM.man)
```

And the ANOVA statistics show the differences among the workloads and their changes in parameter settings:

```
Type II MANOVA Tests:

Sum of squares and products for error:
          Parameter1 Parameter2
Parameter1   7140.827    5846.12
Parameter2   5846.120    9943.84


------------------------------------------

Term: WL_ID

Sum of squares and products for the hypothesis:
          Parameter1 Parameter2
Parameter1      42.32     149.04
Parameter2     149.04     524.88

Multivariate Tests: WL_ID
                Df test stat approx F num Df den Df  Pr(>F)
Pillai           1 0.0618062 2.371602      2     72 0.10058
Wilks            1 0.9381938 2.371602      2     72 0.10058
Hotelling-Lawley 1 0.0658778 2.371602      2     72 0.10058
Roy              1 0.0658778 2.371602      2     72 0.10058
```

Creating predictions with R - disk usage

Predictions involve spotting any unplanned and unwanted activities or unusual system behavior, especially when compared it to the baseline. In this manner, raising a red flag would result in fewer false positive states.

In addition, we always come across disk-size problems. Based on this problem, we will demo database growth, store the data, and then run predictions against the collected data to be able at the end to predict when a DBA can expect disk space problems.

To illustrate this scenario, I will create a small database of 8 MB and no possibility of growth. I will create two tables. One will serve as a baseline, DataPack_Info_SMALL, and the other will serve as a so-called everyday log, where everything will be stored for unexpected cases or undesired behavior. This will persist in the DataPack_Info_LARGE table.

First, create a database:

```
USE [master];
GO
CREATE DATABASE FixSizeDB
CONTAINMENT = NONE
ON  PRIMARY
( NAME = N'FixSizeDB', FILENAME = N'C:\Program Files\Microsoft SQL
```

```
Server\MSSQL14.MSSQLSERVER2017\MSSQL\DATA\FixSizeDB_2.mdf' ,
SIZE = 8192KB , FILEGROWTH = 0)
LOG ON
( NAME = N'FixSizeDB_log', FILENAME = N'C:\Program Files\Microsoft SQL
Server\MSSQL14.MSSQLSERVER2017\MSSQL\DATA\FixSizeDB_2_log.ldf',
SIZE = 8192KB , FILEGROWTH = 0)
GO
ALTER DATABASE [FixSizeDB] SET COMPATIBILITY_LEVEL = 140
GO
ALTER DATABASE [FixSizeDB] SET RECOVERY SIMPLE
GO
```

The `DataPack` table will serve as a storage place for all the generated inserts and later deletes:

```
CREATE TABLE DataPack
        (
          DataPackID BIGINT IDENTITY NOT NULL
         ,col1 VARCHAR(1000) NOT NULL
         ,col2 VARCHAR(1000) NOT NULL
        )
```

Populating the `DataPack` table will be done with the following simple `WHILE` loop:

```
DECLARE @i INT = 1;
BEGIN TRAN
        WHILE @i <= 1000
                BEGIN
                        INSERT dbo.DataPack(col1, col2)
                                SELECT
                                        REPLICATE('A',200)
                                       ,REPLICATE('B',300);
                        SET @i = @i + 1;
                END
COMMIT;
GO
```

Capturing disk space changes with the following query will be very important for the task:

```
SELECT
        t.NAME AS TableName
       ,s.Name AS SchemaName
       ,p.rows AS RowCounts
       ,SUM(a.total_pages) * 8 AS TotalSpaceKB
       ,SUM(a.used_pages) * 8 AS UsedSpaceKB
       ,(SUM(a.total_pages) - SUM(a.used_pages)) * 8 AS UnusedSpaceKB
FROM
        sys.tables t
```

```
INNER JOIN sys.indexes AS i
        ON t.OBJECT_ID = i.object_id
INNER JOIN sys.partitions AS p
        ON i.object_id = p.OBJECT_ID
        AND i.index_id = p.index_id
INNER JOIN sys.allocation_units AS a
        ON p.partition_id = a.container_id
LEFT OUTER JOIN sys.schemas AS s
        ON t.schema_id = s.schema_id
WHERE
        t.NAME NOT LIKE 'dt%'
    AND t.is_ms_shipped = 0
    AND i.OBJECT_ID > 255
    AND t.Name = 'DataPack'
GROUP BY t.Name, s.Name, p.Rows
```

The `Log` table will be filled along with the `DataPack` table in order to gather immediate changes in disk space:

```
DECLARE @nof_steps INT = 0
WHILE @nof_steps < 15
BEGIN
        BEGIN TRAN
                -- insert some data
                DECLARE @i INT = 1;
                WHILE @i <= 1000 -- step is 100 rows
                                        BEGIN
                                                INSERT dbo.DataPack(col1, col2)
                                                        SELECT

REPLICATE('A',FLOOR(RAND()*200))

,REPLICATE('B',FLOOR(RAND()*300));
                                                SET @i = @i + 1;
                                        END
                -- run statistics on table
                INSERT INTO dbo.DataPack
                SELECT
                        t.NAME AS TableName
                        ,s.Name AS SchemaName
                        ,p.rows AS RowCounts
                        ,SUM(a.total_pages) * 8 AS TotalSpaceKB
                        ,SUM(a.used_pages) * 8 AS UsedSpaceKB
                        ,(SUM(a.total_pages) - SUM(a.used_pages)) * 8 AS
UnusedSpaceKB
                        ,GETDATE() AS TimeMeasure
                FROM
```

```
                        sys.tables AS t
                   INNER JOIN sys.indexes AS i
                   ON t.OBJECT_ID = i.object_id
                   INNER JOIN sys.partitions AS p
                   ON i.object_id = p.OBJECT_ID
                   AND i.index_id = p.index_id
                   INNER JOIN sys.allocation_units AS a
                   ON p.partition_id = a.container_id
                   LEFT OUTER JOIN sys.schemas AS s
                   ON t.schema_id = s.schema_id
             WHERE
                          t.NAME NOT LIKE 'dt%'
                   AND t.is_ms_shipped = 0
                   AND t.name = 'DataPack'
                   AND i.OBJECT_ID > 255
             GROUP BY t.Name, s.Name, p.Rows
             WAITFOR DELAY '00:00:02'
        COMMIT;
    END
```

This will serve as our baseline when comparing the results. When we query the `DataPack_Log_Small` table, the results are as follows:

```
DECLARE @RScript nvarchar(max)
SET @RScript = N'
                        library(Hmisc)
                        mydata <- InputDataSet
                        all_sub <- mydata[2:3]
                        c <- cor(all_sub, use="complete.obs",
method="pearson")
                        t <- rcorr(as.matrix(all_sub), type="pearson")
                        c <- cor(all_sub, use="complete.obs",
method="pearson")
                        c <- data.frame(c)
                        OutputDataSet <- c'
DECLARE @SQLScript nvarchar(max)
SET @SQLScript = N'SELECT
                                    TableName
                                   ,RowCounts
                                   ,UsedSpaceKB
                                   ,TimeMeasure
                                   FROM DataPack_Info_SMALL'
EXECUTE sp_execute_external_script
        @language = N'R'
       ,@script = @RScript
       ,@input_data_1 = @SQLScript
       WITH result SETS ((RowCounts VARCHAR(100)
```

```
                              ,UsedSpaceKB  VARCHAR(100)));
    GO
```

As a result, we get a strong and positive correlation between the RowCounts and UsedSpaceKB columns. This can easily be interpreted as: when the value for RowCounts goes up, the value for UsedSpaceKB also goes up. This is the only logical explanation. It would be somehow strange to have a negative correlation. Now, we will try to simulate random deletes and inserts and observe a similar behavior with the following code:

```
DECLARE @nof_steps INT = 0
WHILE @nof_steps < 15
BEGIN
      BEGIN TRAN
            -- insert some data
            DECLARE @i INT = 1;
            DECLARE @insertedRows INT = 0;
            DECLARE @deletedRows INT = 0;
            DECLARE @Rand DECIMAL(10,2) = RAND()*10
            IF @Rand < 5
              BEGIN
                              WHILE @i <= 1000 -- step is 100 rows
                                        BEGIN
                                                INSERT
dbo.DataPack(col1, col2)

SELECT

REPLICATE('A',FLOOR(RAND()*200))  -- pages are filling up differently

,REPLICATE('B',FLOOR(RAND()*300));
                                                SET @i = @i
+ 1;
                                        END
                        SET @insertedRows = 1000
            END

            IF @Rand  >= 5
                  BEGIN
                              SET @deletedRows = (SELECT COUNT(*) FROM
dbo.DataPack WHERE DataPackID % 3 = 0)
                              DELETE FROM dbo.DataPack
                                        WHERE
                              DataPackID % 3 = 0 OR DataPackID % 5 = 0
                  END
            -- run statistics on table
            INSERT INTO dbo.DataPack_Info_LARGE
            SELECT
```

```
                        t.NAME AS TableName
                        ,s.Name AS SchemaName
                        ,p.rows AS RowCounts
                        ,SUM(a.total_pages) * 8 AS TotalSpaceKB
                        ,SUM(a.used_pages) * 8 AS UsedSpaceKB
                        ,(SUM(a.total_pages) - SUM(a.used_pages)) * 8 AS
        UnusedSpaceKB

                        ,GETDATE() AS TimeMeasure
                        ,CASE WHEN @Rand < 5 THEN 'Insert'
                                WHEN @Rand >= 5 THEN 'Delete'
                                ELSE 'meeeh' END AS Operation
                        ,CASE WHEN @Rand < 5 THEN @insertedRows
                                WHEN @Rand >= 5 THEN @deletedRows
                                ELSE 0 END AS NofRowsOperation
                FROM
                            sys.tables AS t
                    INNER JOIN sys.indexes AS i
                    ON t.OBJECT_ID = i.object_id
                    INNER JOIN sys.partitions AS p
                    ON i.object_id = p.OBJECT_ID
                    AND i.index_id = p.index_id
                    INNER JOIN sys.allocation_units AS a
                    ON p.partition_id = a.container_id
                    LEFT OUTER JOIN sys.schemas AS s
                    ON t.schema_id = s.schema_id
                WHERE
                            t.NAME NOT LIKE 'dt%'
                    AND t.is_ms_shipped = 0
                    AND t.name = 'DataPack'
                    AND i.OBJECT_ID > 255
                GROUP BY t.Name, s.Name, p.Rows
                WAITFOR DELAY '00:00:01'
        COMMIT;
    END
```

We have added a DELETE statement, as well as RowCounts, so that the demo will not be so straightforward. By calculating the correlation coefficient, it is obvious, that we again get a very strong and positive correlation.

We will now compare our LARGE test with the baseline by running the same correlation coefficient on different datasets. The first is on our baseline (DataPack_Info_SMALL) and the second one is from our test table (DataPack_Info_LARGE):

```
DECLARE @RScript1 nvarchar(max)
SET @RScript1 = N'
                             library(Hmisc)
                             mydata <- InputDataSet
                             all_sub <- mydata[4:5]
                             c <- cor(all_sub, use="complete.obs",
method="pearson")
                             c <- data.frame(c)
                             OutputDataSet <- c'
DECLARE @SQLScript1 nvarchar(max)
SET @SQLScript1 = N'SELECT
                                    TableName
                                    ,RowCounts
                                    ,TimeMeasure
                                    ,UsedSpaceKB
                                    ,UnusedSpaceKB
                                    FROM DataPack_Info_SMALL
                                    WHERE RowCounts <> 0'
EXECUTE sp_execute_external_script
      @language = N'R'
      ,@script = @RScript1
      ,@input_data_1 = @SQLScript1
      WITH result SETS ( (
                                RowCounts VARCHAR(100)
                                ,UsedSpaceKB  VARCHAR(100)
                                ));
DECLARE @RScript2 nvarchar(max)
SET @RScript2 = N'
                          library(Hmisc)
                          mydata <- InputDataSet
                          all_sub <- mydata[4:5]
                          c <- cor(all_sub, use="complete.obs",
method="pearson")
                          c <- data.frame(c)
                          OutputDataSet <- c'
DECLARE @SQLScript2 nvarchar(max)
SET @SQLScript2 = N'SELECT
                                  TableName
                                  ,RowCounts
                                  ,TimeMeasure
                                  ,UsedSpaceKB
                                  ,UnusedSpaceKB
                                  FROM DataPack_Info_LARGE
```

```
                                            WHERE NofRowsOperation <> 0
                                            AND RowCounts <> 0'
EXECUTE sp_execute_external_script
        @language = N'R'
        ,@script = @RScript2
        ,@input_data_1 = @SQLScript2
        WITH result SETS ( (
                                              RowCounts VARCHAR(100)
                                              ,UsedSpaceKB   VARCHAR(100)
                                              )
                            );
  GO
```

The results are very interesting. The baseline shows no correlation between UsedSpaceKB and UnusedSpaceKB (it is -0.049), whereas our test shows an almost 3x stronger negative correlation (it is -0.109). A couple of words on this correlation: this shows that UsedSpaceKB is negatively correlated with UnUsedSpaceKB; this which is still too small to draw any concrete conclusions, but it shows how a slight change can cause a difference in a simple correlation.

You can gather disk space usage information with T-SQL, by using PowerShell, by implementing .NET assembly, or creating a SQL Server job, or any other way. The important part and the biggest advantage is that, using R and the data collected, now you will not only be monitoring and reacting to the past data, but you will also be able to predict what will happen.

Let's go a step further and assume the following query and dataset taken from our sample created:

```
SELECT
   TableName
  ,Operation
  ,NofRowsOperation
  ,UsedSpaceKB
  ,UnusedSpaceKB
FROM dbo.DataPack_Info_LARGE
```

We will give a prediction on the size of the `usedSpaceKB` based on historical data. Our input will be `TableName`, `Operation`, and `NofRowsOperation` for a given number to predict on. I will be using a general linear model (the GLM algorithm) for predicting `usedDiskSpace`! Before you all start saying this is absurd, this cannot be done due to DBCC caching, page brakes, indexes, stall statistics, and many other parameters, I would like to point out that all this information can be added into the algorithm and would make the prediction even better. Since my queries are very simple `INSERT` and `DELETE` statements, you should also know what kinds of queries are you predicting. In addition, such an approach can be good for code testing, unit testing, and stress testing before deployment.

With the following R code, we can start creating predictions:

```
-- GLM prediction
DECLARE @SQL_input AS NVARCHAR(MAX)
SET @SQL_input = N'SELECT
                                  TableName
                                 ,CASE WHEN Operation = ''Insert'' THEN 1
ELSE 0 END AS Operation
                                 ,NofRowsOperation
                                 ,UsedSpaceKB
                                 ,UnusedSpaceKB
                                  FROM dbo.DataPack_Info_LARGE
                                  WHERE
                                          NofRowsOperation <> 0';
DECLARE @R_code AS NVARCHAR(MAX)
SET @R_code = N'library(RevoScaleR)
                library(dplyr)
                DPLogR <- rxGlm(UsedSpaceKB ~ Operation + NofRowsOperation
+ UnusedSpaceKB, data = DataPack_info, family = Gamma)
                df_predict <- data.frame(TableName=("DataPack"),
Operation=(1), NofRowsOperation=(451), UnusedSpaceKB=(20))
                predictions <- rxPredict(modelObject = DPLogR, data =
df_predict, outData = NULL,
                                predVarNames = "UsedSpaceKB", type =
"response",checkFactorLevels=FALSE);
                OutputDataSet <- predictions'
EXEC sys.sp_execute_external_script
    @language = N'R'
    ,@script = @R_code
    ,@input_data_1 = @SQL_input
    ,@input_data_1_name = N'DataPack_info'
       WITH RESULT SETS ((
                         UsedSpaceKB_predict INT
                         ));
GO
```

Now we can predict the size of `UsedSpaceKB` based on the following data:

```
df_predict <- data.frame(TableName=("DataPack"), Operation=(1),
NofRowsOperation=(451), UnusedSpaceKB=(20))
```

We have a few things to clear out first. The following R code with the `xp_execute_external_script` would work much better as a stored procedure with input parameters for these columns: `TableName`, `Operation`, `NofRowsOperation`, and `UnusedSpaceKB`. Furthermore, to avoid unnecessary computational time for model building, it is usually the practice to store a serialized model in a SQL table and just deserialize it when running predictions. At last, since this was just a demo, make sure that the numbers used in predictions make sense, As we saw in our example, the `UsedSpaceKB` would be predicted much better if absolutely calculated, rather than using the cumulative values. Only later is the cumulative value calculated.

To sum up this rather long demo, let's create a procedure and run some predictions to see how efficient this is. The stored procedure is as follows:

```
CREATE PROCEDURE Predict_UsedSpace
    (
     @TableName NVARCHAR(100)
    ,@Operation CHAR(1)   -- 1 = Insert; 0 = Delete
    ,@NofRowsOperation NVARCHAR(10)
    ,@UnusedSpaceKB NVARCHAR(10)
    )
    AS
    DECLARE @SQL_input AS NVARCHAR(MAX)
    SET @SQL_input = N'SELECT
                                    TableName
                                   ,CASE WHEN Operation = ''Insert''
THEN 1 ELSE 0 END AS Operation
                                   ,NofRowsOperation
                                   ,UsedSpaceKB
                                   ,UnusedSpaceKB
                                    FROM dbo.DataPack_Info_LARGE
                                    WHERE
                                            NofRowsOperation <> 0';
        DECLARE @R_code AS NVARCHAR(MAX)
        SET @R_code = N'library(RevoScaleR)
                        DPLogR <- rxGlm(UsedSpaceKB ~ Operation +
NofRowsOperation + UnusedSpaceKB, data = DataPack_info, family = Gamma)
                        df_predict <- data.frame(TableName=("'+@TableName+'"),
Operation=('+@Operation+'),
                                NofRowsOperation=('+@NofRowsOperation+'),
UnusedSpaceKB=('+@UnusedSpaceKB+'))
                        predictions <- rxPredict(modelObject = DPLogR, data =
```

```
df_predict, outData = NULL,  predVarNames = "UsedSpaceKB", type =
"response",checkFactorLevels=FALSE) ;
                        OutputDataSet <- predictions'
    EXEC sys.sp_execute_external_script
          @language = N'R'
        ,@script = @R_code
        ,@input_data_1 = @SQL_input
        ,@input_data_1_name = N'DataPack_info'
    WITH RESULT SETS ((
                                    UsedSpaceKB_predict INT
                                    ));
    GO
```

Now we need to run the procedure two times in a row:

```
EXECUTE Predict_UsedSpace
                    @TableName = 'DataPack'
                    ,@Operation = 1
                    ,@NofRowsOperation = 120
                    ,@UnusedSpaceKB = 2;
GO
EXECUTE Predict_UsedSpace
                    @TableName = 'DataPack'
                    ,@Operation = 1
                    ,@NofRowsOperation = 500
                    ,@UnusedSpaceKB = 12;
GO
```

Both predictions on used space disk are based on our demo data but can be used on a larger scale and for predictions as well. Of course, for even better predictions, some baseline statistics could also be included. With every model, we also need to test the predictions to see how good they are.

Summary

Using SQL Server R for any kind of DBA task, as we have seen here, it is not always hardcore statistics or predictive analytics; we might also be some simple statistical understanding underlying the connection and relationships between the attribute's queries, gathered statistics, and indexes. Prognosing and predicting, for example, information from execution plans in order to prepare a better understanding of the query of cover missing index, is a crucial point. Parameter sniffing or a cardinality estimator would also be a great task to tackle along the usual statistics.

But we have seen that predicting events that are usually only monitored can be a huge advantage for a DBA and a very welcome feature for core systems.

With R integration into SQL Server, such daily, weekly, or monthly tasks can be automated to different, before not uses yet, extent. And as such, it can help give different insight to DBAs and also people responsible for system maintenance.

In next chapter, we will be covering extending features beyond R external procedure and how to use them.

10

R and SQL Server 2016/2017 Features Extended

SQL Server 2016 and 2017 provide a lot of new and improved query performance capabilities, extensibility features, security features, and built-in/native capabilities that are useful for developers, DBAs, and data scientists. These new features and capabilities can be used together with machine learning services in SQL, bringing a powerful data science solution as well as making the life of the developer/data scientist much easier.

This chapter will walk you through a few unique scenarios to show the combined power of R and other built-in capabilities in SQL Server. These scenarios include JSON built-in capabilities to show how we work with IoT data, PolyBase to illustrate beyond relational data sources, and a large amount of data with the `ColumnStore` index. We will dive into these scenarios and produce data visualization and predictive analysis power in R that we have learned in previous chapters.

Built-in JSON capabilities

In this scenario, we will use the EMS incidents by month from the official city of Austin open data portal (`https://data.austintexas.gov/Public-Safety/EMS-Incidents-by-Month/gjtj-jt2d`). The data essentially contains incident counts, broken down by location and priorities for the city of Austin and Travis County incidents, and the percentage of on-time compliance.

The following are the prerequisites to get started:

1. Download the data from `https://data.austintexas.gov/resource/bpws-iwvb.json` to a local path, such as `C:\Temp\bpws-iwvb.json`.

2. Grant read access to the directory; for example:

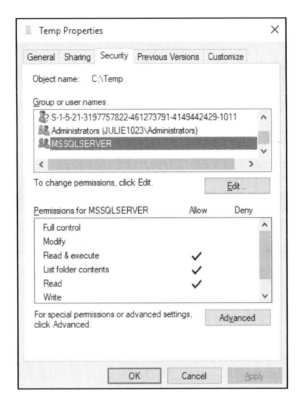

Figure 10.1 Granting access to C:\Temp for MS SQL Server

3. For ease of R visualization, we will use SQL Operations Studio. You can download SQL Ops Studio from: `https://docs.microsoft.com/en-us/sql/sql-operations-studio/download`.

The following is an excerpt of a JSON file:

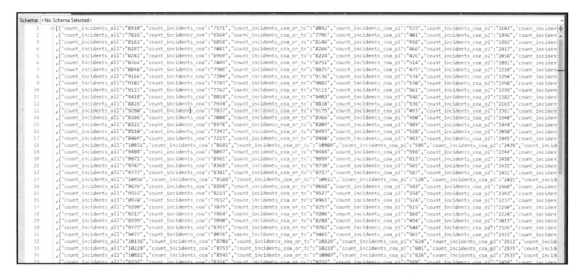

Figure 10.2: Excerpt of bpws-iwvb.json

The schema of the JSON object in this file is fairly straightforward. It's an array of the following 31 properties:

- `count_incidents_all`
- `count_incidents_coa`
- `count_incidents_coa_or_tc`
- `count_incidents_coa_p1`
- `count_incidents_coa_p2`
- `count_incidents_coa_p3`
- `count_incidents_coa_p4`
- `count_incidents_coa_p5`
- `count_incidents_other`
- `count_incidents_tc`
- `count_incidents_tc_p1`

- count_incidents_tc_p2
- count_incidents_tc_p3
- count_incidents_tc_p4
- count_incidents_tc_p5
- month_key
- month_start_date
- percent_on_time_all
- percent_on_time_coa
- percent_on_time_coa_p1
- percent_on_time_coa_p2
- percent_on_time_coa_p3
- percent_on_time_coa_p4
- percent_on_time_coa_p5
- percent_on_time_target
- percent_on_time_tc
- percent_on_time_tc_p1
- percent_on_time_tc_p2
- percent_on_time_tc_p3
- percent_on_time_tc_p4
- percent_on_time_tc_p5

To see a first row of the data and what the value looks like, you can use the following T-SQL code:

```
SELECT *
FROM OPENJSON((SELECT Doc.BulkColumn
                FROM OPENROWSET(BULK N'C:\Temp\bpws-iwvb.json',
SINGLE_CLOB) AS Doc), '$[0]')
```

The following is the output of the previous command:

	key	value	type
1	count_incidents_all	8910	1
2	count_incidents_coa	7571	1
3	count_incidents_coa_or_tc	8892	1
4	count_incidents_coa_p1	533	1
5	count_incidents_coa_p2	2103	1
6	count_incidents_coa_p3	1039	1
7	count_incidents_coa_p4	2938	1
8	count_incidents_coa_p5	958	1
9	count_incidents_other	18	1

Figure 10.3 Inspecting the first row of data in bpws-iwvb.json

The remainder of this section will show you how to use built-in JSON and R capabilities in SQL Server to parse the data and create a visualization to understand the trends of EMS incidents received by ATCEMS. The following screenshot shows the data visualization that we will build from the preceding JSON data via SQL Operations Studio:

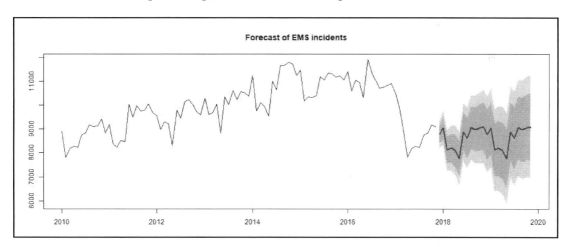

Figure 10.4 Using R to produce a forecast of EMS incidents

Perform the following steps to build the preceding visualization:

1. Open SQL Operations Studio.
2. Using JSON, get the `Date` and incident counts:

```
SELECT
    a.Date,
    a.TotalIncidents,
    a.AustinIncidents,
    a.TravisIncidents
FROM OPENJSON((SELECT Doc.BulkColumn
               FROM OPENROWSET(BULK N'C:\Temp\bpws-iwvb.json',
SINGLE_CLOB) AS Doc), '$')
WITH (Date         DATE     '$.month_start_date',
    TotalIncidents  INT     '$.count_incidents_all',
    AustinIncidents INT     '$.count_incidents_coa',
    TravisIncidents INT     '$.count_incidents_tc'
    ) AS a
ORDER BY a.Date ASC;
```

Here, we are using OPENROWSET and SINGLE_CLOB to read the file stream in clear text.

3. Then, we use OPEN_JSON to extract `month_start_date` as `Date`, `count_incidents_all` as `TotalIncidients`, `count_incidents_coa` as `AustinIncidents`, and `count_incidents_tc` as `TravisIncidents`.

The output should look something like this:

	Date	TotalIncidents	AustinIncidents	TravisIncidents
1	2010-10-01	8910	7571	1321
2	2010-11-01	7826	6564	1232
3	2010-12-01	8182	6858	1290
4	2011-01-01	8287	7081	1185
5	2011-02-01	8241	6969	1255
6	2011-03-01	8764	7449	1302
7	2011-04-01	8848	7506	1319
8	2011-05-01	9166	7704	1432
9	2011-06-01	9102	7743	1339
10	2011-07-01	9121	7762	1349

Figure 10.5: Output of running OPENJSON against the EMS Incident JSON file

4. Now, let's build the `InputDataSet` for the R script with the `Date` and `TotalIncidents` data:

```
DECLARE @input_query    NVARCHAR(MAX);
SET @input_query = 'SELECT
    a.Date,
    a.TotalIncidents
FROM OPENJSON((SELECT Doc.BulkColumn
    FROM OPENROWSET(BULK N'C:\Temp\bpws-iwvb.json',
        SINGLE_CLOB) AS Doc), '$')
    WITH (Date            DATE   '$.month_start_date',
        TotalIncidents  INT    '$.count_incidents_all'
        ) AS a;'
```

5. Let's build the R script that uses the preceding `InputDataSet`:

In this script, we will use the forecast package to perform forecasting based on the existing data in January 2010 and November 2017. More information about the forecast package, including the dependent packages, is available at: https://cran.r-project.org/web/packages/forecast/index.html.

In this specific example, the number of incidents can be seasonal. So, we are going to use a few helping functions that help with forecasting:

- `ts` function to convert the `InputDataSet` dataframe into time series
- `stl` function to decompose a time series into seasonal, trend, and irregular components
- `forecast` function that takes into account seasonality:

```
DECLARE @RPlot            NVARCHAR(MAX);

SET @RPlot = 'library(forecast);
    image_file = tempfile();
    jpeg(filename = image_file, width=1000, height=400);

    #store as time series
    myts <- ts(InputDataSet$TotalIncidents,
        start = c(2010, 1), end = c(2017, 11),
        frequency = 12);
    fit <- stl(myts, s.window = "period");

    # show the plot
    plot(forecast(fit), main = "Forecast of EMS incidents");
```

```
dev.off();

# return the plot as dataframe
OutputDataSet <-  data.frame(
    data=readBin(file(image_file,"rb"),
    what=raw(),n=1e6));'
```

6. Now, let's execute the following script:

```
EXEC sp_execute_external_script @language = N'R'
    ,@script = @RPlot
    ,@input_data_1 = @input_query
    ,@input_data_1_name = N'InputDataSet'
    ,@output_data_1_name = N'OutputDataSet'
    WITH RESULT SETS (( [plot] VARBINARY(MAX)));
```

7. In SQL Ops Studio, the result will be in the VARBINARY data type:

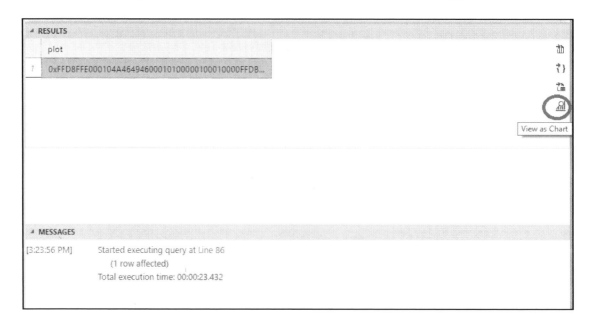

Figure 10.6: View as Chart function in SQL Operations Studio

8. Click on the **View as Chart** icon on the right, then click on the **Chart Viewer** tab on the **Results** pane, and then choose **image** from **Chart Type**. The output should be similar to the following:

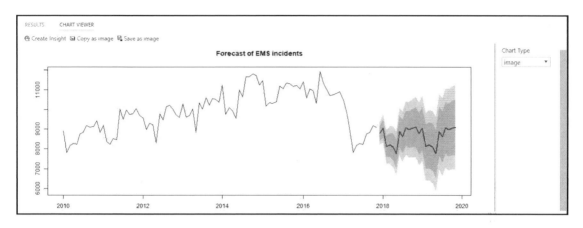

Figure 10.7: Displaying the chart produced by R in SQL Operations Studio

Accessing external data sources using PolyBase

PolyBase allows your SQL Server instance to access data outside of the server/database using T-SQL. In SQL Server 2016, you can run queries on external data in Hadoop or import data from Azure Blob Storage:

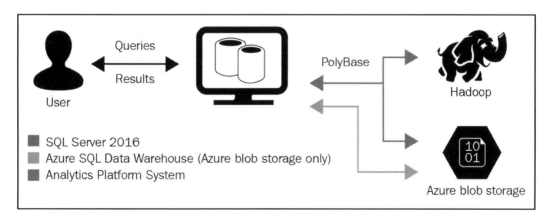

Figure 10.8: PolyBase concept (source: https://docs.microsoft.com/en-us/sql/relational-databases/polybase/polybase-guide)

In this section, we'll use a similar dataset as in the previous section, represented as CSV files in Azure Blob Storage. These CSV files represent the EMS incidents, which will be exposed as an external table in SQL Server. The goal for this walk-through is to understand seasonality and the trending of EMS incidents. We will use R in the SQL Server to do this and view the chart in SQL Operations Studio.

The following are the prerequisites to get started:

1. The SQL Server instance installed with PolyBase. This step is documented at: `https://docs.microsoft.com/en-us/sql/relational-databases/polybase/get-started-with-polybase`

2. Microsoft Azure Storage Explorer installed. Using Azure Storage Explorer, you can upload files, manage containers in your storage account, and get a Primary Access Key from the storage account:

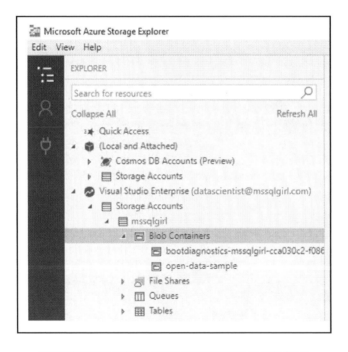

Figure 10.9: Using Microsoft Azure Storage Explorer to connect to Azure Blob Storage

3. EMS Incident by Month downloaded from <insert GitHub link> and uploaded to your Azure Blob Storage.

4. SSMS or SQL Operations Studio installed.

Perform the following steps to create an external table:

1. Enable the advanced option to enable connectivity to Azure Blob Storage on the master database first.

   Having Hadoop connectivity set to 7 allows connectivity to Azure Blob Storage. For more information on others supported data sources, visit:

   https://docs.microsoft.com/en-us/sql/database-engine/configure-windows/polybase-connectivity-configuration-transact-sql

   ```
   USE master;
   GO
   EXEC sp_configure 'show advanced option', '1';
   RECONFIGURE;
   GO
   EXEC sp_configure 'hadoop connectivity', 7;
   GO
   RECONFIGURE;
   GO
   ```

2. Create a master key in your database where you'd like to create an external table connecting to the CSV files in Azure Blob Storage:

   ```
   USE [AdventureWorks2016]
   GO
   CREATE MASTER KEY ENCRYPTION BY
   PASSWORD='MsSQLGirlLovesSQLServer2016&2017:)';
   ```

3. Create the database MsSQLGirlAtAzureBlobStorage:

   ```
   CREATE DATABASE SCOPED CREDENTIAL MsSQLGirlAtAzureBlobStorage
   WITH IDENTITY = 'credential', Secret =
   'Es3duvq+x9G5x+EFbuUmGo0salEi6Jsd59NI20KXespbiBG9RswLA4L1fuqs/59por
   PBay64YkRj/tvQ7XAMLA==';
   ```

4. Create the external data source pointing to a container in Azure Blob Storage. In this instance, open-data-sample is the name of the container, and mssqlgirl.blob.core.windows.net is the Azure Blob Storage location:

   ```
   CREATE EXTERNAL DATA SOURCE OpenDataSample
   WITH (
       TYPE = HADOOP,
       LOCATION = 'wasbs://open-data-
   sample@mssqlgirl.blob.core.windows.net/',
       CREDENTIAL = MsSQLGirlAtAzureBlobStorage
   ```

```
);
```

5. Create the file format of the source files in the container:

```
CREATE EXTERNAL FILE FORMAT csvformat
WITH (
    FORMAT_TYPE = DELIMITEDTEXT,
    FORMAT_OPTIONS (
        FIELD_TERMINATOR = ','
    )
);
```

6. Create the following source files in the container:

```
CREATE EXTERNAL TABLE EMSIncident
(
    [Month Key]                              INT,
    [Month-Year]                             VARCHAR(30),
    [Total Incidents]                        INT,
    [Austin Incidents]                       INT,
    [Travis County Incidents]                INT,
    [Other Area Incidents]                   INT,
    [Combined Austin & Travis Incidents]        INT,
    [Austin P1 Incidents]                    INT,
    [Austin P2 Incidents]                    INT,
    [Austin P3 Incidents]                    INT,
    [Austin P4 Incidents]                    INT,
    [Austin P5 Incidents]                    INT,
    [Travis County P1 Incidents]             INT,
    [Travis County P2 Incidents]             INT,
    [Travis County P3 Incidents]             INT,
    [Travis County P4 Incidents]             INT,
    [Travis County P5 Incidents]             INT,
    [Overall On-Time Compliance]             VARCHAR(10),
    [Austin On-Time Compliance]                 VARCHAR(10),
    [Travis County On-Time Compliance]          VARCHAR(10),
    [Austin P1 On-Time Compliance]              VARCHAR(10),
    [Austin P2 On-Time Compliance]              VARCHAR(10),
    [Austin P3 On-Time Compliance]              VARCHAR(10),
    [Austin P4 On-Time Compliance]              VARCHAR(10),
    [Austin P5 On-Time Compliance]              VARCHAR(10),
    [Travis County P1 On-Time Compliance]       VARCHAR(10),
    [Travis County P2 On-Time Compliance]       VARCHAR(10),
    [Travis County P3 On-Time Compliance]       VARCHAR(10),
    [Travis County P4 On-Time Compliance]       VARCHAR(10),
    [Travis County P5 On-Time Compliance]       VARCHAR(10),
    [Target On-Time Compliance]                 VARCHAR(10)
```

```
)
WITH
(
    LOCATION = '/EMS_-_Incidents_by_Month.csv',
    DATA_SOURCE = OpenDataSample,
    FILE_FORMAT = csvformat
)
```

7. So, now we can do a `SELECT` statement on the external table as an input to the R script:

```
DECLARE @input_query    NVARCHAR(MAX);
DECLARE @RPlot          NVARCHAR(MAX);

SET @input_query = 'SELECT
    CAST([Month-Year] AS DATE) AS [Date],
    [Total Incidents] AS [TotalIncidents]
FROM EMSIncident;'
SET @RPlot = 'library(ggplot2);
    library(forecast);
    image_file = tempfile();
    jpeg(filename = image_file, width=1000, height=400);

    #store as time series
    myts <- ts(InputDataSet$TotalIncidents,
        start = c(2010, 1), end = c(2017, 11),
        frequency = 12);
    fit <- stl(myts, s.window = "period");
    # show the plot
    plot(fit, main = "EMS incidents");
    dev.off();

    # return the plot as dataframe
    OutputDataSet <-  data.frame(
        data=readBin(file(image_file,"rb"),
        what=raw(),n=1e6));'


EXEC sp_execute_external_script @language = N'R'
    ,@script = @RPlot
    ,@input_data_1 = @input_query
    ,@input_data_1_name = N'InputDataSet'
    ,@output_data_1_name = N'OutputDataSet'
    WITH RESULT SETS (( [plot] VARBINARY(MAX)));
```

If you are using SQL Operations Studio, you can view the graph, which should look like the following:

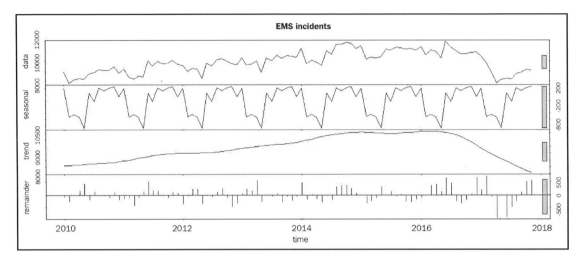

Figure 10.10: EMS incidents time series

The preceding chart suggests that the trend is increasing from year 2010 to 2016, which then significantly decreases in general.

High performance using ColumnStore and in memory OLTP

SQL Server 2016 R Services and SQL Server 2017 ML Services provide advanced analytical capabilities that can also be applied to optimized tables. In this section, we will walk you through comparisons on how to use R Services with:

- A table with a primary key
- A table with a clustered ColumnStore index
- A memory-optimized table
- A memory-optimized table with a clustered ColumnStore index

TIP For more optimization tips and tricks with SQL Server and machine learning, visit:
`https://azure.microsoft.com/en-us/blog/optimization-tips-and-tricks-on-azure-sql-server-for-machine-learning-services/`

Testing rxLinMod performance on a table with a primary key

The following steps will test the performance of `rxLinMod` over 6,096,762 bits of data stored in a table with a primary key. This Air Flights data can be downloaded from `https://packages.revolutionanalytics.com/datasets/AirOnTime2012.xdf` and stored in `C:/Program Files/Microsoft SQL Server/140/R_SERVER/library/RevoScaleR/SampleData`. At the end of the steps, we will record the CPU time:

1. Create a stored procedure that reads the `AirFlights` sample data in an XDF file, and return it as a data frame so that we can insert it into a new table:

```
CREATE PROCEDURE [dbo].[usp_ImportXDFtoSQL]
AS
    DECLARE @RScript NVARCHAR(MAX)
    SET @RScript = N'library(RevoScaleR)
        rxOptions(sampleDataDir = "C:/Program Files/Microsoft SQL
Server/140/R_SERVER/library/RevoScaleR/SampleData");
        outFile <-  file.path(rxGetOption("sampleDataDir"),
"AirOnTime2012.xdf");
        OutputDataSet <- data.frame(rxReadXdf(file=outFile,
varsToKeep=c("ArrDelay", "CRSDepTime","DayOfWeek")))'

    EXECUTE sp_execute_external_script
        @language = N'R'
        ,@script = @RScript
        WITH RESULT SETS ((
            [ArrDelay]          SMALLINT,
            [CRSDepTime]        DECIMAL(6,4),
            [DayOfWeek]         NVARCHAR(10)));
    GO
```

2. Create a table where the `AirFlights` data will be stored. This table represents a row-stored table with a primary key:

```
CREATE TABLE [dbo].[AirFlights]
(
     [ID]              INT NOT NULL IDENTITY(1,1)
    ,[ArrDelay]        SMALLINT
    ,[CRSDepTime]      DECIMAL(6,4)
    ,[DayOfWeek]       NVARCHAR(10)
    ,CONSTRAINT PK_AirFlights PRIMARY KEY ([ID])
);
GO
```

3. Insert the Air Flights data into the `AirFlights` table. In this instance, we are using R services to load the data:

```
INSERT INTO [dbo].[AirFlights]
EXECUTE [dbo].[usp_ImportXDFtoSQL]
```

4. Create a procedure that calls an external script to calculate the coefficient from the linear model prediction of the Arrival Delay:

```
CREATE PROCEDURE dbo.usp_TestPerformance (@TableName VARCHAR(50))
AS
    DECLARE @RScript NVARCHAR(MAX)
    SET @RScript = N'library(RevoScaleR)
                            LMResults <- rxLinMod(ArrDelay ~
DayOfWeek, data = InputDataSet)
                            OutputDataSet <-
data.frame(LMResults$coefficients)'

    DECLARE @SQLScript nvarchar(max)
    SET @SQLScript = N'SELECT ArrDelay, DayOfWeek FROM ' +
@TableName
    SET STATISTICS TIME ON;
    EXECUTE sp_execute_external_script
          @language = N'R'
         ,@script = @RScript
         ,@input_data_1 = @SQLScript
    WITH RESULT SETS ((
                    Coefficient DECIMAL(10,5)
                    ));

    SET STATISTICS TIME OFF;
GO
```

5. Execute the procedure, as follows:

```
EXEC dbo.usp_TestPerformance '[dbo].[AirFlights]'
```

The result should look something like this:

```
SQL Server parse and compile time:
   CPU time = 0 ms, elapsed time = 1 ms.
STDOUT message(s) from external script:
Rows Read: 6096762, Total Rows Processed: 6096762, Total Chunk
Time: 0.075 seconds
Computation time: 0.080 seconds.
(8 rows affected)
 SQL Server Execution Times:
   CPU time = 2797 ms,  elapsed time = 10463 ms.
 SQL Server Execution Times:
   CPU time = 2797 ms,  elapsed time = 10464 ms.
```

Testing rxLinMod performance on a table with a clustered ColumnStore index

The following steps will test the performance of rxLinMod over 6,096,762 bits of data stored in a table with a clustered ColumnStore index. At the end of the steps, we will record the CPU time:

1. Create a table similar to dbo.AirFlights from the previous section. We also want to create a clustered ColumnStore index and insert the data from dbo.AirFlights:

```
CREATE TABLE AirFlights_CS
(
    [ID]              INT NOT NULL IDENTITY(1,1)
  , [ArrDelay]        SMALLINT
  , [CRSDepTime]      DECIMAL(6,4)
  , [DayOfWeek]       NVARCHAR(10)
);
GO

INSERT INTO [dbo].[AirFlights_CS]
(
    [ArrDelay]
  , [CRSDepTime]
  , [DayOfWeek]
)
```

```
SELECT
    [ArrDelay]
    , [CRSDepTime]
    , [DayOfWeek]
FROM [dbo].[AirFlights];
GO

CREATE CLUSTERED COLUMNSTORE INDEX CCI_Airflights_CS ON
[dbo].[AirFlights_CS]
GO
```

2. Execute the following procedure:

```
EXEC dbo.usp_TestPerformance '[dbo].[AirFlights_CS]'
```

The result should look something like the following:

```
SQL Server parse and compile time:
    CPU time = 0 ms, elapsed time = 7 ms.
STDOUT message(s) from external script:
Rows Read: 6096762, Total Rows Processed: 6096762, Total Chunk
Time: 0.075 seconds
Computation time: 0.080 seconds.
(8 rows affected)
 SQL Server Execution Times:
    CPU time = 2235 ms,   elapsed time = 10684 ms.
 SQL Server Execution Times:
    CPU time = 2235 ms,   elapsed time = 10692 ms.
```

Testing rxLinMod performance on a memory-optimized table with a primary key

The following steps will test the performance of rxLinMod over 6,096,762 bits of data stored in a memory-optimized table with a non-clustered primary key. At the end of the steps, we will record the CPU time:

1. Create a file group for the memory-optimized table in the database:

```
ALTER DATABASE PerfTuning
    ADD FILEGROUP PerfTuningMOD CONTAINS MEMORY_OPTIMIZED_DATA;

ALTER DATABASE PerfTuning
    ADD FILE (NAME='PerfTuningMOD',
    FILENAME = 'C:\Program Files\Microsoft SQL
```

```
Server\MSSQL14.MSSQLSERVER\MSSQL\DATA\PerfTuningMOD.ndf')
    TO FILEGROUP PerfTuningMOD;

ALTER DATABASE PerfTuning
    SET MEMORY_OPTIMIZED_ELEVATE_TO_SNAPSHOT=ON
GO
```

2. Create a memory-optimized table version of `dbo.AirFlights`:

```
CREATE TABLE [dbo].[AirFlights_MOD]
(
        [ID] INT IDENTITY(1,1) NOT NULL PRIMARY KEY NONCLUSTERED
        ,[ArrDelay] SMALLINT
        ,[CRSDepTime]      DECIMAL(6,4)
        ,[DayOfWeek]       NVARCHAR(10)
) WITH (MEMORY_OPTIMIZED=ON, DURABILITY = SCHEMA_AND_DATA);
GO
INSERT INTO [dbo].[AirFlights_MOD]
(
        [ArrDelay]
        ,[CRSDepTime]
        ,[DayOfWeek]
)
SELECT
        [ArrDelay]
        ,[CRSDepTime]
        ,[DayOfWeek]
FROM [dbo].[AirFlights]
go
```

3. Execute the following procedure:

```
EXEC dbo.usp_TestPerformance '[dbo].[AirFlights_MOD]'
```

The result should look something like this:

```
SQL Server parse and compile time:
    CPU time = 2 ms, elapsed time = 2 ms.
STDOUT message(s) from external script:
Rows Read: 6096762, Total Rows Processed: 6096762, Total Chunk
Time: 0.072 seconds
Computation time: 0.077 seconds.
(8 rows affected)
 SQL Server Execution Times:
    CPU time = 2109 ms,  elapsed time = 8835 ms.
 SQL Server Execution Times: 2235 ms,  elapsed time = 10692 ms.
```

Testing rxLinMod performance on a memory-optimized table with a clustered ColumnStore index

The following steps will test the performance of `rxLinMod` over 6,096,762 bits of data stored in a memory-optimized table with a non-clustered primary key. At the end of the steps, we will record the CPU time:

1. Create a memory-optimized table with a clustered `columstore` index version of `dbo.AirFlights`:

```
CREATE TABLE [dbo].[AirFlights_MODCS]
(
    [ID] INT IDENTITY(1,1) NOT NULL PRIMARY KEY NONCLUSTERED
    ,[ArrDelay] SMALLINT
    ,[CRSDepTime] DECIMAL(6,4)
    ,[DayOfWeek]        VARCHAR(10)
) WITH (MEMORY_OPTIMIZED=ON, DURABILITY = SCHEMA_AND_DATA);
GO

INSERT INTO [dbo].[AirFlights_MODCS]
(
    [ArrDelay]
    ,[CRSDepTime]
    ,[DayOfWeek]
)
SELECT
    [ArrDelay]
    ,[CRSDepTime]
    ,[DayOfWeek]
FROM [dbo].[AirFlights];
GO
ALTER TABLE [dbo].[AirFlights_MODCS]
ADD INDEX CCI_Airflights_MODCS CLUSTERED COLUMNSTORE
GO
```

2. Execute the following procedure:

```
EXEC dbo.usp_TestPerformance '[dbo].[AirFlights_MODCS]'
```

The result should look something like this:

```
SQL Server parse and compile time:
    CPU time = 3 ms, elapsed time = 3 ms.
```

```
STDOUT message(s) from external script:
Rows Read: 6096762, Total Rows Processed: 6096762, Total Chunk
Time: 0.088 seconds
Computation time: 0.093 seconds.
(8 rows affected)
 SQL Server Execution Times:
   CPU time = 1766 ms,  elapsed time = 8659 ms.
 SQL Server Execution Times:
   CPU time = 1782 ms,  elapsed time = 8662 ms.
```

Comparing results

As you can see from the following quick chart comparison, SQL Server R Services can take advantage of optimized tables very well:

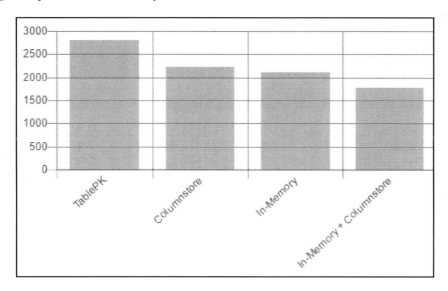

Figure 10.11 Comparing performance of classic primary key, Columnstore, in-memory, and in-memory + Columnstore when used in combination with R Services

For additional information on the performance comparison, you can go to *Tomaž Kaštrun's* article here:

```
https://github.com/tomaztk/Performance-differences-between-RevoScaleR-
ColumnStore-Table-and-In-Memory-OLTP-Table/blob/master/RevoScaleR_vs_
ColumStore_vs_InMemoryOLTP.sql
```

Summary

SQL Server 2016 and SQL Server 2017 are packed with useful features, from JSON, PolyBase, to high performance features, such as the `ColumnStore` index and memory-optimized tables. Most of these features are compatible and can enhance your advanced analytics experience. In this chapter, you have learned the steps for creating forecast and seasonal trends of EMS incidents in Austin and Travis County. We used both JSON data source and CSV files in Azure Blob Storage. Finally, you also have learned how to make use of `ColumnStore` and memory-optimized tables to improve performance of R Services.

Other Books You May Enjoy

If you enjoyed this book, you may be interested in these other books by Packt:

SQL Server 2017 Administrator's Guide
Marek Chmel, Vladimír Mužný

ISBN: 978-1-78646-254-1

- Learn about the new features of SQL Server 2017 and how to implement them
- Build a stable and fast SQL Server environment
- Fix performance issues by optimizing queries and making use of indexes
- Perform a health check of an existing troublesome database environment
- Design and use an optimal database management strategy
- Implement efficient backup and recovery techniques in-line with security policies
- Combine SQL Server 2017 and Azure and manage your solution by various
- automation techniques Perform data migration, cluster upgradation and server consolidation

SQL Server 2017 Integration Services Cookbook

Christian Cote, Matija Lah, Dejan Sarka

ISBN: 978-1-78646-182-7

- Understand the key components of an ETL solution using SQL Server 2016-2017 Integration Services
- Design the architecture of a modern ETL solution
- Have a good knowledge of the new capabilities and features added to Integration Services
- Implement ETL solutions using Integration Services for both on-premises and Azure data
- Improve the performance and scalability of an ETL solution
- Enhance the ETL solution using a custom framework
- Be able to work on the ETL solution with many other developers and have common design paradigms or techniques
- Effectively use scripting to solve complex data issues

Leave a review - let other readers know what you think

Please share your thoughts on this book with others by leaving a review on the site that you bought it from. If you purchased the book from Amazon, please leave us an honest review on this book's Amazon page. This is vital so that other potential readers can see and use your unbiased opinion to make purchasing decisions, we can understand what our customers think about our products, and our authors can see your feedback on the title that they have worked with Packt to create. It will only take a few minutes of your time, but is valuable to other potential customers, our authors, and Packt. Thank you!

Index

V

version control
  using 231
Visual Studio Team Services (VSTS)
  build definition, creating 235
  build, automating for CI 243
  build, deploying to local SQL Server instance
    240
  continuous delivery, setting up 246
  continuous integration (CI), setting up 233
  reference 251
  test phase, adding to build definition 241
  URL 213
Visual Studio
  about 91, 95
  URL 198, 212
  URL, for VSTS project 231
  used, for operationalizing R code 198
visualizations
  R integration 89

W

WideWorldImporters database
  URL 70
workloads
  creating 275, 276, 278, 280
  extensibility framework workloads 190
  external packages 192
  fast batch prediction workloads 191
  permissions, managing 190
  replaying 275, 276, 278, 280
  roles, managing 190
write-ahead log (WAL) 258

X

XDT Transform
  about 248
  URL 249
XP_CMDSHELL
  using 58

91082181R00187

Made in the USA
Lexington, KY
18 June 2018